Multinational
Corporate Strategy

Multinational Corporate Strategy

Planning for World Markets

James C. Leontiades
Manchester Business School
University of Manchester

Lexington Books
An Imprint of The Free Press
New York   London   Toronto   Sydney   Tokyo   Singapore

Lexington Books
An Imprint of The Free Press
A Division of Simon & Schuster Inc.
1230 Avenue of the Americas
New York, N.Y. 10020

Printed in the United States of America

printing number
1 2 3 4 5 6 7 8 9 10

Library of Congress Cataloging in Publication Data

Leontiades, James C.
  Multinational corporate strategy.

  Bibliography: p.
  Includes index.
    1. International business enterprises—Management.
2. Corporate planning. I. Title.
HD62.4.L46   1985   658.4′012   83-48686
ISBN 0-669-07381-4 (alk. paper)
ISBN 0-669-16038-5 (pbk. : alk. paper)

To My Parents

Contents

Figures   xiii

Foreword   xvii
H. Igor Ansoff

Preface   xix

Part I   The Multinational in a Changing Environment   1

1. **The Internationalization of Business and Business Strategy   3**

   Internationalized Industries   4

   Forces of Change   5

   Corporate Strategy   7

   International Strategy   8

2. **Differing Approaches to Multinational Strategy   11**

   Early Experience   11

   Planning in the Multinational   12

   Strategic Planning Modes   13

   Levels of Strategic Planning   19

3. **The Practice of Strategic Planning in a Multinational Company: An Evolutionary View   21**

   Early Internationalization   22

   The International Division   23

   Regional Coordination   24

Strategic Planning at Ford of Europe   25

Planning Development   31

Nature of Strategy   31

Conclusion   35

Part II   Strategy at the Regional/Global Level   37

4.   International Portfolio Strategy   39

Portfolio Strategy   40

International Resource Allocation   46

Assessing International Portfolio Performance   48

Portfolio Interdependence   49

5.   Global and National Competitive Strategies   51

Four Generic International Competitive Strategies   52

Competitive Strategy and Structure   56

Geopolitical Aspects   56

6.   Implementing Strategic Change   59

The Competitors   59

Changing Conditions   61

Implementing a Global Niche Strategy   62

Market Share and Return on Investment   63

Areas of Vulnerability   63

International Sources of Competitive Advantage   66

7.   Marketing Strategy: The International Headquarters Role   69

Headquarters Functions   70

Market Intelligence and Data Gathering   70

Marketing Strategies   77

8. **International Marketing Policies   85**

International Product Policy   85

International Pricing Policy   89

International Distribution Policy   92

International Promotion Policies   93

9. **International Plant Location and Logistics   95**

Foreign Investment Decision Process   95

Screening National Locations   96

Plant Location and Regional/Global Logistics   101

Conclusion   107

Part III   Strategy at the National Level   109

10. **National Entry Strategy Appraisal   111**

Strategic Appraisal—Objectives   112

Environmental Appraisal   113

Resource Appraisal   124

Company Values, Tradition, and Philosophy   126

11. **National Entry Strategy Decisions and Options   129**

Planning Entry Strategy   129

Generic Entry Strategies   130

Logistics Methods for Market Entry   133

Investment in Foreign-Based Facilities   134

Low-Equity Foreign-Based Operations   135

Strategy Evaluation and Selection   136

12. **National New Product Introduction   141**

New Product Introduction at Kellogg's   141

Comparative Market Analysis   145

Time Shift Comparisons   149

Special Situations in Developing Countries   150

Summary   152

13. **Anticipating and Managing Political Risk   153**

Political Risk: A Definition   154

Forecasing Political Risk   155

Managing Political Risk   161

Conclusion   166

Part IV   Coordinating Strategy across National Borders   167

14. **Strategic Planning Systems and Other Coordinative Mechanisms   169**

Annual Planning Cycle   170

Formal and Informal Planning   171

Resource Allocation: Capital Budget Planning   171

Beyond Capital Budgeting   174

Discretionary Coordination   175

International Policy   177

Strategic Planning in a Highly Integrated Multinational   177

Developing a Multinational Company Culture   181

15. **Changing the Organizational Structure   185**

Export Organizations   185

Early Multinational Organizations   188

Global Structures   193

Matrix Structures   196

Hybrid Structures   198

Strategy and Structural Change   198

Implementing Organizational Change   200

International Coordination: The Broader Context   201

Notes 203

Index 215

About the Author 229

Figures

Figures

1–1.   Definitions of Strategy and Strategy Formulation   8

1–2.   International Strategy: Matching the Firm to Its International Environment   10

2–1.   Planning Scope of Railroad Administrative Units   13

2–2.   Control and Strategy in the Multinational: Three Alternative Modes   15

3–1.   Composition of the Worldwide Car Market   27

4–1.   Strategic Business Units Defined by Product and Geography   42

4–2.   International Growth/Share Portfolio   43

4–3.   Political Risk/Profitability Portfolio   45

4–4.   International Comparison of Changes in Relative Market Share   46

4–5.   Growth/Share Matrix   47

4–6.   Regional/Global Portfolio   48

4–7.   Border Effects Influencing Perception of Firm's International Portfolio   50

5–1.   Four Generic International Competitive Strategies   53

5–2.   Conceptual View of the Distribution of Global and National Competitive Strategies in an Industry   58

7–1.   Product Life Cycle   74

7–2.   Product Life Cycles in Different Countries   74

7–3.   Global View of Product Life Cycles   76

7–4.   Stages of International Product-Market Development, World Automobile Markets   78

7–5.   Leader and Follower Strategies   81

8–1.   International Product Development Policies   87

8–2.   Experience Curve Pricing   91

8–3.   Experience Curve Pricing Strategy   91

9–1.   Rating Scale for Screening National Environments   97

9–2.   Portfolio Screening of National Location Opportunities   100

9–3.   International Change in Product Cycle and Plant Location   106

10–1.   Entering a New National Environment: Areas of Strategic Appraisal   113

10–2.   Checklist for General National Business Conditions and Investment Climate   115

10–3.   Comparative Product-Market Analysis   116

10–4.   Mapping   123

10–5.   Appraising the Business Environment in New National Product-Markets   124

11–1.   Four Generic National Market Entry Strategies   131

11–2.   Entry Strategy Planning Process   139

12–1.   Marketing Interaction and Transfer in a Multinational   146

12–2.   International Comparison for New Product Introduction   148

13–1.   Typology of Political Risk   155

13–2.   Checklist of Political Risk Indicators   161

13–3.   Hedging Strategies   163

14–1.   Planning Cycles in a Multinational   170

14–2.   Format for Capital Appropriation Request   173

15–1.   Domestic Functional Organization with Export Department   186

15–2.   Mother-Daughter Structure   190

15–3.   Divisional Structure   192

15–4. Global Product Structure   194

15–5. Global Area Structure   195

15–6. Matrix Structure   197

15–7. Multinational Company Strategy and Structure   199

15–8. International Coordination Mechanisms   201

Foreword

Jim Leontiades' book is a timely and needed addition to the literature on multinational strategy formulation. It is timely because, more than ever, each business firm must plan its strategy within a multinational perspective. This applies to firms that seek their opportunities in nations and regions new to them. But as Jim so insightfully points out, an ever-growing number of industries are becoming multinational and global in scope. This means that firms that have no ambitions for multinational expansion must nevertheless take account of multinational competitive forces in planning their domestic strategy.

The book is a needed addition to the literature because it joins an unfortunately small number of books that take a comprehensive perspective of the key elements of a multinational strategy. In a clear expository style, Jim combines significant lessons to be learned from experiences of successful multinationals with insight into the variables that determine success in multinational competition, and with practical suggestions for formulation of a multinational strategy.

Successful multinational firms will find in this book a well-organized summary of the variables and relationships that they take into account in their daily management.

Firms that have burned their fingers in their initial efforts to become multinational will almost certainly find an explanation for their difficulties and suggestions for overcoming them. The book is "must" reading for managers who are planning to launch their firms on the turbulent seas of multinational competition.

H. Igor Ansoff
Distinguished Professor of Strategic Management
U.S. International University
San Diego, California

Preface

This book is directed at managers and students of management interested in the international aspects of strategy, particularly with reference to multinational companies. The immediate stimulus behind the material presented here stems from my involvement with the project method of teaching employed at the Manchester Business School. This brought me into contact with a large number of companies grappling with problems associated with international expansion and competition.

The gap between the published material dealing with decision making in this context and the managerial task at hand was very noticeable. For problems falling squarely within the prescribed boundaries of established disciplines, such as international economics, international finance, and marketing, powerful analytical tools are provided. But only a relatively small proportion of the major international business decisions seemed to fall into this category.

Finding an optimal solution within a narrowly defined discipline is seldom the issue. In practice, a major problem is often one of determining whether a problem, in the sense of a genuine need or opportunity, actually exists. If it does, a wide number of options are generally available, of which only a few are known at the outset. Discovering and identifying others is a crucial part of the overall task. Inevitably much of the necessary information is missing. Guidance is needed on gathering and integrating additional data. Gradually progress is made toward a compromise solution that reconciles the requirements of the problem at hand with the often-conflicting needs of other parts of the organization and commitments made under previous decisions.

All of this will have a familiar ring to those already acquainted with the growing body of work developed under the heading of corporate strategy. The emphasis is on the relationship of the firm to its external environment. It does not pretend to provide theory-based solutions for finding the right answer. Prescriptive comments are directed at providing guidelines for what is essentially a search process.

This stress on the firm's external environment and the firm's adjustment to it lends itself to decision making within international and multinational companies.

Operating as they do across very different national territories, the relevance and need for such adjustment is obvious.

One aim of this book is to apply the latest methods and techniques of corporate strategy to the special situation of multinational firms. The geographic mobility of such companies means that environment itself becomes a variable and thus part of management's strategic decision making. Also, by definition, multinationals are sited in multiple national environments. Both of these points raise options and issues quite different from those found in purely domestic firms. Another aim has been to focus the material presented around a number of decision areas particularly relevant to the management of such companies.

The organization of the material presented here seeks to avoid the confusion that stems from the different perception of what constitutes a firm's environment. Although it is easy to slip into the habit of seeing companies as decision-making entities, this can be very misleading. The collection of individuals comprising any organization inevitably will have different roles and responsibilities in the decision-making process, and this will condition their perception of the company, its environment, as well as their priorities as to what is best. In multinational companies, these differences are accentuated by geographic distance, national loyalties, and barriers. It is noticeable that management in the multinational firms' international headquarters has a different view of the world than is generally to be found in its individual operating units abroad, that is, the firm's national subsidiaries.

These differences are not accidental; they are part of the specialization of decision-making labor in multinationals. Both points of view are important. Failing to make the distinction between the more global interpretation of strategic decision making at headquarters and the more nationally oriented interpretation within the firm's national operating units can be a source of misunderstanding. Not a little of the friction among managers in such companies may be traced to these differing perspectives. Making this distinction explicit is useful at arriving at a fuller understanding of decision making in this form of enterprise.

Part I begins with an examination of the growing internationalization of industry and the forces behind this trend. A framework is provided in chapter 2 for interpreting the relationship between strategy and various control relationships in multinational firms. Chapter 3 provides a step-by-step examination of the evolution of strategy and structure within one multinational firm.

Part II concentrates on regional and global strategy—that is, strategy as seen from international headquarters. International portfolio strategy, as well as competitive, marketing, and logistics strategy for the multinational firm, are treated at length.

Part III presents an analysis of the international aspects of strategic decision making at the national level. This includes appraisal of new national environments, entry strategy, and new product introduction from a national subsidiary.

The final chapter in this part deals with political risk appraisal and strategies for managing national political risk.

Part IV examines various methods for coordinating strategic decision making within multinational firms. A number of coordinating mechanisms are considered, including annual cycle planning, capital budgeting, strategic planning systems, and various organization structures.

I am indebted to the many managers at Ford of Europe who gave so generously of their time in providing the material used in the several examples based on that organization—in particular, Robert A. Lutz, Erick Reickert, Peter Smith, John Waddell, Bill Hayden. Also, Peter Slater, Ford Motor Company Limited.

I also thank Valerie Acton for deciphering my notes and preparing the manuscript.

Part I
The Multinational in a Changing Environment

1

The Internationalization of Business and Business Strategy

O ne of the most important phenomena of the twentieth century has been the international expansion of industry. Today virtually all major firms have a significant and growing presence in business outside their country of origin.

A number of factors have contributed to this expansion. Dramatic improvement in the means of communication and transportation has reduced the barriers of distance between countries. When the Singer Company, one of the early multinationals, was incorporated in 1863, ocean travel was still largely by wooden ship. The first transatlantic telegraph cable did not come until a few years later, and telephone communication across the Atlantic was more than eighty years away. Today travel between countries is measured in hours rather than days. Japan's NEC Corporation has a decision room in its Tokyo office equipped with electronic systems that provide face-to-face communication in minutes with staff in various parts of the world.

Equally significant are the changes in the world economy. At one time, the U.S. market comprised the bulk of the total world demand for telephones, automobiles, petroleum, radios, and various household appliances. This is no longer the case. As other national companies expand and develop, the United States and many other traditional industrial countries, considered individually, represent a shrinking proportion of world demand. Industrialization, which at one time was confined almost exclusively to Western Europe and North America, has spread to include a host of additional countries, creating in its wake new opportunities and new competitors.

The growing importance of international business has not been lost on governments. Along with the expansion of traditional exports, they have observed with rising interest, and some apprehension, the growth of the multinational firm. During the immediate post–World War II period, the expansion of this form of enterprise was largely associated with the foreign direct investment of U.S. firms.

Participation in such companies today is much more evenly distributed. In more recent years, Japan and a number of European countries have led the growth rate in foreign direct investment. For the most part, developing countries remain recipients of such investment, though this is by no means universal. A small number of developing countries have launched their own multinational companies.

Above all, there has been an increase in international competition. The nation-state has become too narrow a definition of the firm's competitive sphere in an increasing number of industries.

Internationalized Industries

These changes in the international expansion of business bear a certain resemblance to industrial development in the latter part of the nineteenth century. Prior to that time, limitations in transport, communication, and organizational structure meant that the firm's effective operating environment was local rather than national in scope. The rise of the national firm did not appear in the United States until the 1890s. The appearance of companies operating on a national basis changed and widened the geographic scope of management's perception of its business environment. Planning limited to a purely local geographic area came to be seen as inadequate. Management's horizons broadened to encompass the rise of national competitors, national suppliers, and a changing industry structure that transcended previous boundaries.

A knowledge of local conditions remained essential, but, over time, the various elements comprising the firm's sphere of competition and its operating environment came to be seen in most industries in national rather than local terms. Firms operating on a less than national scale remained; however, they underwent a drastic change in their relative competitive posture within the industry as national companies emerged to dominate product areas as diverse as chemicals, packaged foods, oil, steel, agricultural equipment, and home appliances.

Much the same thing is happening today on an international level. With the rise of companies operating globally and regionally, the geographic scope of many industries has widened beyond national boundaries. In certain areas, the internationalization of industry has progressed to such a degree that the inadequacy of a purely national definition is evident. For example, it is difficult to interpret the oil and petrochemical business in other than an international context. The major oil companies produce their raw material in countries far removed from their downstream activities. Crude oil produced from the Middle East, Alaska, Indonesia, and the North Sea is coordinated with markets, refining operations, and chemical plants in the United States, Japan, Europe, and elsewhere. Refinery capacity is optimized on an international rather than a national basis. The price of oil is a global price, and the major oil companies calculate their competitive standing in terms of global sales and market share. The basis of their strategic advantage and survival is to be found not in any individual country but in their ability to coordinate and link resources and activities internationally. Smaller firms adjust their strategy to fit into this international industry structure. Strategists attempting to interpret the oil industry on a national, country-by-country basis are in much the same position as the famous blind men of India, trying to describe an elephant by each focusing on an individual portion of its anatomy.

Similarly, the aircraft industry, once comprised of several nationally based industries, is now clearly international in scope. Greatly expanded research and development costs have reduced the competitors to a handful. The major jet engine producers—General Electric, Pratt and Whitney, Rolls Royce, and Snecma of France—compete directly with each other, regardless of national location. Company success and survival depend on international performance measured in terms of international sales, profitability, and market share. Firms in this industry cannot survive without an international orientation and perception of the business environment.

Although the degree of industry internationalization varies, strong trends in the same direction are readily observable in an increasing number of products and services, including electronic components, office equipment, fast-food franchising, advertising, banking, pharmaceuticals, computers, automobiles, medical services, and insurance.

Forces of Change

Three major forces of change are behind the growing internationalization of industry. The first is economic development. The modern era has witnessed unparalleled economic growth in the industrial nations of the world, as well as many of the developing countries. Capital and resources generated by this economic upsurge have contributed to the rise of new international competitors, such as those from the newly industrialized countries of Singapore, Hong Kong, South Korea, Brazil, and others. Today many Western firms find themselves in direct competition with companies whose names they were scarcely aware of a few years ago.

Economic growth has also brought about a convergence among the industrial countries of the world in terms of product demand and production methods. Machines and products that find a ready market in one part of the world are often the same ones in demand elsewhere. This greater homogeneity makes national markets more accessible to international competitors.

The second major force is a lowering of institutional barriers to international mobility. Since World War II there has been a gradually declining trend in many of the institutional barriers impeding cross-border business activity. The various trade groups such as the European Community and the Andean Group have been effective in reducing tariffs and other border barriers on a regional basis.

On a more global level, the General Agreement on Tariffs and Trade (GATT) has been instrumental in reducing tariffs and quotas, as well as establishing rules of procedure governing international trade. The International Monetary Fund has helped overcome barriers associated with currency convertibility. Numerous other international bodies have contributed toward more uniform industrial standards. The multinational firm itself, by providing an enterprise form uniquely equipped for certain types of international business, has provided another powerful impetus toward more closely linked, international industries.

Perhaps the most powerful internationalizing force of all has been the impact of technology. Equally important to its effect on travel and communications is the higher technological content in many products and services and the associated pressures on many firms to do business on an international scale in order to achieve the volumes necessary to cover soaring research and development costs. As early as 1968, a report by the Organization of Economic Cooperation and Development (OECD) noted: "The efficient exploitation of advanced technologies calls for both technological resources beyond national boundaries and access to markets that are international in scope."[1] Since then, the potential economies associated with defraying research and development costs over an international rather than a national sphere of operation have, if anything, increased.

The change factors have not always moved in the same direction. At times tariffs and institutional barriers have increased, and they may be expected to do so again. Not infrequently, economic growth has been negative. Technological change has introduced a number of inventions, such as the electric steel furnace and the centrifugal process for refining uranium, that have reduced the scale required to attain minimum unit cost. But these may be seen as deviations about a long-term trend whose direction is toward the rationalization of industry on an international scale. The geographic scope of the industry for most companies will continue to widen beyond national boundaries, fundamentally changing the strategic posture of companies (domestic as well as international) in a manner that requires management to interpret its business environment on a regional or even global basis.

This growing movement of industry across national boundaries poses new opportunities and new threats. Managers accustomed to interpreting their business and environment on a national basis, focusing only on national competitors and opportunities, are increasingly vulnerable to changes of an international nature. The following examples are illustrative of some of the pressures.

Company A is a European subcontractor of components to a major automobile producer located a few miles away. Over the years, it has formed a close relationship with this firm. But now the automobile producer has notified its suppliers that it can obtain the same components from the Far East at reduced cost. Company A is faced with the choice of establishing facilities in one of the newly industrialized countries with low wage costs or possibly losing a major part of its business.

Company B is a moderate-sized producer of specialized equipment for wire cable manufacturers. It has been extremely successful in its home territory, capturing over 60 percent of this narrow market. Opportunities for further expansion are limited, particularly considering the slow growth in what has now become a mature product area. International expansion offers new opportunities for this firm in countries where the demand for its product is expanding, but preliminary investigation reveals that its competitors have already established themselves in the most promising national markets.

Company C was caught off balance when it discovered, one day, that a foreign competitor had emerged out of the blue with a bid to acquire one of its largest domestic distributors.

Company D is an advertising firm that has seen several major domestic clients expand abroad, where they have retained foreign advertising companies. These advertising firms, having established close relationships with the client in its international operations, are now actively bidding for company D's account with the parent company.

Such incidents are indicative of a restructuring of industry along more international lines. They are signals to management to adopt a more global concept of the firm's environment and competitive sphere, one that goes beyond international business in the sense of isolated international trade and investment initiatives to fundamental issues of overall strategy.

Corporate Strategy

Corporate strategy as a modern concept traces back to the writings of Igor Ansoff, Peter Drucker, and Kenneth Andrews, particularly their assertion that the most important task of top management is one of corporate direction, identifying what business the firm is in and what business it should be in. From the outset, corporate strategy has dealt with fundamental changes in the firm's business. Unlike long-range planning, it did not address future change within the context of the firm's existing business. The firm's business boundaries became a variable, the responsibility of forward-thinking management to plan for and alter if necessary.

Recent literature has interpreted this to mean that strategy deals with the relationship between the firm and its external environment (see figure 1–1). Managers thinking strategically about their business will need to identify and familiarize themselves with the firm's business environment. They will need to appraise and assess their actual and potential customers, competitors, suppliers, legal and political constraints, and so on. They will require a close knowledge of their own firm's capabilities and resources. The task of the strategist is to find a relationship or match between the firm and its environment that is consistent with the characteristics of that environment, as well as the firm's own objectives, resources, and capabilities.

Authors	Definitions
Andrews (1965)	"Strategy is the pattern of objectives, purposes or goals and major policies and plans for achieving these goals stated in such a way as to define what business the company is in or is to be in and what kind of company it is or is to be."
Ansoff (1965)	"To use an engineering term, the strategic problem is concerned with establishing an 'impedence match' between the firm and its environment or, in more usual terms, it is the problem of deciding what business the firm is in and what kind of businesses it will seek to enter."
Mintzberg (1979)	"Strategy formulation therefore involves the interpretation of the environment and the development of consistent patterns in streams of organizational decisions. . . ."
Steiner and Miner (1977)	"Strategy refers to the formulation of basic organizational missions, purposes, and objectives; policies and program strategies to achieve them; and the methods needed to assure that strategies are implemented to achieve organizational ends."
Bowman (1974)	"The institutional sphere deals essentially with the relationship between the organization and its environment. This is the area of corporate strategy."
Hofer and Schendel (1978)	"The basic characteristics of the match an organization achieves with its environment is called its strategy."
Porter (1980)	"The essence of formulating competitive strategy is relating a company to its environment."

C.R. Christensen, K.R. Andrews and J.L. Bower, *Business Policy: Texts and Cases* (Homewood, Ill.: Richard D. Irwin, 1973), p. 107; H.I. Ansoff, *Corporate Strategy* (New York: McGraw-Hill, 1965), pp. 5, 6; H. Mintzberg, *The Structuring of Organizations* (Englewood Cliffs, N.J.: Prentice-Hall, 1979), p. 25; A. Steiner and J.B. Miner, *Management Policy and Strategy*, (New York: Macmillan, 1977), p. 7; E. Bowman, "Epistemology, Corporate Strategy and Academe," *Sloan Management Review* (Winter 1974): 35; C.W. Hofer and D. Schendel, *Strategy Formulation: Analytical Concepts* (St. Paul: West Publishing Co., 1978), p. 6; M. Porter, *Competitive Strategy* (New York: Free Press, 1980), p. 3.

Figure 1–1. Definitions of Strategy and Strategy Formulation

International Strategy

The changes in industry indicate that for many firms, the environment that provides the context of their strategic analysis is becoming more international rather than national; however, it is an oversimplification in such cases to speak only in terms of global strategies. A close understanding of individual national environments as separate and distinct units of analysis remains essential—first, because there are many industries where the international links do not yet apply. A number of industries, such as brewing, building materials, and engineering equipment too bulky to be economically moved long distances, and tailored to individual specifications, can still be viewed as predominantly national in scope though, even here, there are distinct international elements (for example, brewing companies that have expanded internationally). Second, international strategy that fails to take account of the inevitable national peculiarities is courting disaster. In planning a new manufacturing facility in Belgium, a major U.S. manufacturing firm determined that the premium it would have to pay its employees for working at night was an additional 10 percent over the union wage for the day shift. The firm made its calculations justifying the plant (part of a European-wide manufacturing strategy) accordingly. Subsequently management was surprised to learn that legislation in that country required that all companies paying a nightshift premium were also required to pay the same premium to the day shift. Also, there are countries where tariffs and institutional barriers are such that business has to operate on a predominantly national basis. In many of the developing countries, competition and strategic options are closely constrained within national boundaries.

Finally, the major features that comprise any given national environment tend to be interrelated. For example, the market for a given product within a country is typically related to that country's overall economic performance; this in turn is influenced by its political, financial, and legal institutions, as well as cultural attitudes and priorities. In other words, each country represents a unique subsystem requiring individual assessment and interpretation.

This means that international management requires a dual perspective of its environment. As indicated in figure 1–2, strategy within the internationally oriented company matches the firm against its environment at two distinct levels. There is the strategic perspective that looks at each national environment as an individual system of political and institutional features, competitors, customers, and other facets. The question posed for management here is, What is our strategy for this country?

A different perspective is required in addressing multiple national environments and the question, What is our strategy in this group of countries? National environments are but subsets of a broader regional and/or global frame of reference. The two perspectives ultimately must be coordinated, though the emphasis placed on each, and the degree of coordination, will differ widely among companies. The organization of this book reflects these two distinct levels of strategic analysis.

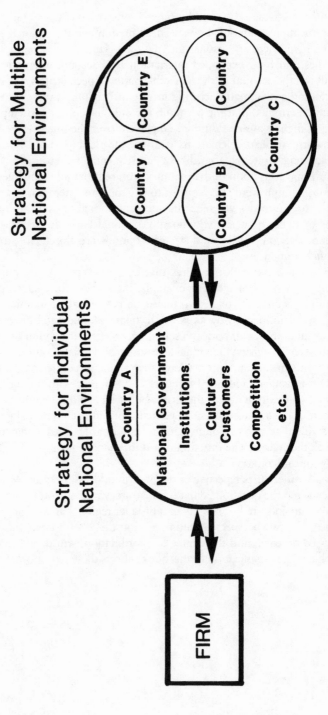

Figure 1–2. International Strategy: Matching the Firm to Its International Environment

2
Differing Approaches to Multinational Strategy

E xpansion of industry across national boundaries has been closely associated with the growth of multinational companies. The distinctive attribute of these firms, their ability to establish, control, and manage facilities on foreign soil, has enabled them to circumvent tariffs and a number of other barriers to international business. Many multinationals have established national subsidiaries in forty to fifty countries and conduct some type of business (including exporting and licensing) in over one-hundred national territories. The Shell Company has over eight-hundred operating companies in different parts of the world. The most challenging aspect of strategy for such firms, one might almost say the dilemma, is how to reconcile the infinite detailed knowledge required for successful operation in a particular national territory with the breadth of coverage required if the firm is to have an overall corporate strategy that gives pattern and direction to its worldwide operations.

One response to the complexity of managing in multiple national environments is to treat each as a separate and distinct entity. Strategy for any particular country is made almost independently of the firm's interests and operations in other parts of the world. Corporate strategy, for the firm as a whole, is comprised of a series of national strategies. However, some of the major forces of change in the world today are bringing major pressures to bear in the opposite direction—toward a more integrated strategic approach that sees each national environment as part of a larger international system.

The choice is sometimes summed up under the familiar centralization–decentralization dichotomy: what balance should management strike between the two, and what are its implications for strategy? Although this statement of the issue may be a useful first approximation, the terms *centralization* and *decentralization* are overly general, difficult to define, and subject to misinterpretation. This chapter sets out a framework for interpreting the different international control options within the multinational company and their implications for strategy.

Early Experience

The problem of increasing complexity with geographical expansion is not unique to multinational companies. Writing on the historical development of U.S. business firms and their administration, Alfred Chandler and Fritz Redlich point to analogous situations involving the geographic expansion of industrial organizations within the United States. They note that "geographical dispersion was the initial step in making modern industrial enterprise because it made necessary the distinction between headquarters and field. . . . The leading men at headquarters had also to coordinate the activities of the several field-units."[1]

This distinction was also illustrated in the expansion of the railroads. As U.S. railroads grew and extended their geographic coverage early in the nineteenth century, the administrative task became more complex. They reacted by establishing a dual-level structure: a central office headquarters with overall responsibility and operating subunits (for example, the Pennsylvania railroad had three such subunits: the lines east of Pittsburgh, those west of Pittsburgh, and those to St. Louis) with their own administrative structure.[2] The general manager of each railroad subunit serving a given geographic area became responsible for the day-to-day administrative tasks within that unit. The central office headquarters was responsible for ensuring coordination among subunits. The central office was also "to consider the major strategies of new construction and of purchase and sales of lines," that is, questions affecting the entire system.[3] The differing planning perspectives of the two levels are illustrated in figure 2–1.

This suggests that planning for complex environments does not proceed immediately to a single grand design that attempts to match all aspects of the firm to every feature of its environment. Rather, it proceeds on a piecemeal basis, breaking down the overall task into more manageable units of analysis. Plans developed for these units are then coordinated into a broader perspective, ultimately matching the entire firm to its overall environment.

Within larger firms, different parts of the corporate hierarchy tend to specialize on different levels of strategic planning. Managers close to particular operating environments are often responsible for developing substrategies that are then incorporated into a broader strategy by management at company headquarters.[4]

Planning in the Multinational

This hierarchical approach to strategy formulation is clearly evident in multinational companies. A multinational company's staff in France will typically approach planning from the perspective of what is the best strategy for operations in France. Working on a day-to-day basis within that country, the staff members are in the best position to interpret the many intricate and complex features that will influence the firm's strategic adjustment to that particular national environment; however, they are unlikely to have an equally close knowledge of other countries.

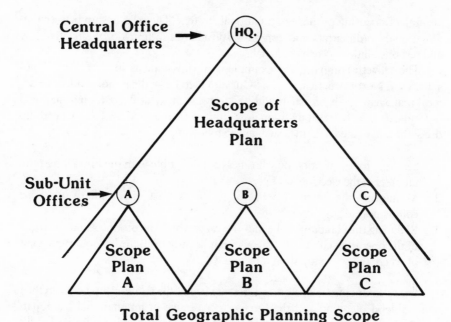

Total Geographic Planning Scope

Figure 2–1. Planning Scope of Railroad Administrative Units

Usually a separate management group will be charged with planning that takes a broader view of the company's businesses in several countries. They will have a different, multicountry perspective, addressing questions such as these:

Should we increase our investment in certain countries while reducing it in others?

Is there advantage to be gained from coordinating our businesses in one part of the world with those in others?

Should we standardize our products internationally?

Strategic Planning Modes

Multinational companies vary widely in the priority they place on the different levels of strategy formulation. In practical terms, this difference is reflected in the relationship between international headquarters and the multinational firms' various national subsidiaries. Typically the former is concerned with strategy at the regional and/or global level, while the latter takes a narrower view of its environment, focusing primarily on national strategy. The relationship between international headquarters and company subsidiaries in terms of the relative role and responsibilities of each is crucial.

The Olivetti company, for example, with investments in twenty U.S. subsidiaries in North America, states, "Our aim is to leave them independent under local management." Consistent with this view, strategy at Olivetti's international headquarters, in Ivrea, Italy, is mainly limited to resource allocation portfolio decisions and related activities such as the following:

1. Selecting for acquisition new businesses compatible with the firm's long-term interests in the electronic office,
2. Monitoring the financial performance of its existing subsidiary operating companies,
3. Reducing the company stake in those cases where the products and strategies of the operating companies diverge significantly from the headquarters' view of where the company should be going.[5]

Other companies take a quite different view of the relationship between their national-level planning and the broader perspective of international headquarters. At Texas Instruments, strategic planning tends to be highly centralized at the company's Dallas headquarters. Strategy formulated there includes:

1. A regional and global analysis of competition
2. A core of product designs that are standardized around the world
3. Centralized and coordinated R&D to avoid costly duplication
4. Production rationalized on a global basis to make maximum use of volume-related efficiencies on an international scale
5. Global pricing policies[6]

Strategy here relies much more on a global and regional view of the firm's environment. Planning at the national level still plays an important role, though its scope and responsibility are reduced. The emphasis is on strategies that coordinate subsidiaries regionally and globally. The three modes shown in figure 2–2 define three different headquarters-subsidiary relationships, or control structures, and their associated implications for strategy.

Holding Company Mode

Multinationals that adopt this mode will place maximum emphasis on a national view of strategy. Strategic plans will be based on the perceptions of locally based staff in the firm's various national subsidiaries; these have both the freedom and the responsibility to formulate strategy within the national territory of their lo-

	Strategic Planning Role	
Control Structure	Regional/Global Level (International Headquarters)	National Level (Subsidiary)
Holding Company Mode 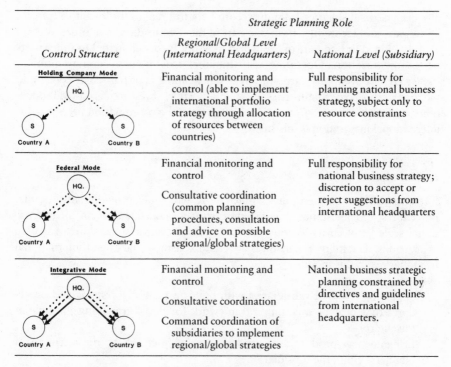	Financial monitoring and control (able to implement international portfolio strategy through allocation of resources between countries)	Full responsibility for planning national business strategy, subject only to resource constraints
Federal Mode	Financial monitoring and control Consultative coordination (common planning procedures, consultation and advice on possible regional/global strategies)	Full responsibility for national business strategy; discretion to accept or reject suggestions from international headquarters
Integrative Mode	Financial monitoring and control Consultative coordination Command coordination of subsidiaries to implement regional/global strategies	National business strategic planning constrained by directives and guidelines from international headquarters.

Figure 2–2. Control and Strategy in the Multinational: Three Alternative Modes

Note: Dotted lines: financial monitoring and control; dashed lines: consultative coordination; and solid lines: command coordination.

cation. International headquarters in this type of structure acts as a banker, monitoring the financial performance of the subsidiaries and controlling the allocation of resources (portfolio strategy). There is no direct attempt to coordinate the strategic planning of the national subsidiaries. Within the resources available to them, they are treated as autonomous units. Strategy in this type of multinational proceeds on a country-by-country basis, with each national subsidiary developing its own strategy, subject only to financial resource constraints from international headquarters.

The holding company mode places the primary responsibility for strategic planning at the national level with subsidiary managers and staff in direct contact with the local national environment. Their freedom and independence of action minimizes reaction time, contributing to rapid response to national needs and opportunities with a minimum of red tape and bureaucratic control from international headquarters, the latter often far from the scene of the action. Its disadvantages stem from these strengths. The independence of the firm's internationally dispersed subsidiaries from any central control makes it difficult to transfer know-how and techniques from one part of the organization to another. A good idea developed in one part of the world may not be disseminated to other parts of the organization. Operating with minimal cross-national communication, these may not even be aware of it. This shortcoming is of particular concern in the more technological industries, where duplication of research is costly. Production also has to proceed on a national basis, since the coordination necessary for international integration is missing.

Federal Mode

International headquarters plays a much more active role, providing institutional procedures and assistance that facilitate strategy coordination on an international scale between its various subsidiaries; however, it stops short of issuing instructions. The following features are characteristic of the role of international headquarters in this mode:

1. Supplying national subsidiaries with uniform planning systems and procedures that provide a common framework for decision making throughout the enterprise.
2. Bringing new product ideas and production methods to the attention of planners within the subsidiaries.
3. Providing information and advice on international trends in world trade, international shifts in business activity, changes in foreign supply sources, and other relevant matters outside the scanning horizon of national subsidiary managers.
4. Facilitating the transfer of company experience and products from one national subsidiary to another.
5. Providing technical advice and service.

The decision on what use, if any, to make of this information and assistance lies with the firm's national subsidiaries, which remain free to make their own strategic decisions.

The advantage of this approach is that it opens up opportunities for cross-national coordination while retaining the independence of management within the multinational firm's various national businesses to plan strategy for which they bear clear responsibility. But this discretion also means that certain strategies requiring close coordination between the firm's national businesses may not be practicable where each subsidiary has complete freedom to accept or reject such moves. The more frequent contact with headquarters in this structure may also be a source of friction, particularly since headquarters staff members are less closely in touch with local conditions.

Integrative Mode

The multinational firm's various national subsidiaries are not operated as independent entities or subject only to voluntary international coordination. National plans are viewed as parts of an internationally integrated system that can be coordinated at the instruction of international headquarters in pursuit of regional and global objectives.

Financial monitoring and control, together with common planning systems, advice, and assistance, are supplemented by "command coordination", directives from international headquarters that specify the role of the various subsidiaries within the overall strategic plan. National strategy formulation within the national subsidiaries is limited to those areas not covered by headquarters directives.

By interpreting the environment on a global basis, such multinationals are able to spot opportunities and threats that may be beyond the horizon of any of the subsidiaries. The firm adopting this mode is able to bring the full weight of its resources to bear on selected competitors or markets. It can make more effective use of its mobile resources by shifting them from countries where they are underutilized to parts of the world where demand exceeds supply. By coordinating the selection of its products (which products shall we produce?), it is able to select among the best available within its worldwide network. It is able to ensure the use of experience attained at high cost in one country in another territory where it may be relevant. Production facilities in different countries can be integrated into the production of common products, achieving economies of international scale (where they exist).

In its emphasis on the wider strategic perspective, this mode also incurs a number of major disadvantages. Perhaps the greatest is the behavioral impact on managers and staff within its national subsidiaries, which now have to operate within the bounds of numerous guidelines and constraints from headquarters. Strategic planning continues at this level, though within limits imposed by the need for conformity with the wider strategy.

Frictions and frustration may arise from a fundamental difference in planning perspectives. Management within the national subsidiaries inevitably notes that it is in a better position to judge the needs of its national environment. Headquarters is seen to be out of touch. From the perspective of headquarters, management within its national units takes a too narrow view of the world. By not looking beyond its restricted horizons to the wider possibilities, it is in danger of suboptimizing.

This conflict of interest and perception is often readily observable in major decisions taken for the good of the total system but that inevitably have an adverse effect on some parts of that system while benefiting others. For example, during the selection of its worldwide line of 360 computers, IBM headquarters had to choose among a number of product designs submitted by its various national operating units. The final selection inevitably led to the rejection of certain product proposals, the result of years of hard work. Careers and budgets were affected.

Not least of the difficulties is the potential bureaucratic effect of a large headquarters staff. Linking the firm's various international businesses requires intensive communication between headquarters and the various subsidiaries. Forms, paperwork, international meetings, and executive travel multiply.

Variability of Modes

The distinctions noted in figure 2–2 are rarely so clear-cut. Even multinationals adopting the holding company mode rarely limit their relationship with their subsidiaries entirely to questions of resource allocation and financial performance. The type and degree of control exercised by international headquarters over the strategy of its subsidiaries will vary, even within the same firm, according to a number of factors.

Function. The degree and type of control exercised by international headquarters will vary by function. In particular, certain functions requiring close contact with the local national environment, such as sales, distribution, and promotion, often will be accorded a high degree of autonomy, even within those multinationals adopting a predominantly integrative mode. Research typically is carried out under close headquarters control to avoid duplication.

Operating Unit. The firm may wish to discriminate among its subsidiaries regarding the degree of control and integration with headquarter's plans. A successful operation may be subject to less direction from international headquarters, for example, than one that has experienced severe setbacks and requires financial and other assistance.

Territory. National differences in trade barriers, government policy, customer preferences, and other factors require a change of planning mode in different countries and regions. For example, a number of firms operate a highly integrated regional approach to planning within the tariff-free European Community while allowing more autonomy and independence to their operations in other parts of the world.

Attitudes and Outlook of Management. The attitudes and capacity for international cooperation among managers at different levels of the hierarchy and working in different parts of the world is perhaps the most important ingredient of all. Where managerial understanding, flexibility, and company culture are conducive to a meeting of minds across organizational and geographic boundaries, formal control relationships become less important.

Levels of Strategic Planning

In all but the smallest firms, strategy involves a hierarchy of plans and planning activity. At the lower level, strategic planning addresses segments of the environment, considered as discrete planning units. At a higher level, planning takes a broader view, ultimately encompassing all such units.

For domestic firms, the distinction or boundaries separating one unit of analysis from another for planning purposes may be provided by differences in customers, product lines, technology, or other characteristics. For companies with operations in different parts of the world, geographic distinctions are introduced. These are usually in the form of national boundaries, although there is nothing sacrosanct about these. It is conceivable that in some situations, other territorial distinctions—for example, climatic conditions or religious differences—would serve equally well or better. But historically and in practice, the fact that national boundaries represent different political jurisdictions, each with its own laws, currency, and other institutions, has acted to insulate national business operations in one country from those in another. Due to the lowering of tariffs and other barriers, this insulating property has diminished in many regions, such as the European Community, but for the most part, national boundaries still provide a natural line of demarcation.

We will proceed on the assumption that national boundaries are the relevant geographic distinction used by internationally oriented companies to define their environmental units. Strategy that is directed at matching the firm to the threats and opportunities of a single geographic unit, such as a particular national environment, will be referred to as strategy at the national level. Strategy that takes a regional or global perspective encompassing several such units will be referred to as strategy at the regional/global level.

3
The Practice of Strategic Planning in a Multinational Company: An Evolutionary View

> When Russia and China and India and South America come into consuming power, what are you going to do? Surely you don't think that Britain and America will be able to supply them? Surely you don't visualize Britain and America as nothing but vast factories to supply the world? A moment's thought will make clear why the future must see nation after nation taking over its own work of supply. And we ought to be glad to help the work along.
>
> Henry Ford[1]

T his chapter takes a close look at strategy formulation in practice. We will be interested in examining the following issues in the context of strategic planning by one firm, Ford.[2]

1. How does the multinational enterprise determine the relative importance of strategy formulation at the two planning levels? In some companies, regional and global strategic planning plays a major role. In others, strategic planning takes place predominantly at the national level.
2. How does the approach to international strategic planning change over time? Planning is closely related to learning. Present plans are based on the best available evidence and knowledge. As the firm accumulates experience, this changes. The novice company in a particular national environment is in a quite different situation from the experienced firm. Where the former may be swamped by the complexity of the new environment, the latter is able to rely on accumulated knowledge and planning routines based on previous experience to reduce complexity and open up new possibilities. In other words, the firm's plans and planning methods will evolve over time. The right approach at one stage of its development may not be right for another.
3. How do multinational companies reconcile the differing perceptions, attitudes, and aims of planners and managers in different countries? In their study of decision making in a firm, Cyert and Marsh found that informal negotiations and maneuvering between different coalitions of managers played a significant role.[3] Even within a purely national enterprise, we may expect decision making to reflect disparate interests and backgrounds.

The fact that managers within the multinational type of enterprise are located in business units separated by geographic distance and under the influence of different cultural and institutional forces greatly complicates the problem of consensus formation and decision making. Such international barriers and influences are bound to affect strategy formulation; to what degree and how this effect is evidenced in practice is a matter of major interest. This chapter provides insight into these issues by reviewing the development of strategic planning in one multinational enterprise, the Ford Motor Company and, particularly, its European operations.

Early Internationalization

Ford went international a few weeks after its incorporation; the sixth car produced by the firm was sent to a Canadian distributor in 1903. Early internationalization followed the classic pattern. Initial expansion abroad was based on agents and dealers. Within a few years, the company had sales agents in England and twenty-two dealers marketing its products in France, Germany, Belgium, Spain, Holland, Denmark, Sweden, Poland, Austria, and Russia.

Ford's initial strategic advantage in Europe, as in its home market, was based on a light, efficient car design complementing Henry Ford's concept of mass production techniques and the lower prices these made possible. Compared to the individually handcrafted European cars, the early Ford product appeared relatively crude and unrefined; however, there was little doubt of its durability and engineering excellence. By 1912, the Ford Model T was the best-selling automobile in Europe.

The company's product and manufacturing strategy, the central pillar of its success, was oriented about the U.S. home market. Communications between the firm's Detroit headquarters and the rapidly growing sales of its foreign agents and distributors were hampered by the technological limitations of that period. The company's representatives in the various countries initially had to devise their own plans with a minimum of control and support from the parent company.

With success abroad and an increasing commitment to foreign investment in the form of sales companies and assembly and manufacturing operations, the parent company began to exercise greater control. In the 1920s, the English manufacturing plant and other European assembly and sales companies were directly linked to the parent company. According to a Ford publication documenting the European history of the firm during that era, "Detroit gave the orders and controlled operations with 100% ownership."[4]

Closely defined rules were set out in the "Ford bible," the company manual containing precise instructions on company procedures on accounting, sales, production, and purchasing. These instructions, based on U.S. experience, dictated standards, such as which side of the car the steering wheel should be on, sometimes at odds with European conditions.

Ford policies on unions and plant location were also applied to Europe. One story has it that Henry Ford refused to lay the foundation stone for a new plant in Rotterdam, one of Europe's major ports, because the proposed site was insufficiently close to water, as set out in company policy. Ford turned away as the mayor and other civic dignitaries waited; "No water, no plant" was his explanation. Two years later, a Ford plant opened at a new location, suitably located the requisite distance from navigable water.[5]

A proposed strategy to coordinate European operations from Europe rather than from the United States was forwarded as early as 1928. The aim was to unify Ford's European activities under the leadership of the company's operations in England. It was a bold plan that eventually proved impracticable due to the introduction of sharply increased tariffs and other trade barriers in the early 1930s. Under the impact of such protectionist measures, the company's manufacturing plants in England, Germany, and France began independent manufacture of their own products. The onset of World War II completed the fragmentation. Ford operations in the various countries became subject to national government control and the pursuit of national objectives.

The International Division

An international division was formed in 1946, inheriting the Ford holdings that emerged from the war. Shortly afterward, management determined that there was excessive overlap and confusion among the firm's different European operations. Some insight into the postwar fragmentation of Ford's European businesses can be gained from their financial structure. The parent company owned 59 percent of Ford of England, which in turn owned 60 percent of Ford of Denmark, which owned 60 percent of Ford of Sweden, which owned 60 percent of Ford of Finland.[6]

Fragmentation was also reflected in product planning. In the early postwar years, each Ford major manufacturing plant in Europe went its own way. Design and development proceeded independently in the United States, England, and Germany.

Product planning was very informal. Terry Beckett, who eventually became managing director of Ford's operations in the United Kingdom, describes product planning in the early 1950s:

> The managing director would simply call in his key men, the engineer, the production boss and so on—and tell them "I want a new car in two years' time, about the size of the Morris Minor. We'll want 400 a day, the weight should be perhaps 1,600 pounds. The engine displacement 800 to 1000 cc's, acceleration

from 0 to 60 in 26 seconds and a touring fuel consumption of 40 plus. Now I want some styling and engineering ideas from you. Let's meet again in a month's time."[7]

The growing movement toward European economic integration eventually gave renewed impetus to closer coordination among Ford's European plants. The proposals for a tariff-free Europe, incorporated in the 1957 Treaty of Rome establishing the European Community, were reinforced by developments in the automotive market. Competition had become intense, putting pressure on profit margins. European car models were changed more frequently; production processes themselves had become more sophisticated and highly technical. Ford's duplicate design and production facilities in England and Germany offered a clear opportunity for rationalization.

Regional Coordination

In 1967 Ford established a European regional headquarters at Warley, Essex, on a site once occupied by the East India Company. Ford of Europe, the official title of the new organization, was responsible for coordinating Ford's fifteen European national operations into a regional network, producing a single European line of cars. This strategy differed sharply from those of its European competitors, which produced their products mainly within their respective national markets, servicing other European markets primarily through exports. Product design was geared primarily to conditions and requirements of the same national home territory. The Ford regional approach differed also from that of its U.S. competitor, General Motors, which continued to produce separate product lines in England and Germany with separate distribution networks and brand names.

Under the new Ford approach, products would be designed from the outset for a region rather than a country and also would be produced on a regional basis. Production of standardized components would be concentrated in several European countries and transshipped to assembly plants. From there the finished product went to a dealer network operating in each country under the Ford name. Duplication of research, design, and development would be minimized, and longer production runs for standardized products would make possible lower unit costs.

Some problems became quickly evident. The new regional strategy required that the many different nationalities that made up Ford of Europe work together, not just by communicating through letter and telephone but side by side on joint projects and assignments. Different national factories and facilities also became interdependent. A stoppage in one plant could seriously affect the functioning of other, previously independent operations. This last quality became the source of some early frictions and reservations about the Europeanization program.

Two years after the establishment of Ford of Europe, the London *Times* reported that an internal management struggle was threatened within the new regional organization.[8] The immediate problem was a strike in Ford's British plants, which had brought its other European plants, dependent on British supplied components, to a halt. A request was received from Ford's Cologne plant to produce parts which were formerly arriving from Britain. Comments were voiced about falling morale and Anglo-German frictions which threw doubt on the wisdom of the whole enterprise.

Within a few years, the situation had changed significantly. The major doubts and frictions of a national character sharply diminished. Much of this shift was due to increased face-to-face contact between the various nationalities. Travel between the firm's various facilities had become routine. Ford established its own airline, operating a regular service to its European plants. Eventually executives of different nationalities began working together on a first-name basis. The initial tensions turned out to be, in the words of one Ford manager, "strictly temporary."[9]

Strategic Planning at Ford of Europe

In the early days of Ford of Europe there was no set procedure for producing an overall strategic plan for the region. Formal strategic planning focused on a few special areas, such as new product development and capital facilities. The nature of strategy formulation at that time is best illustrated by specific example.

Planning Product Strategy: The Global Perspective

In 1976 the Ford Motor Company launched the Fiesta, its first truly small car and the first entry of any U.S. producer into the small car segment of the market, referred to in the trade as the B car segment. Investment and development costs ultimately reached $1 billion, the largest single investment up to that time in Ford's history.

The sequence of events that culminated in this radical change in Ford's product strategy can be traced to a management presentation in Dearborn, Michigan, on September 15, 1972. Henry Ford II and a group of top executives were listening to a management presentation of changes taking place in world automotive markets. One major change was the market share of the North American market relative to the rest of the world. Historically the former had made up the bulk of total world automotive sales, but in the late 1960s, automotive sales in North America for the first time accounted for less than half the total. Moreover, it was clear that this was part of a long-term trend. Sales in Canada and the United States were shrinking steadily relative to growth in the rest of the world. Company projections of the world automotive market indicated that this trend would continue. Europe was rapidly emerging as the world's largest single regional market (figure 3–1). Two more points were also brought out: outside North America, Ford's market share had dropped from 12 percent in 1961 to 9.2 percent in 1971, and two new small B cars had been introduced in Europe, the Fiat and Renault, which upset the industry's traditional view of low profitability for this type of product.

Another important consideration for Ford was that the type of B cars preferred in the various countries used to vary widely in terms of size of performance and comfort; for example, Italians seemed to prefer the higher performance, less comfortable models, while the reverse specification sold well in the French market.

These product differences were reinforced by the national orientation of the present B car manufacturers. Although sales to other countries were considered important, products were designed primarily to meet the needs of their respective national markets. This meant that the European B car market traditionally had been split along national lines. By themselves, none of these national subcategories could support sufficient volume to offer an attractive opportunity for a major outside producer. The introduction of the new Italian and French B cars threatened to alter these distinctions. These new B entries commanded a much higher price and were potentially more profitable. They were also much closer together in performance and internal dimensions.

Threats and Opportunities

The coming together of the previously fragmented B car segment of the European car market offered special opportunities for Ford. To a much greater extent than any of the other B car producers, Ford was now established, organized, and equipped to market its products on a European-wide basis. A Ford B car would reinforce the company's position in the French, Italian, and Spanish markets, an area of historic weakness. A Ford B car would also contribute to trading up. It was evident that many first-time buyers of a small car eventually trade up to a larger, more profitable model within the same manufacturer's range. This benefit was not available to Ford at the time. There was also a distinct possibility that a Ford B car produced for Europe might eventually reinforce the company's product line in Latin America and the United States, either through exports or actual production in those countries.

Difficulties were also evident. Could the company design and produce a new European car sufficiently attractive to compete with the formidable new B cars at a profit? Even with the higher price of the new B cars, it would require a reduction in costs of about $100 below those of Ford's smallest European model at the time, the Ford Escort. Considering the rigorous efforts that had gone into keeping Escort costs down, this was a formidable challenge. Moreover, where would the company find the capacity and other resources required to produce

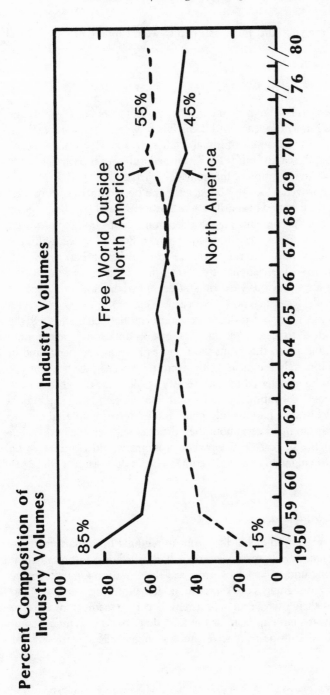

Note : Excludes East Bloc Countries

Figure 3–1. Composition of the Worldwide Car Market

and market a new model? Ford European plants were running at close to full capacity.

World Headquarters: Initial Budget Approval

The analysis presented to Ford management contained suggested dimensions and other characteristics for a European Ford B car. These were in the nature of recommendations on paper, the result of initial studies by a new section of Ford's Product Planning and Research staff (PP&R) formed only five months earlier to carry out an intensive investigation of the small car market.

Management approved a healthy budget for the development and market testing of a concept B car aimed primarily at the European market. The program now had the blessing of the company's highest decision-making body to proceed.

Developing the new-concept car, now code named Bobcat, posed a number of exceptional problems. Ford had no previous B car on the market; hence, unlike most other new model development projects, the objective was not to develop a replacement for a previously existing model but to develop a concept for a completely new model for which no Ford precedent existed.

The cross-national mode of product development that characterized the progress of Bobcat added to the complications. Work on Bobcat had begun some five months earlier, and up to this point the Bobcat program had been sited in the United States. Ultimately the project, if it were to proceed past the concept stage, would have to be transferred to Europe. Above all, a car designed for the European market required continual contact with that market from the outset. The head of the PP&R staff had already made numerous trips to Europe. He talked to Ford's European managers about their product requirements. Although the concept stage of the Bobcat's development program would continue to be based in Dearborn, Michigan, the time had come to begin discussions with Ford's European operations.

European Regional Headquarters

When the PP&R team arrived at Ford's European regional headquarters in autumn 1972, the product development team there had heard only informally that a new study was being undertaken on a proposed B car. At the time, they were heavily involved in redesigning Ford's Escort model. Not long ago they had stopped all work on their own version of a new B car. A member of Ford of Europe's Advanced Car Planning team at the time describes the technical comment made by Ford of Europe product engineers on the PP&R proposal for Bobcat:

> In some cases it was necessary to say—"Don't do that." We know from experience that usage and corrosion patterns in Europe are such that this particular

component design will entail heavy warranty costs. Part of the comment was at this nitpicking level. There was plenty of time to correct this type of feature. More serious at this stage were questions such as braking/steering stability and turning circle. American engineers could not understand why we in Europe were concerned on this score. They did not understand European driving conditions, the different physical environment. They were designing the car on a very logical basis. For example, they would look in a book for certain legally required standards and plan the product to fit them. We said, the European buyer won't accept that and it has nothing to do with legal reasons. No American can understand why we want a 30 foot turning circle. Most American roads are 40 feet wide. The braking stability standard used in the United States assumed road lanes 14 feet wide, versus 7 feet commonly found in Europe.[10]

From the view of the parent company PP&R staff, however, it would be misleading to suggest that they were either unaware of or did not appreciate these differences. They had brought the Bobcat to Ford of Europe at this stage of the program knowing that they would need assistance in tailoring the car to the European driving environment and European tastes.

Planning at the National Level

The Ford of Europe planning teams were particularly concerned that sales of the new B car might be at the expense of one of the company's existing models, the Escort. Partly in response to this, the Ford of Europe product development group put forward two smaller alternative B car proposals, one 120 inches in length and the other 130 inches, as compared to Bobcat's 140 inches.

Proposed specifications for these three different-sized B cars were sent to all of the Ford of Europe national subsidiaries. Each subsidiary made its own forecasts of projected sales in its market for each proposed model. These forecasts were assembled and aggregated by the Ford of Europe regional headquarters marketing staff into an overall company consensus estimate of projected sales for the three alternative car concepts. Taking into account expected volume, prices, and the degree to which each model represented incremental sales (those over and above those obtained by the Escort). Bobcat was clearly the major opportunity.

Operation Eagle

Planning the expansion of production facilities, code named project Eagle, was another important strand in the Ford international strategy. Initially project Eagle and Ford's new B car were separate and distinct projects, but gradually they became linked. It made sense to locate the new production facilities in a country that would reinforce the firm's strategy to gain a larger sector of the B car market and to strengthen its position in the Mediterranean countries. A new plant in

Spain producing components for the new car would not only provide needed production capacity, it would also establish Ford with a Spanish base to overcome the sizable tariffs that government imposed on imports into the country. The Spanish government, clearly interested in the employment and exports such a facility would provide, indicated that it would be prepared to negotiate existing tariffs and other legislative restrictions that could hamper cross-national operations between a new Spanish plant and other Ford European production facilities.

The calculations for the new Ford plant were complex. Return on investment was not only linked to negotiations with the Spanish government; it also depended on the success of Bobcat sales across Europe. It required a coordinated flow of components not only among Ford plants in Spain, Germany, Britain, and France but also from the many outside suppliers who would provide 1,793 of the new car's 3,000 components. How would Ford's production methods work in the agrarian Spanish society? Sociologists were hired to advise the company. A number of Ford executives were sent to language school to learn Spanish.[11]

Thirty possible sites for the plant were examined. Eventually a 640-acre site, planted in onions and artichokes, was selected. Nineteen months after groundbreaking, the first engine for the Bobcat, now called by its production name, Fiesta, came off the new assembly line.[12]

Interaction of Regional and National Planning Perspectives

Ford's regional headquarters ultimately had direct responsibility for the design and development of the new car, as well as the planning and coordination of production facilities on a regional basis.

Market research in connection with the new product design was also the primary responsibility of Ford of Europe, though carried out in close cooperation and consultation with national planning staff. An early phase of the market research included market surveys of several thousand households in five European countries. Subsequent tests were in the form of product clinics showing proposed designs, along with competitor products, to carefully selected groups. In some clinics, interviewees were flown from different national locations to central points where their reaction to the different product proposals could be assessed. The objective was to arrive at the best product design for Western Europe.

Ford's national subsidiaries had primary responsibility for planning the national marketing and distribution of the new product. Planning here focused on questions of distribution marketing, including national promotion, pricing, incentive schemes, and introduction dates.

Close coordination was required between the regional-global and national planning staffs on a number of points. Not all of these were susceptible to clear-cut distinctions based on lines of authority. There was inevitably an area where the two planning perspectives overlapped calling for the use of discretion and common sense in determining the relative contribution of each. For example,

Ford regional staff, based on their market research, developed a European-wide theme to be used in the promotional campaign that would launch the new product. When the theme was presented to the various national subsidiaries, most accepted it with adaptations as to language and details; however, a number of subsidiaries believed that the theme was not suitable for their national territories and subsequently developed their own promotional campaigns. In general, planners at the national level were considered the authorities on local national market characteristics. Their advice was sought and almost invariably taken whenever questions relating to national conditions arose. The role of regional planning was to synthesize and coordinate the various national contributions into a single regional perspective.

Planning Development

The Bobcat project may be seen as part of a continuous, evolutionary development in Ford planning. Prior to this project, strategic planning at Ford of Europe, in the sense of formal planning, turned largely about new capital facilities, product planning, and market sales forecasts.

The size and complexity of the Bobcat project stimulated and contributed to further development in Ford planning procedures. In the late 1970s, Ford of Europe introduced systematic strategic planning on an annual basis. Plans drawn up by the various European subsidiaries at the national level, concerned largely with marketing strategy in a particular country, feed into the regional strategic plan for Ford of Europe, which sets out the firm's strategy, covering manufacturing, logistics, and product and marketing strategy on a regional basis. The regional strategic plan eventually is submitted to Ford world headquarters, providing an input into the overall global corporate strategy.

The various planning levels—national, regional, and global—are further linked through a number of mechanisms, which include interlocking membership on company boards. Ford of Europe executives may be members of the board of directors of one or more national subsidiaries, as well as members of the Ford of Europe board of directors and/or the board of the parent company. In addition, there are various special project teams moving between the different organizational levels, special assignments, international corporate meetings and conferences, and the constant flow of executives from one part of the organization to another.

Nature of Strategy

The Ford experience tells us something about the nature of strategy formulation in multinational companies. Much of what is eventually seen to be the strategy of the company is not necessarily perceived as such initially. Ford's plant in Spain may, with the benefit of hindsight, be viewed as part of the firm's overall strategy to expand its market penetration in southern Europe (the Bobcat project was sometimes referred to as Ford's southern strategy). This was not the case at the outset. The proposal for a new plant was first put forward to provide additional capacity for Ford's existing products. Only later did it become connected with the production of the new car and a Spanish location. The new product itself was stimulated by observation of global product trends and competitor products. Developing links among previously independent projects and activities is an important aspect of strategy formulation.

It is also apparent that cross-national strategy involves matters not readily susceptible to technical analysis. There is considerable dependence on the exercise of judgment and even intuition. Ford's decision to go for international sourcing of production, transshipping the components, and assembling them in different countries presented a number of major uncertainties. Would the new European Economic Community implement tariff reductions? What would be the union reaction to jobs presumed lost to foreign plants? There were also questions of government controls, exchange rates, and other factors, many of which remain areas of major uncertainty.

National differences and traditions impose additional problems in intracompany coordination. Coordination among the firm's business operations in different countries is not simply a matter of organizational structure and hierarchical authority. Perhaps equally important is the frequent opportunity for face-to-face contact, cross-border job assignments (both long term and short term) shared responsibilities, interlinking systems and routines (such as plans at the various levels), and informal contact among nationalities. Ford's experience indicates that nationally based frictions in working situations tend to subside as cross-border contact increases.

The relationship between strategic planning at the different levels within the firm is subject to change over time. During the initial period of Ford's expansion, planning at the regional/global level was minimal. The complexities of planning for diverse national environments was, in effect, contracted out to agents and distributors located within the various national markets. Subsequently the firm tried to impose a higher degree of central authority through the adoption abroad of its U.S. policies and procedures (the era of the Ford bible). This ethnocentric approach was soon abandoned for a much looser form of control.

This early period stands in sharp contrast to the internationally coordinated planning and operations that have characterized Ford's European planning in later years. Over time the emphasis has shifted toward planning carried out at regional and global headquarters within a framework that closely integrates national plans into a regional perspective.

The change is one that has been observed in other international companies. A high degree of autonomy at the national business level is frequently associated with early international expansion. In a number of firms, there is a subsequent tendency toward increasing emphasis on strategic planning that adopts a wider multicountry perspective. As in the case of Ford, movement in this direction is not necessarily uniform, nor is it necessarily desirable in all cases. Ford's shift toward a regional/global strategy appears to have been conditioned by a number of factors.

Corporate Knowledge of the International Environment

Initially knowledge of foreign environments was very limited. The small Ford New York staff established at the outset had to deal with countries in Latin America, Asia, and Africa, as well as in Europe. Although certain individuals may have had extensive knowledge and experience abroad, the company lacked a coherent data base on diverse local national conditions specific to its own interests.

Since the early 1900s, the company has built up a corps of managers experienced in the various requirements of different national automotive markets. Environmental knowledge has been accumulated in both a personal sense (managers trained and experienced in interpreting different national environments) and an institutional sense (referring to the firm's buildup of an extensive store of data on automotive markets, government requirements, production methods, and market information essential to present planning). Over time the firm has developed a data base that consolidates information on a regional/global basis and managers able to process this information for purposes of strategy formulation.

National Barriers

This refers particularly to barriers in the form of tariffs and other obstacles to cross-border transfer and communication. Early tentative moves toward higher regional coordination were frustrated by the protectionist era of the 1930s. Without the lowering of tariffs brought about by the formation of the European Community, it is doubtful that Ford's regional strategy, based on international coordination of its European operations, would have been practicable.

Tariffs are only one of a large number of national barriers relevant to the issue. Differences in national industrial standards and legislation, price controls, customer preferences, work practices, currency fluctuations—in fact, any impediment that hinders interaction among the firm's business operations in different countries—will favor an emphasis on strategy formulated at the national level. This also includes differences in national preferences and tastes. Consumer preferences with respect to automotive products were found to be sufficiently similar to support a common product line, but there is no assumption that this will be true for food, clothing, housing, or other products. National differences in taste may be so great that they obviate multicountry strategies based on common products.

Technology

A central feature of Ford's European strategy is the prospect of competitive advantage through lower costs, which in turn depend on efficiencies of large-scale (European-scale) production. This requires an extensive headquarters staff at Ford's regional offices, in addition to the staff at Ford's U.S. world headquarters. Are the added costs and red tape worth it? To a large degree, that will be technically determined by the efficiencies of large-scale production.

It appears that this technological relationship has been changing. There is a perception, evident in both the statements and the actions of the industry, that the minimum efficient size (MES) required to make full use of efficiencies of scale is increasing. At one time, it was widely accepted that the MES was 250,000 automobiles for assembly plants and 500,000 units for plants producing automotive engines; however, such estimates refer only to production cost, excluding research and development costs, as well as market research and advertising.[13] These latter categories represent mainly fixed costs, which are rising sharply upward, increasing MES well beyond these figures and even beyond the volumes attainable by producers like Ford on a European regional scale.

In 1984, Bob Lutz, executive vice-president of Ford International Automotive Operations, stated, "There has to be a global strategy because it is getting so incredibly expensive to create new car model lines."[14] Already there is a degree of coordination on product development among Ford's major regions: North America, Latin America, Asia Pacific, and Europe. In the future, it appears probable that the emphasis on integration will shift more toward the global level, marking a further evolution in Ford's strategy.

Ford's major competitors are moving in much the same direction. General Motors' engine production in Australia supplies its operations in Western Europe and South Africa, and engines produced in Brazil supply North and South American plants. The GM tradition of quasi-independent national subsidiaries has undergone major change, particularly in Europe, to accommodate a much greater emphasis on regional/global coordination.

Smaller competitors in the industry, most of which were at one time considered large enough to attain MES internally, are rapidly forming international networks of collaborative agreements designed to spread their costs over a larger volume.[15]

Organizational Structure

Ford's organizational structure has been influenced by its strategy, confirming Alfred Chandler's research.[16] It is also evident that a particular organizational structure may facilitate or impede the firm's ability to identify and formulate certain strategies. In Ford's case, the establishment of a European regional headquarters provided the necessary organizational basis for a much more active regional strategy.

It is doubtful that the international division structure that preceded the establishment of Ford's regional headquarters was capable of either planning or implementing the type of regional coordination that developed and produced the Bobcat. To quote a Ford senior executive, "Ford International had a few marketing and a few finance men, but no in-depth expertise of local national situations. That, plus 3,000 miles, makes a hell of a barrier."[17]

Structure is also interpreted to include such factors as ownership. Management determined that joint ownership of the various national businesses was incompatible with its proposed European strategy. Equity in its European subsidiaries held outside the company was bought out shortly before Ford moved toward a regional/global emphasis.

Conclusion

The Ford situation outlines a development sequence situation that many managers and students of international expansion will recognize. The lack of environmental knowledge during initial expansion makes it highly probable that the firm will rely heavily on local national planning, for example, by agents and distributors. As the organization develops its internal know-how and organization structure, it becomes better equipped to take a more global view of its opportunities. The relative attractiveness of these strategic opportunities, and hence the incentive toward more emphasis on a regional/global strategy, will depend on a number of factors external to the firm, including technology, and particularly its impact on the economies of large-scale production, and national barriers to cross-national coordination and transfer.

Part II
Strategy at the Regional/Global Level

4
International Portfolio Strategy

Management in the larger companies has become increasingly preoccupied with issues of portfolio strategy. Impetus for this approach was provided by the movement toward corporate diversification, the rise of conglomerates, and the need for board-level executives to obtain a comprehensive overview of the firm's various businesses.

At the heart of corporate portfolio strategy is the allocation of resources among alternative businesses. The fact that multinationals are able to allocate their resources across different national locations opens up a number of portfolio strategies associated with the geographic location of their businesses. An example is provided by a major agricultural firm, which had the problem of dealing with a sales pattern dominated by the growing season; most of the demand for its product was concentrated in the summer months. An expansion of the company's operations to Australia with its reverse seasonal cycle dramatically improved the distribution of the firm's cash flow, profits, and sales over the year.

The Nestlé company's situation is representative of the multinational with an international portfolio of businesses. Nestlé breaks down its various products into seventeen product groups, ranging across areas as diverse as cosmetics, soups, and pharmaceuticals. The different product lines are marketed in over fifty-five different national territories. Managers with regional or global strategic responsibility in this type of firm will address questions such as these:

Do our present businesses generate sufficient cash flow to meet our future investment requirements?

Are we overcommitted in country X?

Should we devote more resources to businesses in countries that represent a high potential for future growth?

Are we getting too involved in countries with high political risk?

These and similar decisions that relate to the firm's international portfolio of businesses are the subject of this chapter.

Portfolio Strategy

As in the more familiar portfolio comprised of financial bonds and shares, portfolio strategy deals with resource commitments that can be varied to secure a balance of attributes across the firm's various business units considered collectively. This overview of the firm's various businesses opens up new strategic opportunities. An acquisition too risky on its own becomes desirable if balanced against the firm's other businesses of a more conservative nature. A business deficient in liquidity may be quite acceptable for the firm with liquidity to spare elsewhere in the organization. Portfolio strategy is concerned with the allocation and redistribution of the firm's resources across its various business units in a way that advances the firm's overall corporate objectives.

Planning a portfolio strategy requires four steps:

1. Identifying the firm's various business units. Unlike the financial analyst, the business strategist does not deal with neatly defined assets. A crucial part of the task is to identify which of the firm's various operations shall be considered as a business. The businesses within the firm's portfolio are sometimes referred to as strategic business units, or SBUs. They comprise a particular segmentation of the firm's overall operations into discrete business units.

2. Assessing the present balance of the portfolio. Portfolio strategy requires an assessment of the existing distribution of the firm's SBUs along different portfolio parameters, such as risk, return, cash flow, and growth. Matrices and bubble charts are often used to enable strategists to visualize better the relationship of multiple business units to each other.

3. Identifying the future desired balance of the portfolio. If the present balance is not optimal, the firm will want to consider how this should be changed; for example, if in fact it feels overcommitted to high-risk business, it will want to shift resources toward business areas with lower risk levels. Changing the balance of the portfolio concerns the redistribution of resources among the firm's business units, including divesting present businesses and adding new ones.[1]

4. Implementation. Provision is made either to maintain the existing portfolio or to reallocate resources among existing (and possibly) new SBUs. If major changes are called for, these may well require corresponding adjustment in the specific objectives and strategies of individual SBUs.

Any company that chooses where its international resources shall be deployed and how much shall be invested in businesses in different parts of the world faces a portfolio planning situation. In a study of portfolio planning, Philippe Haspeslagh found that 45 percent of the Fortune 500 industrial companies (most of which qualify as international or multinational) had introduced portfolio planning to some extent.[2] Many firms employ the method without the terminology. The chief executive of one major firm states that the policy of his company is "to build the widest geographical spread of active subsidiaries, thereby balancing and protecting the interests of the shareholder."[3]

Analysis of the firm's international portfolio addresses many of the same issues as portfolio strategy within a domestic company, but a number of new aspects are introduced specific to its international context.

Consider for instance the definition of the firm's SBUs. This is based on identifying significant differences (significant for purposes of strategy) that distinguish one part of the firm's overall business operations from another.

In multinational and international companies, geographic differences, and more specifically national location, play a major role in defining the SBU building blocks of the firm's international portfolio. Hence, a company engaged in one type of business activity in, say, West Germany would treat that as separate and distinct from essentially similar activities in Thailand, Japan, or Chile.

Figure 4–1 provides an illustration of SBUs in a multinational company. Viewed along the horizontal axis, they are differentiated by international geographic location. Along the vertical axis, they are separated (in this case) by differences in their product lines. Other distinctions frequently used by domestic firms to separate their businesses, such as customer differences and technology, might also have been used here.

The international dimension introduces special questions of portfolio strategy for such companies, which may be summed up under three headings. The first is how the international portfolio of businesses relates to regional and global opportunities. The rapid internationalization of industry carries with it the danger that some firms will not move swiftly enough into new areas of opportunity, allowing competitors to establish a strong position that effectively preempts the most favorable of these.

Figure 4–2 depicts a growth-share matrix as used by the Norton Company to interpret its international portfolio of SBUs. The bubbles, or circles, are proportional to company sales within the indicated national territory. The vertical axis measures the market growth rate for each country in real terms. The horizontal axis measures Norton's market share in these countries relative to the market share of major competitors, with the midpoint (1.0) indicating equal market shares. The matrix indicates that the SBUs in this portfolio are concentrated within countries whose markets in these businesses are experiencing slow growth.[4]

Undoubtedly there are powerful reasons behind the present location of the firm's businesses. Managers using this type of analysis have to keep in mind the reality behind the portfolio symbols. Each SBU represents a complex situation involving careers, historical connections, and traditions, as well as certain resources not readily transferable. Nevertheless, certain reallocation decisions in

Country / Product Group	Country 1	Country 2	Country 3	Country 4
Product Group A	SBU A1	SBU A2	SBU A34	
Product Group B	SBU B1	SBU B2	SBU B3	SBU B4
Product Group C	SBU C1	SBU C23		SBU C4
Product Group D	SBU D1	SBU D2	SBU D3	SBU D4
Product Group E	SBU E1	SBU E2	SBU E3	SBU E4

Figure 4–1. Strategic Business Units Defined by Product and Geography

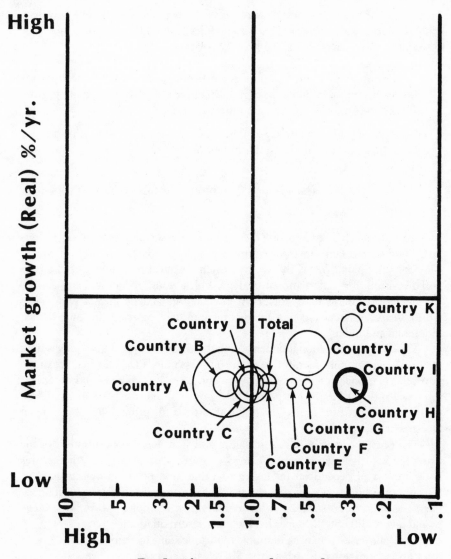

High

Market growth (Real) %/yr.

Low

Country K
Country D | Total
Country B
Country A
Country C
Country J
Country I
Country H
Country G
Country F
Country E

10 5 3 2 1.5 1.0 .7 .5 .3 .2 .1

High

Low

Relative market share

Source: R. Cushman, "Norton's Top-Down, Bottom-Up Planning Process," *Planning Review* 7 (November 1979): 7. Published by Robert J. Allio & Associates, Inc., for the North American Society of Corporate Planning, copyright 1979.

Note: Circles proportional to SBU company sales.

Figure 4–2. International Growth/Share Portfolio

response to the rise of business opportunities in new territories are not only generally desirable but necessary if the firm wishes to maintain its position within the industry. These may take any one of the following forms:

Redistribution of resources among the firm's present SBUs, switching resources from those that are less promising in terms of the companies portfolio objectives to those that appear more promising;

Establishment of new SBUs, possibly in new national locations (this may be through acquisition or the establishment of the firm's own new businesses); or

Divestment of SBUs that appear less promising to free resources for new SBUs.

Sears Roebuck and Company divested itself of its equity in retail operations in Colombia and Peru, investing more heavily in the larger markets of Brazil, Mexico, and Spain.[5] BASF, the West German chemical firm, announced a proposed revision of its international strategy, which would reduce its Latin American operations following a slowdown in economic activity in that part of the world. Instead it intends to step up investment in Asia, especially in South Korea, Indonesia, and India.[6]

The second international dimension that introduces special questions is how the present geographic distribution of the business units affects the balance of the portfolio. National differences in government, economic climate, and other features will influence the firm's portfolio.[7] Figure 4–3 illustrates an international portfolio, defined in terms of political risk and profitability (return on investment).

The portfolio matrix shown in figure 4–3 indicates a concentration of the firm's SBUs in the low risk-return category (lower right quadrant). Whether this is desirable will depend on management values and portfolio objectives. This type of portfolio balance may be acceptable for a company pursuing a conservative or safe portfolio strategy. A less conservative "gambler" portfolio strategy would favour SBUs in the upper left high risk-return quadrant.

In certain cases, it may be desirable to include some indication of future portfolio projections—that is, where the SBUs will be in the next five years. Such projections are indicated in figure 4–3 by arrows, the direction and length of the arrow pointing out the projected future position of its SBU. These indicate that several of the firm's business units (in the Middle East, Argentina, and Nigeria) are expected to incur a higher level of political risk in the next five years. Management may wish to take action to counter this expected added risk, either by reducing the magnitude of its exposure in these areas, expanding its SBUs in the less risky countries, or some combination of the two.

Political Risk

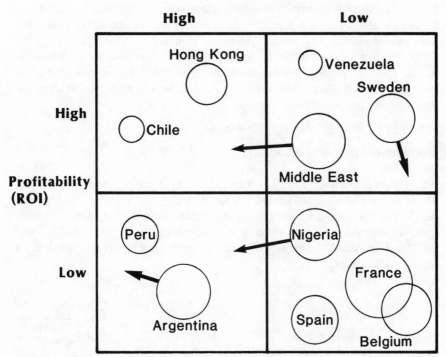

Note: Circles are proportional to SBU sales; arrows indicate projected change in SBU position in five years

Figure 4–3. Political Risk/Profitability Portfolio

International portfolio strategy may properly address the spread or concentration of the firm's business units: is the firm spreading itself too thin geographically, given its available resources? This can be a vital strategic issue, particularly for smaller firms and those just embarking on international expansion.[8]

The third question for international portfolio strategy is how the company's SBUs are positioned relative to the competition. Strategy requires that management have a clear picture of the firm's position regarding its competitors. In the case of multinational companies and competitors, the comparison is one between international networks of business units—that is, a comparison of international business portfolios. Interpreting the competitor's international portfolio may provide insight into the company's strategy. For example, a competitor's success in gaining market share in the larger, more sophisticated national markets has distinct implications for its ability to achieve economies of scale and experience not available to firms that may have confined themselves to smaller national markets.

The competitor's portfolio may be displayed on the same matrix chart as the firm's own SBUs. Figure 4–4 provides a comparison of the growth of two multinational companies in the same seven national markets over the past five years. Company X has grown more rapidly in Italy, Sweden, and Canada, while competitor Y has performed better in the United States, Mexico, Singapore, and Japan, growing faster than company X and, hence, increasing its market share relative to company X in those countries.

International Resource Allocation

Application of portfolio strategy on an international scale encounters a number of constraints. To illustrate, we can refer to the well-known scheme developed by the Boston Consulting Group (BCG). As shown in figure 4–5 excess liquidity from "cash cows" in the firm's low-growth businesses can be used to fund "stars" and "problem child" businesses that require additional assets to capitalize on high growth opportunities.

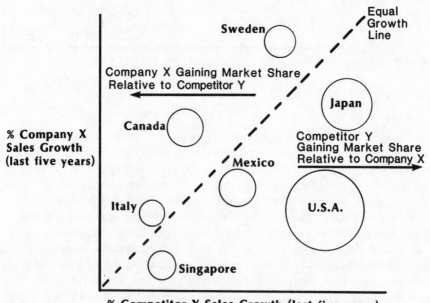

Note: Circles are proportional to latest total industry sales in territory.

Figure 4–4. **International Comparison of Changes in Relative Market Share**

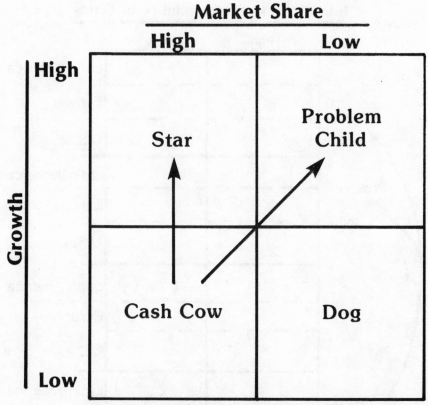

Arrows indicate preferred allocation of cash resources

Source: Adapted with permission from Barry Hedley, "Strategy and the Business Portfolio," *Long Range Planning*, vol. 10 (February 1977), Pergamon Press Ltd.

Figure 4–5. Growth/Share Matrix

Figure 4–6 depicts the BCG portfolio classification viewed on a regional and global basis. The company finds it has a potential problem even though its international portfolio includes a good mix of businesses in the various categories. The firm's cash-rich businesses, from which it might expect to finance its stars and problem child businesses, are located mainly in certain Latin American and European countries where financial controls, money market conditions, or other considerations severely limit the export of capital earnings.

These constraints are familiar to companies experienced in international operations. Questions of cross-border resource transfers—such as, Can we repatriate our earnings?—are a routine part of the foreign investment decision process.[9]

International Transferability of Funds

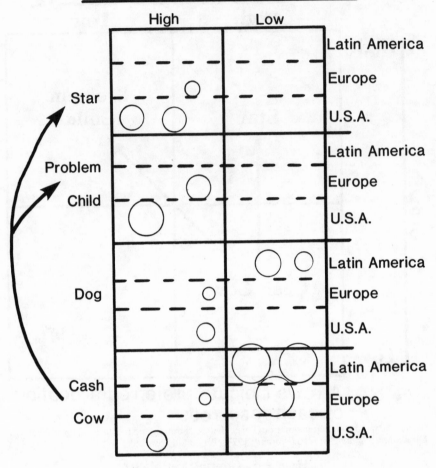

Figure 4–6. Regional/Global Portfolio

Though this cross-border aspect is of limited relevance to domestic firms, it represents an important dimension of the international firm's portfolio strategy.

Assessing International Portfolio Performance

The impact of national location on the firm's international business portfolio is not limited to shifting resources across national borders. National location will also affect the perceived performance of the firm's businesses. From the portfolio manager's point of view, the performance of the firm's various businesses, considered internationally, might be quite different from their performance assessed nationally. For example, a business that is earning a 10 percent return on investment in terms of national currency might show a quite different profit performance as viewed from abroad, depending on the rate of exchange and accounting conventions used to translate earnings into another currency.

Since portfolio strategy is based on a collective view of the firm's international businesses, it is virtually certain that for some purposes, the evaluation of the portfolio performance will require translation of the earnings and other results of the individual SBUs into a common reference currency, which permits comparability between units in different countries.[10] Most often, the currency of the parent company's home country is used as the reference currency, though it is by no means certain that this should always be the case, particularly where ownership of the corporation is international and, as in some cases, its headquarters is subject to change from one country to another.[11]

Figure 4–7 indicates some of the border effects that may modify SBU performance as perceived across national boundaries internationally from the international headquarters' portfolio planning perspective. Seen from international headquarters, the national performance of foreign-based SBUs will be affected by exchange rate fluctuations, capital controls, repatriation of earnings regulations, and even unofficial government attitudes. These will also affect international headquarters' perception of risk and other variables. The importance of such modifications, although long recognized, has not been explored systematically for purposes of portfolio strategy.

Portfolio Interdependence

The freedom to allocate resources among different business units may assume a degree of independence among SBUs that in many cases does not exist. To put it another way, functional interdependence among SBUs can hamper portfolio strategy.[12] If we suppose, for example, that one SBU supplies a vital component to other SBUs, it may not be possible to shift resources in line with portfolio objectives without bringing the entire system to a halt. Such interdependence is a very realistic proposition for many such firms.

Portfolio strategy works with a minimum of such constraint in multinationals operated as international holding companies, the firm's various business units characterized by a high degree of independence. This does not imply that the portfolio approach cannot be used in the more integrative multinationals, operating their businesses as parts of an interdependent system. Even in these situations, typically there will be a certain degree of flexibility at the margin—that is, some reallocation will be possible, though it is likely to be limited. Second, restrictions due to interdependence will have much less, if any, application regard-

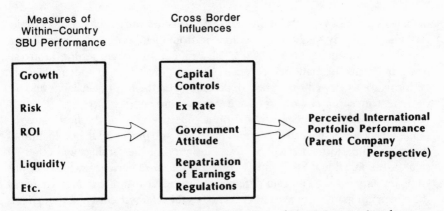

Figure 4–7. Border Effects Influencing Perception of Firm's International Portfolio

ing new commitments of capital and other resources as these are made available through depreciation, profits, or new investment. This means that, over time, even the more highly integrated multinationals will be able to implement a portfolio strategy, albeit incrementally.

5
Global and National Competitive Strategies

S uccessful strategies are built on positions of strength not readily duplicated by others. In the more internationalized industries, top management is faced with two quite different interpretations of competitive strategy, national and global.

National competitive strategies are those that seek to develop competitive strength based on the firm's presence and operations in a specific national environment. Assessment of the firm's competitive performance is also nationally based; the most obvious reflection of this is the measurement of market share only on a national basis.

Global competitive strategies are based on an international perception of the firm's environment and resources. Multinationals adopting a global strategic approach seek to develop international competitive strengths not available to the purely domestic firm or to other multinationals operating on a country-by-country basis. Such international strengths may be based on (1) efficiencies of international scale and volume, that is, products and production processes geared to international rather than national markets—where available, these efficiencies may enable global competitors to reduce unit costs below those of more nationally oriented firms; (2) the international transfer of lessons, ideas, and experience from one country to another; (3) an international image and reputation; (4) shifting financial and other resources from one part of the world to support operations in another; (5) superior access to place economies, such as low-cost raw materials, skills, labor, and other inputs; and (6) the ability to provide an international service. All of these depend on the firm's ability to coordinate its resources internationally.

Global as used here does not usually refer to every country. A firm pursuing a global strategy interprets its major areas of opportunity (such as markets) and competition on a world basis. It also mobilizes its own resources internationally, though this may include only a limited number of countries, toward these globally defined threats and opportunities. It is possible for such firms to operate a global strategy in some parts of their international network of operations while adopting a more national competitive stance in other parts of the world. This chapter outlines the major characteristics of both orientations.

Four Generic International Competitive Strategies

The trend toward industry internationalization does not mean that all firms should adopt a more global competitive posture. Even within the more international industries, there will be geographic, product, and technological segments where a national approach can prove effective. Figure 5–1 identifies four generic international competitive strategies differentiated according to geographic scope and market share objective.

Global Strategies

Global High Share Strategies. Companies pursuing global high share strategies are usually the giants of the industry. The competitive strategies of firms such as Shell, General Motors, IBM, Electrolux, and SKF reflect a global interpretation of competitors and opportunities. Operations are coordinated across national boundaries to secure a major share of the global market.[1]

A number of characteristics are associated with global high share strategies:

1. Pricing, product range, promotion, and other elements of the marketing program are geared to mass markets.
2. A high priority is placed on the firm's international market share position.
3. Products are usually characterized by a high degree of international standardization.
4. Production facilities are operated as part of a regional or global network, where possible, to reduce unit costs.
5. Design and research expenditures are high in absolute terms by industry standards but low on a per unit basis, reflecting their ability to defray such costs across multiple national markets.
6. Products are at the forefront of industry development but not necessarily pioneering or representing radically new technology.
7. Such firms are often wary about alliances with other firms (such as joint ventures or licensing) in what they consider to be their core products and markets, though exceptions increasingly are being made in those countries that are difficult to enter and with promising new suppliers that have developed new products and/or techniques.

The growing effectiveness of the more global competitors is readily observable in a wide number of industries. During the early days of television, the orientation of Zenith, Motorola, and other U.S. firms in the industry was predominantly toward the national market. The United States accounted for the bulk of their business. Japanese producers adopted a different approach; they quickly

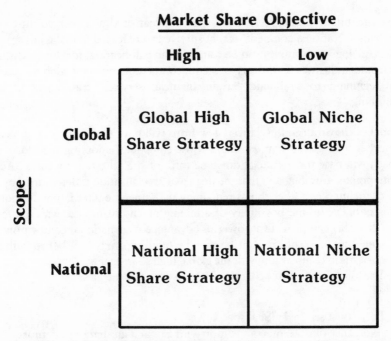

Figure 5–1. Four Generic International Competitive Strategies

moved toward a more international orientation with design and production aimed at international markets.

In 1960, Japanese exports of television (monochrome) sets to the United States accounted for only 1 percent of total Japanese production. By 1970, the Japanese were exporting more sets abroad (61 percent of production) than sold at home. Two-thirds of such exports went to the United States.[2] The Japanese achieved economies of international volume that enabled them to undercut their U.S. competitors. Eventually they established production facilities in countries of Southeast Asia, providing further advantage through lower wage costs.

The same theme is detectable in the development of the European industry for major household appliances such as washing machines and refrigerators. During the 1960s, a number of Italian producers of these products expanded to achieve international scale. With the lowering of trade barriers, competition became more regional and global than national. Firms that remained predominantly national producers found themselves under extreme competitive pressure from the international Italian producers such as Zannusi and Candy, which were undercutting their prices as well as Sweden's Electrolux company. A number were driven to financial collapse. Many were amalgamated and merged into other companies. National competitors that survived were forced to realign their strategies. Analogous examples can be found in the ball bearing, forklift trucks, and electronics industries. In the service sector, competitors pursuing global strategies are beginning to dominate certain financial services, transportation, and publishing.

Global Niche Strategies. Relatively few firms will have the resources required to achieve a high global market share. Most companies adopting the global approach will base their strategy on some form of specialization, or niche. Adam Smith pointed out long ago that the degree of specialization is determined by the size of the market. Other things remaining the same, the internationalization of industry opens up the possibility of attaining much greater size within a given specialty. This can provide a powerful advantage over national competitors. At the same time, the choice of niche may be (and hopefully will be) such that it avoids head-on competition with the global high share giants.

The following features characterize global niche strategies:

1. Focus on a selected global specialty.
2. Avoidance of head-on competition with global high share competitors.
3. Selection of a specialty that is relatively insensitive to price competition (part of the defense against global high share competitors).
4. Capitalizing on possible complementarities relative to the products and technologies of larger competitors, such as producing computer peripherals that are plug compatible with IBM computers.
5. Extensive resort to alliances with other firms to defray costs of research and to gain access to new territories and technologies.
6. Maximum utilization of international competitive advantages. Although the narrower product-market scope will limit certain efficiencies of scale and volume open to larger global competitors, such firms are often able to capitalize on the international strengths within their chosen speciality.

The global specialization on which such strategies are based may take any of the following forms:

1. Specialization by technology. Certain technologies and subtechnologies do not lend themselves to the very high-volume targets of the global high share strategies. This was a major consideration in Ferranti's decision to concentrate on the development of the technology (the collector diffusion process) necessary to the production of so-called custom-built chips. The firm was able to develop a particular technological niche that gave it a position of leadership within the chosen speciality.[3]

2. Specialization by product. Rolls Royce concentrates on luxury motor cars, which it markets globally.
3. Specialization by geography. Focusing company efforts in those countries that because of tariffs, government attitudes, and regulations or other reasons provide a uniquely favorable environment.
4. Specialization by stage of life cycle. Some firms specialize in certain stages of the product life cycle.[4]
5. Specialization by stage of production. Many companies choose to specialize on a particular stage of production, such as the final assembly of the product.
6. Specialization by market segment. Specialization may be focused on particular customer segments; for example, Christian Dior aims its products at a specific global customer category.

National Strategies

Competition and objectives are defined nationally. National strategies are by no means confined to domestic companies. Multinationals that operate their subsidiaries largely as independent units (holding company mode) formulate competitive strategy on a country-by-country basis. In some cases, strategy will revolve about a single national territory, usually the company's home market, with operations in other parts of the world considered as extra or supplementary to the major national market. Here again there is a distinction to be made between strategies directed at a major share of the market and those aimed at a niche, though in this case the niche refers to a special segment of the national market.

National High Share Strategies. These aim at a high national market share through the use of nationally based competitive strengths. Marketing programs and objectives are geared to achieving high volume and lower cost, measured in terms of other national competitors. Their national status offers access to the usual advantages of size on a national level, but they remain vulnerable to the even larger scale of operations that characterize global strategies. Hence their success often depends on countering the more global competitors by making maximum use of the following:

1. National entry barriers. Where local national production facilities exist, tariffs, quotas, and other border restrictions provide significant entry barriers to competitors.
2. Local national government preference in terms of purchasing arrangements, subsidies, research expenditures, and so on.
3. Close contact and knowledge of national conditions, including customers, industry regulations, national institutions (such as unions and industry associations), and competitors.

4. Flexibility of response to local conditions, capitalizing on shorter lines of communication and freedom to tailor products and services to only one set of national conditions.
5. Customer preference for dealing with local national firms.

National Niche Strategies. These utilize the advantages of specialization within a particular national environment against both national and global competitors. Particularly with reference to the latter, the size of the national target market is such that it is below the threshold considered large enough to attract direct competition. There are certain exceptions to this, as in the case of niches in areas with major growth potential.

Firms pursuing national niche strategies also resort to the defensive strategy features outlined above such as tariffs, government preferential treatment, and other national barriers to entry.

Competitive Strategy and Structure

Multinational companies may be grouped into two camps. First are those that have developed a competitive strategy focused primarily about a particular individual national territory or those whose subsidiaries in different countries are implementing nationally oriented strategies. In both instances, the firm's competitive posture is essentially that of a national, domestic company. The other approach attempts to build competitive advantage by making use of the firm's network of international operations to develop advantages of international scale, experience transfer, and other competences based on the firm's international system of resources and capabilities.

The firm's control structure plays an important role in its ability to implement the different strategies. Multinationals adopting the holding company mode fall necessarily in the first camp since they are not organized to implement the cross-national coordination required by the second. The latter requires a more integrative type of organization, with a high degree of responsibility for competitive strategy at the regional/global level.

Geopolitical Aspects

Given the diversity of national and regional environments, some firms find that no one strategy can be applied uniformly on a world basis. In countries where tariffs, local content programs, financial control, or other problems impede cross-border transfers, companies may find that they have little choice but to pursue a strategy that is predominantly nationally oriented. In other parts of the world, they may find that they are able to implement the cross-national coordination necessary to develop a more global competitive approach.

Some parts of the world are more receptive to global strategies than others. There is an observed tendency for multinational companies in both manufacturing and service industries to invest in facilities located in the larger world markets.[5] It might be thought, then, that these will be among the first to feel the impact of more global competition. But this is not necessarily the case since the ability of multinationals to mount such strategies in these countries may be constrained by the presence of national barriers. A number of Latin American countries with quite large national markets in certain industries have high national barriers that effectively insulate them from international competition. The barriers in question may include government incentives and practices that favor nationally oriented firms, as well as the more familiar tariffs and quotas. Any of these may impede the ability of multinational firms to implement global strategies; they will also curtail the competitive impact of international competition through trade.

According to this view, the impact of global competitive strategies is likely to be felt first in those national product-markets that are large and have low barriers to foreign products and companies. These are also likely to comprise the center of world demand, particularly in the newer, more technologically intensive products. For example, Japan, the United States, and the member countries of the European Community account for over 75 percent of total world demand for integrated circuits. Securing a position as a global competitor will require active participation in one, and very likely more than one, of these national markets (upper left-hand corner of figure 5–2). A number of smaller markets that offer an exceptionally favorable environment to international trade and investment, such as Hong Kong and Singapore, may also feature in the move toward a more global competitive stance at a relatively early stage.

Countries with high barriers to foreign companies and products offer less congenial sites for the cross-border transfer and coordination required by global strategies. Countries with both small national product-markets and high barriers are the least likely sites of all for such strategies.

Many multinationals that adopt a global strategic approach in the countries represented in the upper left-hand corner of figure 5–2 may choose to employ national strategies (in the same industry) within countries represented on the lower right, though the situation is constantly changing. There has been a long-term decline in many national barriers. Economic growth is increasing the size and attractiveness of national markets once considered too small. Increased technological input in the research, production, and design of goods and services increases fixed costs, making the efficiencies associated with large-scale international production more attractive.

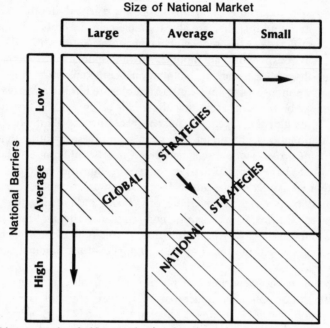

Note: World countries classified by size of national market and national barriers in a given industry.

Figure 5–2. Conceptual View of the Distribution of Global and National Competitive Strategies in an Industry

In these circumstances, many firms are finding that the effectiveness of strategies and features that once protected them from more global competitors is diminishing. This is often accompanied by an industry shake-out as competition intensifies and a more global strategic approach spreads to countries once dominated by firms pursuing national competitive strategies.

6

Implementing Strategic Change

Many of the most successful international competitors have demonstrated a marked ability to change from one strategic orientation to another. American Express carved out a global niche based on its travelers' checks and then used this to expand internationally across a wide range of financial services. The growth of Japanese firms in machine tools, television, and motorcycles has followed a sequence that moved from national high share strategies to global niche to global high share. There will also be occasions when limitations imposed by new national barriers or corporate resources may call for a reorientation of strategy toward a more national focus. During the late 1970s, Chrysler found that it was not able to keep up with global competition. Production facilities in France, Spain, and England were divested. The company's decision to concentrate its resources on competing within the North American market and Mexico contributed to the turnaround and revival of profitability in the early 1980s.

This ability to change from one view of the firm's competitive arena to another is by no means universal. Because such change requires a break with the past, it may be difficult to perceive. There is a danger that some companies, particularly those with strong national associations and strategies focused about a traditional national territory, will fail to recognize the need for reorientation toward a more global approach. They cling to traditions and methods based on past success long after these have become obsolete.

The following case study will provide insight into such situations and the process of introducing major changes in competitive strategy. It focuses on competitive strategy in the international computer industry.

The Competitors

ICL

ICL, previously known as International Computers Ltd., provides an example of a firm that historically has based its competitive strategy around a strong national position. The company was established in 1968 after a series of mergers actively supported and partly financed by the British government. The government's objective has been to pull together a number of previously independent firms, including International Computers and Tabulators, English Electric (GEC), and English Electric Computers, into a company that would form the nucleus of a national computer industry.

ICL's major strategic problem since its inception has been to survive against the international giants of the computer industry, particularly IBM. Despite the multiple mergers that led to its founding, ICL was still considerably smaller than its major competitors. Its smaller size constituted a considerable disadvantage in financing the scale of investment required to develop new computer products, involving many millions of dollars and rising annually. Given the magnitude of this expenditure, a new product introduction cycle of some four to five years requires a very large customer base. Computer software and customer service are also subject to major economies of scale.

Although technically a multinational, ICL accounts for only a minor share of industry sales outside its home national territory (one source estimates the firm's international sales at less than 3 percent of total world sales).[1] ICL's overseas subsidiaries are limited largely to marketing activities, with the exception of small-scale production in India and, more recently, in North America.

In spite of its small international size, ICL managed to carve out a strong competitive position as the leading supplier of computers within the British markets. Company strategy capitalized on its strengths.

A major strength was ICL's government support. Support from the British government took the form of government equity ownership (the government took an initial stake of 25 percent in the new company) together with subsequent loans and research grants. Most contentious of all was the British government's active preference, as reported in the press, for ICL products. One well-known economic journal stated that the added cost to the taxpayer in one such purchase of a single ICL computer system amounted to £50 million over and above that of a competitive IBM product.[2]

Second, ICL had a close relationship with other British firms, both suppliers and potential customers. Many of the leading computer firms were involved in one way or another with the series of mergers that established ICL. Plessey Limited, a major supplier of electronic components and purchaser of computers, held an 18 percent equity interest in the new company. The newly merged companies comprising ICL included managers from leading national electronics firms who still retained informal links with their former employers.

A third advantage was geographic concentration. Concentration of the firm's major efforts on a single national territory avoided the inefficiencies of a widely dispersed customer base. It also enabled ICL to tailor its products precisely to the needs of its potential national customers. ICL was able, with very limited resources, to develop a number of excellent products. Close contact with universities and government research agencies, together with its own efforts, enabled ICL to produce a range of mainframe computers (notably the 2900 series) that some judged to be equal or superior to those of IBM.

Finally, ICL had a simplified management structure. Concentration of facilities and the bulk of company management within a single national territory avoided many of the problems associated with the more complex organizational structures employed by ICL's more internationally dispersed competitors.

ICL capitalized on these strengths to become the major supplier of computer systems in Britain, enjoying a 25 percent annual growth rate for most of the 1970s.

IBM

Unlike ICL, IBM had large-scale manufacturing and marketing operations outside its home market. In Europe alone, the company has fifteen manufacturing plants and nine research and development laboratories employing over 100,000 persons, of whom fewer than 500 are U.S. citizens. Extensive research and manufacturing is also conducted in Japan and Latin America. IBM coordinates internationally dispersed operations where this will yield efficiencies, while allowing scope for national subsidiary autonomy in other areas.

Research centers are coordinated globally to avoid duplication, enabling IBM to make maximum use of its R&D budget by allocating costs over the firm's global sales. It also reduces R&D expenditure as a percentage of sales relative to competitors while funding an R&D budget higher in absolute terms. IBM's R&D expenditures in 1982 were in excess of $2 billion (higher than ICL's total sales volume for that year), yet they represented only 6 percent of company worldwide sales, low by industry standards and considerably lower than ICL's R&D to sales ratio.[3]

Common-base models are produced on a regional basis. The three major regions are the United States, Europe/Middle East/Africa, and America/Far East. Within the two international regions, national subsidiaries specialize in various computer components, subsequently assembled into a regional product. The regional base models are then adapted to meet specific national requirements. For example, the IBM 4700 finance system has to be modified in Japan to print and display Japanese Kanji characters.

Changing Conditions

By 1980, the competitive environment had changed significantly for both IBM and ICL. The high growth rate associated with ICL's computer sales disappeared. Profits, which had never kept pace with the robustness of its sales performance, turned into heavy losses, recording a £50 million net loss in 1981. It soon became evident that ICL's competitive position was deteriorating to the point where collapse was imminent, barring government aid. This was eventually forthcoming in the form of a £200 million government loan guarantee, which enabled the firm to pay outstanding creditors and provided a breathing space for a basic reassessment of strategy.

Contributing to the decline of ICL's fortunes were a number of factors. Having tackled the major international producers in head-on competition across a wide range of products, ICL was experiencing difficulty in keeping pace with product development. Its mainframe computer, the 2900, originally had been an excellent product, but by 1981 it was less competitive.[4] It had become superseded as early as 1979 when IBM launched its 4300 series, incorporating new technology and offering much improved computing power. It is doubtful that ICL could have matched the 4300 even if the entire amount of government aid had been applied toward R&D. As it was, financial stringency forced ICL to cut back on new product development.

The British computer market, on which the firm was now so highly dependent, entered a severe recession beginning in 1979 that drastically reduced demand. At the same time, the value of the pound sterling on the foreign exchanges almost doubled during the 1979–1980 period, putting ICL at a disadvantage relative to firms' pricing costs and products in dollars and other currencies.

-Government preferential purchases of ICL products were also in jeopardy. The European Community was preparing legislation that would require all European member governments to make their purchases through a system of open tender. Government preferential treatment for national producers would be prohibited. The prospect of such legislation reinforced IBM's own lobbying efforts to persuade the British government to give it equal treatment in tendering for the government computer contracts.[5] For its part, the government had to consider that IBM had located major facilities in Britain and could contribute significantly to national objectives in developing high technology.

Implementing a Global Niche Strategy

The new management chosen to pull ICL out of its deteriorating competitive position made the following decisions:

1. A partnership agreement with Fujitsu, the large Japanese electronics firm, to supply ICL with microcircuits and related technology.[6]
2. An agreement to market Fujitsu mainframe computers in Europe under an ICL brand name, Atlas.[7] This enabled ICL to cancel a number of big computer projects, with substantial savings in resources. It was still able to present a full range of computers to its customers while redirecting its own resources toward more specialized areas and lowering the amount spent on R&D to less than 10 percent of sales.[8]

3. An agreement with the U.S. firm Three Rivers to produce its new small computer. This is part of the new strategy reflected in the managing director's statement that he intended to make ICL "big in small systems."[9]
4. A joint venture with Mitel Corporation of Canada in telecommunication equipment.
5. An increased emphasis on international expansion, particularly toward Europe and the United States.
6. A change in policy to make the firm's new products plug compatible with those of IBM.

ICL has used its nationally based strengths, and particularly its U.K. and European marketing system, to forge links with foreign producers. These links have enabled it to shift the focus of its efforts in a more international direction while attempting to avoid direct competition with the global giants of the industry by specializing in telecommunications and the production and development of smaller computers.

There has been a return to profitability. The overall change in strategy seems to be working, though it is too early to say if this improvement will be lasting.

Market Share and Return on Investment

Throughout this period, IBM's return on investment (ROI) in Great Britain was generally higher than ICL's, despite its smaller share of the national market. Indeed, IBM's British subsidiary was recording record profits during the early 1980s (over 40 percent ROI in 1980 and 1981), just as ICL was on the verge of bankruptcy. At first glance, this runs counter to the body of literature that argues that there is a positive relationship between market share and ROI; that is, the firm with the higher market share is expected to have the highest return on investment.

Among the reasons forwarded in support of the positive relationship between market share and ROI is the advantage of economies of scale, usually associated with the firm with the highest market share.[10] Where the company is international in scope, however, national market share may not be very relevant. Particularly when, as in the case of IBM, company operations are purposely designed to make maximum use of international economies of scale, international rather than national market share may be more indicative.[11]

Areas of Vulnerability

All strategies have areas of vulnerability. A firm's sources of strength in one type of contest may prove a weakness in another. The ICL-IBM case study illustrates some of the potential weaknesses of nationally oriented competitive strategies. Next we consider the vulnerabilities of global competitive strategies.

Vulnerabilities of Global High Share Strategies

Political. Companies pursuing such strategies are likely to occupy a position of major economic influence and high visibility. Although their actions are perhaps no different from that of other competitors, their size and impact on national policies make them particularly vulnerable to government action and, in extreme cases, active intervention.

Size. The larger international scale of operations connected with global high share strategies carries with it the usual diseconomies of large-scale organizations. Within the multinational, these are aggravated by geographic dispersion, national barriers, cultural differences, and other factors.

International Interdependence. Coordination across national boundaries introduces a high order of interdependence among the firm's operations in different countries. Stoppage due to unions, government, or internal breakdown in one part of an internationally coordinated system threatens the entire network, not just operations in the country where the stoppage takes place. To some degree, adverse effects can be limited through multiple sourcing of components providing alternative sources of supply, but this is not always possible and it is frequently costly.

Hazards of International Standardization. International standardization of products and components means that certain compromises will have to be made to arrive at a product acceptable to the maximum number of customers. The danger here is that the product that suits customers in one country will not suit those in another.

Neglected Niches. Not even the largest firm can pursue all avenues of opportunity. Global high share strategies achieve success through careful selection of those products and markets calculated to generate high volume. Inevitably numerous promising opportunities that do not meet the volume threshold requirements will be passed over. Many of these will provide a breeding ground for potential new competitors.

Vulnerabilities of Global Niche Strategies

The success of global niche strategies depends on identifying and defending a particular international segment of the business. Firms pursuing these strategies are vulnerable on several counts.

First, specialization defenses are broken. The defendability of a particular area or niche rests on not attracting excessive interest from firms with superior resources and a special competence within the chosen specialization that is not readily matched by others. Both defenses may be undermined by changing industry conditions. A firm that is too successful in developing its particular specialty is likely to attract the attention of major competitors. Firms that underestimated the potential of the specialty during the early development stages now become active competitors, competing head on within the same special segment. For example, Ferranti, having specialized in custom-built chips, now finds that the area is attracting major interest from international major league competitors such as Texas Instruments.

The firm's relative competence within a specialty may also be overcome by competitors. A specialization strategy relies on certain distinctive attributes to protect it from direct price competition. For example, BMW has preserved its special niche within the motorcycle industry, catering for customers willing to pay a price premium for high-quality craftsmanship in the larger big bike segment. This was a particularly effective specialist strategy so long as the other major international firms, such as Honda, Yamaha, and Suzuki, focused their attention on the small and medium motorcycle segments that comprised the high volume, high share portions of the international market. More recently, these giant firms have upgraded the size and quality of their products, bringing them much closer to those of BMW. Hence the distinctiveness of the BMW niche has narrowed over time. At some point, it may cease to provide a barrier against the Japanese products sufficient to overcome their lower costs.

Second, technology makes the niche obsolete. Particularly in the more technological industries, a specialization strategy requires the latest in technology. In many cases, the firm adopted the specialty in the first instance in order to conserve and focus its limited technological resources. However, innovation is notoriously hard to point toward specified goals. It is possible that a competitor may produce or develop a new production method or device that will undermine the firm's competitive strategy.

Third, global niche strategies frequently rely on alliances to complement the firm's own resources and offset potential weaknesses. These are not without potential danger. With time, allies may learn and assimilate the competence that provides the basis for the firm's specialization. For example, Fujitsu may, through its agreement with ICL, acquire sufficient knowledge of ICL's marketing methods and distribution in Europe to enter that market on its own as a direct competitor to ICL.

Worst of All Worlds

It is also possible to reap the worst of all worlds, particularly in the case of the multinational firm's adopting a national competitive strategy. It is quite conceivable that it will be perceived as foreign by the host government, failing to acquire any preferential advantage from that source, while also not developing any of the international competitive strengths and advantages associated with the more global strategies. Analogously, the multinational pursuing a global competitive strategy may fail to achieve the specialization required for successful competition within a global niche and also find that it lacks the resources required to implement a global high share strategy.

International Sources of Competitive Advantage

It is worth considering in some detail the types of competitive advantages available to multinational companies implementing global strategies.

Economies of International Size and Volume

Operations on an international scale open up the possibility of greater efficiencies of scale and accumulated volume (the experience curve effect). The investment required to produce the design of a single integrated circuit may run into millions of dollars. Once it is developed, the extra cost required to apply the same design across a larger volume of integrated circuits produced and marketed internationally rather than nationally is virtually nil.

International Sourcing

A better source of supply was one of the earliest motives behind international expansion. This expansion focused initially on raw materials and the extractive industries. More recently, offshore manufacturing plants have been established by many firms to employ labor in countries with lower costs and to increase the availability of certain scarce skills.[12]

Experience Transfer

The multinational firm is in direct contact with a wide variety of different national environments. Experience in one country may provide it with a strategic advantage in another.[13]

Ability to Service Customers' Needs Internationally

The ability to provide an internationally coordinated servicing of customer needs can prove another source of competitive strength. International banks, such as Citibank and Bank of America, are able to use their international network of subsidiaries to provide international cash management services that cannot easily be matched by domestic banks or international banks whose branches operate with little or no international coordination. Much the same applies to international advertising firms using their international affiliates to provide regionally or globally integrated promotional campaigns.

International Resource Focus

The firm that is able to shift resources, skills, technology, and products from one part of the world to another is in a position to bring the full weight of its international network to bear on specific competitors and/or opportunites. It is able to exert and sustain competitive efforts that entail negative returns in some territories and that are beyond the capabilities and resources of individual subunits of the firm acting on their own.[14]

International Corporate Image

With improvements in international communication, discrepancies from one country to another in product safety, quality standards, pollution control, and similar areas may severely damage the firm's reputation and credibility. A coherent and consistent international corporate image can prove an asset. Companies like Sony, Shell, and General Motors rely on their international reputations to help them tap financial markets in many parts of the world, thereby lowering capital costs. Such a reputation can facilitate negotiations with government as well as new product introduction.

Efficiencies of Internalization

One school of thought holds that many, if not all, of the advantages are due to the ability of the multinational firm to consummate international transactions and transfers internally on a within-company basis, as between one national subsidiary and another. The same transactions between independent units, such as domestic companies operating through international markets, may encounter obstacles, such as lack of confidentiality and inadequate information that may hamper the efficient international utilization of resources.[15]

7

Marketing Strategy: The International Headquarters Role

> Marketing . . . is the whole business seen from the point of view of its final result, that is from the customer's point of view.
>
> Peter Drucker[1]

Paraphrasing Peter Drucker, we may define international marketing as the whole business seen from the point of view of the international customer. As is often the case with definitions, this leaves a number of questions unanswered. Who is the international customer? What is meant by the whole business? Does this refer to the firm's national business or the corporation considered globally?

Within the management ranks of multinational companies, there is no other area more contentious and subject to dispute. Some experienced marketing executives deny that there is any marketing activity that can be designated as international. Extensive investigations into the marketing programs of multinational companies indicate that many managers view marketing strategy as a local problem, one that should "be left to the local management in each country."[2] This nationally oriented view of international marketing has received wide acceptance. However, the evidence indicates that international headquarters in a great many multinational firms plays an active marketing role quite distinct from that carried out at the national level.[3] The confusion that persists on this point may be a matter of semantics.

A major Swiss-based multinational food company that strongly espouses marketing decision making at the national level points out that conditions in each country are different. Therefore it places primary responsibility for marketing on a national manager responsible in each country for the firm's marketing program and strategy in that national market. This company considers its marketing to be nationally rather than internationally managed. The same company has a number of policies and coordinative activities carried out at the regional or global level. International headquarters is responsible for company brands and packaging. Furthermore, the national executive in charge of managing the firm's marketing at the national level reports to a regional executive with multicountry responsibility for coordinating certain aspects of the firms marketing throughout his or her region.

Are these international headquarters' coordinative decisions and policies part of the firm's international marketing program and strategy? The view here is that they are. The aim of this chapter is to consider the role of international headquarters in formulating marketing strategy at the regional/global level. This may include decisions that affect international customers directly. More often it will consist of decisions, coordinative activity, and policies that provide a broad framework and point company marketing strategy in specific directions but leave considerable freedom for the national operations to tailor their marketing to local national conditions. Whatever the terminology used to describe this activity, it is a vital and growing part of a firm's overall international marketing strategy.

Headquarters Functions

International headquarters has two main functions regarding international marketing strategy. As all good generals are aware, the first requirement for any strategy is to "know the terrain", that is, gathering and interpreting information. At one time, this knowledge could be acquired personally and at first hand through visual inspection. Today management relies extensively on information gathered by others. Second, the increasingly international nature of business enterprise and competitive activity has increased pressure on the upper reaches of the management hierarchy to come to grips with the question of providing a measure of coordination among the firm's various international marketing activities.

Market Intelligence and Data Gathering

Organizations cannot possibly assimilate all of the new, virtually limitless information constantly generated by their external environment. Their perception of the outside world is thus necessarily very different from the real world as information is selected, filtered, and made manageable. Within the multinational firm, this task is compounded by the wider geographic scope of the firm's external environment and the additional variables, such as national attitudes, culture, financial, economic, and social data, that call for management attention.

The particular competence of international headquarters is its access to market intelligence from multiple national environments. Its perspective may be compared to that of a weather satellite. The local weather station has a more intimate first-hand view of weather conditions, but the satellite is often able to identify cross-national patterns and trends not observable at the local level.

Management at international headquarters will rely for much of its marketing information on data gathered by its national business units, such as foreign subsidiaries, in direct contact with national customers and markets. Some data will also be gathered directly by international headquarters staff, for two reasons: it may serve as a useful cross-check since both international headquarters and the firm's national subsidiaries and representatives may be expected to have their own biases and there will be gaps to be filled in, such as information from countries where the firm has no nationally based operations.

The chief task of international headquarters in this respect is to identify, organize, and process highly selective bits of information to give management a global perspective of the firm's market environment. This does not necessarily require the resources of a multinational company or extensive headquarters staff.

The General Engineering Company is a small European producer of industrial equipment that it markets through a direct sales force calling on potential customers throughout the world. Economic change in the firm's different world markets not infrequently gives rise to sudden shifts in demand from one country to another. In the past, such changes sometimes caught the company unaware, with its sales force not optimally distributed. Too many sales representatives would find themselves in countries with declining sales, while not enough would be available to handle requirements in areas of increasing demand.

In order to improve its market intelligence, the company established a new position of sales office manager. The purpose of the new post was to assemble and centralize information gathered by its sales force during their trips abroad and use it to compile a picture of changes in the firm's overall environment.

At the core of the new information system was an estimate by each sales representative of future expected sales in his or her territory and the probability that such sales would be consummated. For example, a 50 percent probability of sale in connection with a machine worth $100,000 would be translated into an expected present value of $50,000. Based on this information, management was able to compare and assess the prospect for many sales in different parts of the world. Emerging trends such as a recent decline in European sales and an increase in North America were identified more rapidly and the firm's sales force redeployed to take advantage of such changes.

Interpreting International Markets

Interpreting international markets requires some scheme for classifying the enormous amount of multicountry data soon generated by even a modest effort. International classification schemes are by no means limited to market analysis. Economists group countries according to their level of economic development. Political scientists classify them by political systems. Health and medical researchers use international classifications based on infant mortality, incidence of disease, length of life, and other categories. The aim is to identify relatively homogeneous groups or segments.

Customers are likely to differ in terms of product preference, buying behavior, physical and psychological characteristics, habits, and other characteristics. Such differences may be used to probe beneath the aggregate or average characteristics of the market and to subdivide it into segments that have certain characteristics in common, particularly regarding their response to the firm's marketing initiatives.

The particular scheme of segmentation chosen to a large degree will determine how the firm sees its markets and, hence, its marketing strategy. International segmentation schemes encompass customers in more than one country. Developing a practical international segmentation of the firm's markets calls for close attention to a number of points.

Data Availability. Segmentation often relies on published information that may be readily available within the firm's domestic market but is much more difficult to secure for foreign markets. In many cases, the company will have had many years to build up a stock of information for its domestic market, detailing customer characteristics, economic status, geographic distribution, and other features. Despite considerable progress by international agencies, such data are not uniformly available for all countries. For example, data on population distribution by per capita income are not available for many African and Latin American countries or, in some cases, are published after a lag of four or five years.

Data Comparability. Certain economic and demographic information such as gross national product, balance of payment figures, and total national population is now published in a form that permits international comparison. But there are still many data categories that, because of differences of definition or measurement methods, are not comparable across countries, even though they may be similarly labeled.

Strategic Insight. Numerous segmentation schemes that satisfy statistical criteria of homogeneity and fit are worthless for purposes of strategy. An international segmentation that classifies international markets according to per capita hospital beds may prove extremely useful for firms associated with medical services but of no use at all to companies dealing with animal food supplements.

Product Life Cycle

Since strategy formulation at international headquarters is vitally concerned with international trends, patterns, and other indicators of possible future developments on a regional or global scale, segmentation schemes that reflect a dynamic interpretation of the firm's international markets are particularly useful. One such aproach is based on the international application of the product life cycle concept.

The notion that products go through a type of growth cycle, moving from early introduction or birth to maturity and eventual decline, is a familiar marketing concept. Figure 7–1 illustrates the classic product life cycle pattern as usually portrayed within a particular national market. Although four life cycle stages are indicated, there is nothing sacrosanct about this number. Some authors identify as many as seven or eight stages.[4]

Figure 7–2 illustrates the product life cycle for the same type of product at different stages of its development in countries A, B, and C. Though often associated with durable goods such as television sets, washing machines, and telephones, the concept is also applicable to services. The development of certain financial services such as leasing, the use of automated teller machines by banks to dispense cash, and the increase in credit cards and fast food outlets displays analogous growth patterns.

The most useful feature of the life cycle concept is its emphasis on impending change. It highlights the fact that the future will be different from the past and rarely predictable as a straight-line projection of it, though essential similarities may exist. Second, it alerts management to the strategic importance of timing. The right strategy for one phase of the life cycle may be inappropriate at another stage. Third, and perhaps most important from the standpoint of international strategy, it provides another basis for intercountry comparisons.

It is evident that product cycles will be in different stages of their development in different countries. New products will not all be introduced simultaneously around the world (though some may be), nor will they move through their various stages at precisely the same rate. In particular, there will be major differences between the industrial countries and the developing nations due to differences in average income, technological capability, and other factors. Changes in the market for a particular product in country A may be subsequently reproduced in country B. Two national product markets that are quite different at the same time may be found to have certain essential similarities if compared at the same stage of their development cycle.

The ability of international headquarters to classify (or segment) its different national markets according to their stage of life cycle development for its particular products or services has evident implications for international marketing strategy in a number of areas.

Marketing Experience Transfer. Experience is the most valuable and costly asset many companies possess. Experience developed in one country may provide the basis for competitive advantage in other countries following a similar development cycle. Research by the Marketing Science Institute indicates that international companies are in fact able to identify and transfer use of marketing techniques developed in one country to other countries, following a similar development pattern.[5] Individual accounts of such experience transfer also support this thesis.

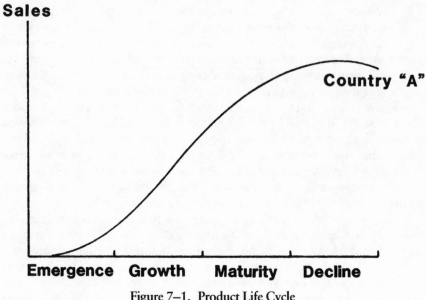

Figure 7–1. Product Life Cycle

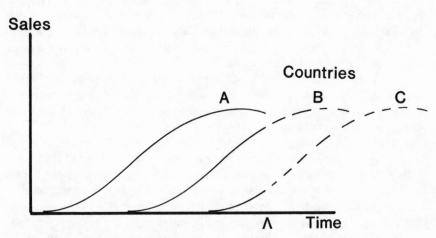

Note: Solid line: actual; dashed line: projected.

Figure 7–2. Product Life Cycles in Different Countries

Working and traveling in Europe in the period following World War II, Richard C. Brown, director of corporate marketing for Scott Paper, noted that there were certain parallels developing there with the market for his company's product in the United States. Although paper tissues there were still sold in drugstores and associated with medicinal use, there were signs that the market was on the verge of rapid growth, developing into a mass market.

Paper products in the United States had reached the mature stage, as indicated by a high per capita consumption pattern and a marked decline in growth rate. However, much of the marketing strategy that Scott Paper had used so successfully to place its products on the U.S. market in the past was found appropriate in the new European context. In its use of the mass media, the focus of the promotional campaign on female shoppers, and the use of supermarkets to distribute the product, Scott Paper was able to make effective use of much of the experience it had developed in the United States.[6]

This is not to imply that experience obtained in one country is always transferable. In the case of Asian and Latin American countries, the U.S. experience is not applicable. In these countries, Scott Paper leans heavily on comparisons with some of its successful operations in countries such as the Philippines.

Better Resource Utilization. By identifying emerging new markets, the firm is able to redeploy its products and services from declining markets, delaying obsolescence, by transferring them to new national territories. For example, Volkswagen was able to produce and market its famous Beetle in Argentina, Brazil, and Mexico long after it had been phased out in European and North American markets.

Timing. Market research indicates that the timing of new product introduction is a crucial determinant of success. Premature introduction can lead to many new product failures. New product introduction that is too late can also be costly. Research supports the widely held view that the first successful new product on the national market has a distinct advantage over subsequent similar products.[7]

By providing insight into international shifts in demand and product trends, the international application of the product life cycle contributes toward better market forecasting and hence improved timing of new product introduction.[8]

Figure 7–3 shows a variation of the product life cycle used by one company. The same product may simultaneously be in different stages of its product cycle in different parts of the world. For example, carbon double-edge blades are in a declining stage in the United States but in a growing stage in Africa and Asia. The figure reflects a pattern (as of 1974) that suggests a systematic shift in product life cycles. Assuming this holds in the future, it can provide a useful indicator as to the direction of international product transfers and the life cycle stage razor products are likely to encounter in various parts of the world, assisting management in matching the firm's portfolio of products to international markets.

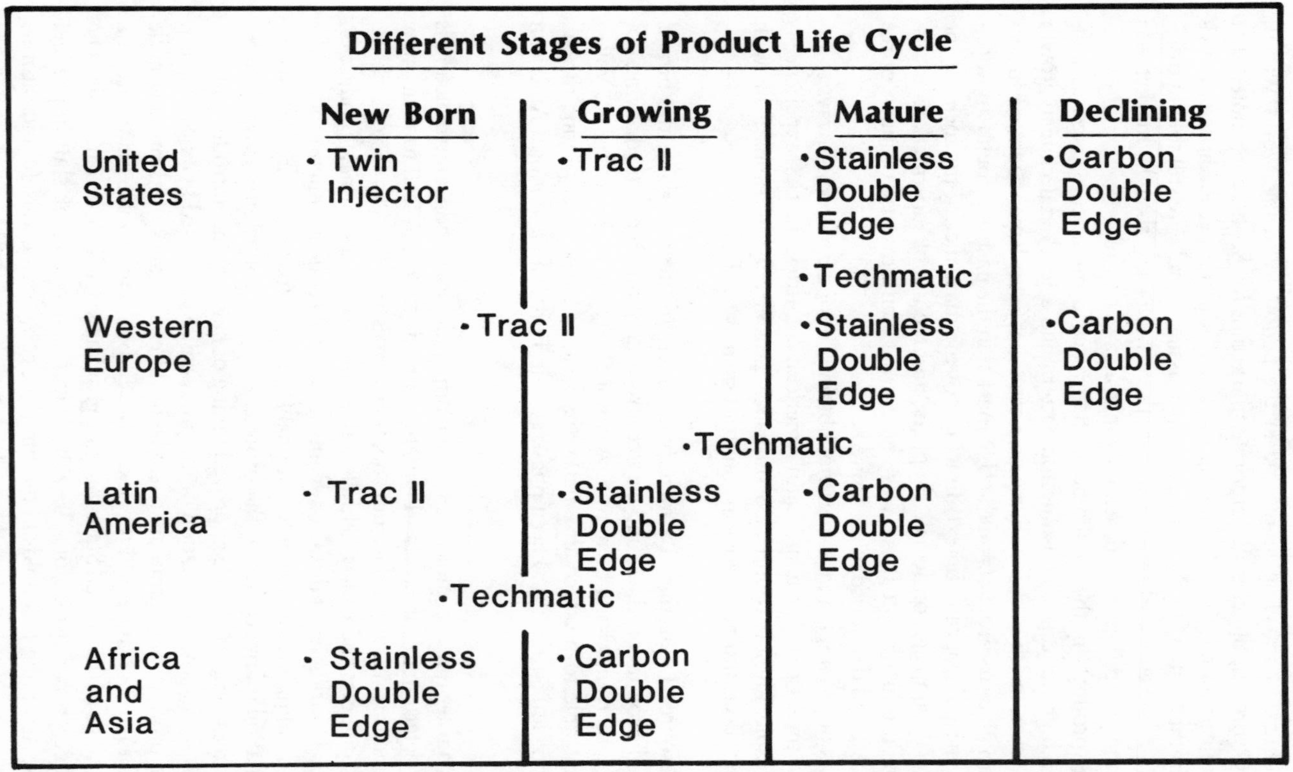

Different Stages of Product Life Cycle

	New Born	Growing	Mature	Declining
United States	• Twin Injector	• Trac II	• Stainless Double Edge • Techmatic	• Carbon Double Edge
Western Europe	• Trac II	• Techmatic	• Techmatic • Stainless Double Edge	• Carbon Double Edge
Latin America	• Trac II • Techmatic	• Stainless Double Edge	• Carbon Double Edge	
Africa and Asia	• Stainless Double Edge	• Carbon Double Edge		

Source: From a 1974 speech entitled "The Outlook for Personal Care Products over the Remainder of the 1970s." Reprinted with permission of The Gillette Company.

Figure 7–3. Global View of Product Life Cycles

Assessment. There is by no means unanimous agreement as to the usefulness of the life cycle. Some companies refuse to employ the concept on the ground that is can become a self-fulfilling prophecy. A downturn in sales, which may be due to any number of other reasons, can all too readily be ascribed to the life cycle. Products with many years of profitable life may thus be abandoned prematurely.

Furthermore, all life cycles are not the same. Chester R. Wasson points out that in the field of industrial products, there are several life cycle development patterns.[9] Differences are particularly evident in the early stages. For example, some thirty years passed before the initial development of the first man-made fiber and the commencement of the growth stage. On the other hand, nylon began its rapid growth phase shortly after its introduction.

Some of the reservations about the life cycle may be traced to problems of definition. It is often difficult to identify a life cycle pattern in the case of products or services defined in broad, generic terms. Clothing may have a cycle so long as to be undetectable. Similarly, generic product definitions such as beer and bread are difficult to employ. But once a particular type of clothing, beer, or bread is specified, life cycle patterns become more evident, such as life cycles in fashion clothing, diet bread, and packaged beer.[10]

Marketing Strategies

Stages of Product-Market Development

The classification scheme illustrated in figure 7–4 can be used by the firm on a do-it-yourself basis to segment its world markets. The central idea here is that the product is part of a more comprehensive development pattern. The entire national market for that product, including distribution and promotion, goes through stages of development.

Two steps are involved in its construction. In step 1, countries are classified according to the stage of market development in each country for the product in question (in this case, automobiles). This classification is not necessarily the same as the country's national economic development. Greece and Mexico, for instance, may be in the same stage of economic development nationally, but this is not very meaningful to the firm interested in the market for television receivers if Mexico has television transmitting facilities and Greece does not. Countries at the same level of national economic development may be at different stages of development in the market for specific products. Accordingly, countries are first classified according to the development of their market for a specific product into the five categories:

1. Premarket: Includes all countries where there is virtually no market for the product.

Stages / Variables	I Pre-Market	II Less Developed Markets	III Take-off Markets	IV Early Mass Markets	V Mature Mass Markets
Product Source	Occasional imports	Regular imports	Domestic assembly and partial manufacture imported parts	Domestic mass production	Domestic research design and mass production "New style"
Product Characteristics	Assorted types	Luxury products	Moderate size product designed for local production and broad appeal	Utility product designed for new mass market infrequent design changes	Specialized products, frequent model change, wide range, many options
Price	No discernable trend	High price category (Low volume)	Moderate price	Low price category (High volume)	Broad range of base prices directed at all market segments
Distribution	No company facilities	Single company appointed distributor	Multiple retail outlets serviced by local plant staff	Manufacturer sells to wholesale and retail outlets	Close co-ordination of factory and retail level electronic ordering
Service Facilities	No company facilities	Low volume personalized service by distributor	Local plants supply parts and training to outlets	Geared for high volume low cost service	Training and equipment for wide range of specialized products
Brand	Foreign brands	Foreign brands	Foreign brands produced domestically and identified with Host country	Domestic brands	"Families" of domestic product brands tied in with single company brand
Advertising and Promotion	None	Point of sale and personal contact	Wide use of printed mass media	Extensive use of all mass media (less emphasis on personal contact)	Research directed use of all mass media. Specialized campaigns for major market segments

Source: Adapted with permission from J. Leontiades, "Planning Strategy for World Markets," *Long Range Planning* 3, no. 2 (December 1970): 43, Pergamon Press Ltd.

Figure 7–4. Stages of International Product-Market Development, World Automobile Markets

2. Less developed markets: National markets with a low volume and relatively stable growth rate.
3. Take-off markets: Markets that have entered a period of rapid growth but cannot yet be termed mass markets.

4. Early mass markets: National markets that have just reached the high unit volumes that characterize a mass market.
5. Mature mass markets: National mass markets in which the product is now widely disseminated and growth has slowed.

In step 2, each group of markets falling into one of the five categories is examined further to locate the dominant, or typical, trends within that group in distribution, advertising, pricing, and so on (the market strategy areas shown on the left-hand side of the matrix).[11]

Looking down any of the stage columns, the user sees a profile of the features that are characteristic of the markets for that product within that stage. Looking across, the user sees characteristic changes in market features between stages.

One of the most important market variables for the multinational firm is product source. Whether the product is imported, assembled, or produced locally can exert a powerful influence on consumer attitudes. Perhaps even more important is the fact that the firm's other strategy alternatives so often depend on this. It would be futile to attempt a mass market strategy by lowering profit margins and using mass media if the product is imported and incurs very high tariff and transportation costs. On the other hand, once the market has reached a certain stage of development, many firms find that direct investment and the alternatives it opens up are required if the company is to maintain its position. Planning foreign direct investment often turns about the ability to identify and forecast the movement from one market stage to another.[12]

The number and type of stages that are useful in describing the development patterns of a specific product group may not be equally relevant for others. Both the strategy variables on the left-hand side of the matrix and the stages indicated at the top can be altered in the light of the firm's own interests and the nature of its markets.

An interesting side effect of this method is the interpretation it conveys of what has come to be termed Americanization. The stages approach indicates that the similarity between the two geographic areas is due more to the fact that similar market situations (such as mass markets) call for a similar business response than any imitative process. As industry markets continue to develop in Australia, Latin American, and Japan, they too are showing evidence of this same similarity.

Lead-Lag Strategies

A logical inference is that firms located in those countries where the first product life cycle for a given product originates, called leader countries, have an advantage over firms in follower countries.

Firms located in leader countries are generally first in the new product area developing on their own doorstep.[13] The fact that they are in on the ground floor of product developments subsequently adopted by other countries gives them a lead in reaping the advantages associated with experience transfer, timing, and better resources utilization. They also have a potential advantage where economies of scale are present, not only from their early sales of the product within their own market but also from their added sales to follower countries. Even where tariffs and other national barriers make necessary the establishment of locally based production facilities and otherwise act to reduce economies of international production, the firm is generally able to reap economies associated with spreading the cost of research and development over a wider base.

Hence, location in a lead country may provide a powerful initial advantage, enabling such firms to develop competitive capabilities that are based on the lead country market, using these to penetrate foreign national markets where they have a competitive edge over local firms relatively unfamiliar with the product. They are thus well placed to establish themselves in a strong position within the international industry for the product as demand grows and to develop global competitive strategies. In the process, they are able to preempt the rise of other global competitors, particularly from countries less economically developed. These are less likely to be the first into the new product area. The best they can hope for, according to this scenario, is survival as national competitors behind protective barriers.

History shows, however, that the initial lead country advantage is not necessarily decisive. Although firms in leader countries have access to the advantages indicated, they frequently have to contend with certain disadvantages. Leader countries are frequently (though not invariably) those with higher levels of industrialization and economic development where wages tend to be higher than in the less developed countries. Also, the fact that a firm has invested in new products earlier than others carries a potential drawback. Such firms have to pioneer new methods and techniques at substantial cost and risk, which with time may prove to be available to late developers at very little cost. The fact that a firm is one of the first in the field may also mean that it has its investment tied up in machinery, techniques, and distribution methods that are relatively outmoded.

In short, there are advantages and disadvantages associated with both situations. The essence of any strategy is the ability to make the most of the strengths associated with an initial starting position and resources. Figure 7–5 sets out a profile of winning strategies for firms in both lead countries and follower countries.

Winning Lead Country Strategy

Innovator firms in lead countries should capitalize on their early proximity to an emerging product life cycle to develop their marketing techniques and accumulate experience together with economies of scale, taking advantage of these strengths to enter follower national markets as these appear, preempting the rise

Stages of Product Life Cycle

	I	II	III	IV
Leader Strategy	Identify and produce new product emerging in lead country where firm has production facilities.	Establish secure base in lead country market. Develop and refine production and marketing methods.	Identify and enter follower national markets where product is in early stage of life cycle, capitalizing on experience and resources from lead countries to preempt local competition.	Consolidate advantages derived from international operations to secure position of global leadership.

Establish production facilities in low-wage countries.

	I	II	III	IV
Follower Strategy (Identify new product cycles emerging in lead country markets.)	Begin production in follower country making maximum use of government protection and local contacts to preempt foreign competition.	Identify and enter other follower countries in early stage of life cycle, capitalizing on experience and other competitive advantages developed in first country.	Enter national markets of lead countries. Exploit new market niches and recent innovations in production and marketing as well as opportunities due to firms leaving mature industry.	Consolidate advantages derived from international operations to secure position of global leadership.

Establish production facilities in other countries.

Figure 7–5. Leader and Follower Strategies

of local national competitors there. They should aim for a position of dominance as a global competitor in their product area, shifting resources progressively toward growth areas and developing economies of scale and volume that will give them a position of leadership. Eventually this may require that some of the firm's productive facilities are shifted to developing countries to make optimal use of lower wages costs, quite independent of market potential in those countries. (In most cases, such firms will have already established foreign production facilities in a number of lead countries.)

Strategies for Firms in Follower Countries

The potential power and effectiveness of follower country strategies has been demonstrated by firms from many countries, particularly those from Japan. Taking advantage of their lower wage costs and government protection (now greatly reduced), Japanese firms were able to compete effectively in their own market with firms from the Western leader countries in product areas as diverse as earthmoving machinery, motorcycles, television sets, pharmaceuticals, hand tools, and watches.

Japanese exports of these products generally began to less developed countries in Southeast Asia where the simpler Japanese products often had an advantage over the more complex products of lead country firms. Production facilities were also established in these countries. Eventually lead country companies were challenged in their own territories. Japanese entry strategy into North American and European markets took full advantage of new opportunities and niches. Japanese television sets aimed at the smaller product segments, where Japanese producers had developed the greatest competence and which had become neglected by domestic lead country producers in North America and Western Europe. Japanese motorcycles developed a new niche as fun transportation, for executives and others previously not associated with such products. Timepieces were incorporated with hand-held calculators and other devices, again opening up new market niches.

Such follower firms made full use of their lack of prior commitments and investments. While the Swiss watch industry was reluctant to abandon its investment in traditional spring-actuated watches, Far East producers captured a major part of the world market by concentrating on electronic timepieces. These were distributed through a number of outlets such as camera and radio shops previously unassociated with this product. Makita, the Japanese hand tool producer, exploited the rise of new types of distribution outlets, such as discount home centers, to gain market share over the more traditional hardware store distribution outlets of Black and Decker.[14]

Japanese production facilities eventually were deployed to Southeast Asia to take advantage of lower wage costs and, in a growing number of instances, into the United States and other lead country markets to overcome entry barriers and transport costs. Having established themselves in international markets, these firms were able to use the efficiencies of international scale and volume to reduce further their unit costs relative to competitors, thus consolidating their positions as global industry leaders.

Winning Follower Country Strategy

A winning follower country strategy requires first the development of an international scanning capability able to spot the development of a new product abroad, preferably one that will soon be suited to the firm's own national market. Production of such products in the firm's own national location is begun before lead country firms have a chance to preempt the market. Protection against foreign competition is often available from the government in the form of tariffs and other preferential treatment. During this stage, the firm follows a national competitive strategy. Once the firm has developed a strong position in its own national market, it is in a position to look abroad, identifying less advanced follower national territories. It uses its domestically developed experience and production base to enter these other national follower markets, gaining further experience and expanding production and gaining the associated economies. Eventually it is in a position to enter lead country national markets making maximum use, where possible, of its generally lower wage costs, any market niches overlooked by the major competitors there (which may have grown so large that they purposely avoid smaller market opportunities), opportunities opened up by local firms withdrawing or placing less emphasis on the now-mature industry, and the latest techniques and opportunities, particularly those neglected by leader firms due to prior commitments in technologies, outlets, and market segments that have been superseded by later developments.

As wages in follower countries increase, they too will seek to deploy production facilities to other follower countries with even lower wage costs. Deep penetration of lead country markets may also require establishment of production facilities in those countries.

Location and Strategy

In both strategies, company location plays a key role. It is assumed that companies introduce their new products in countries where they have local production facilities. The advantage of companies in lead countries is based on their proximity to the national markets that embark on the product life cycle in advance of follower countries. Companies in follower countries begin by marketing to their own national market, where they have locally based production facilities.

The influence of location on the firm's international strategy is indeed crucial, but it does not always follow that firms introduce new products first into their home markets or those countries where they have already established production facilities. Japanese television producers exported color television sets to the United States five years before they introduced them in Japan, judging their home market was not yet ready for the product.[15] For similar reasons, Hitachi decided to market its video discs in the United States before introducing the product into Japan.[16]

In both instances, the Japanese firms were able to overcome the handicap usually associated with introducing a product for the first time in a country where the firm does not have its own production facilities. Given the improvements in international communications and company ability to scan and interpret foreign markets, we are likely to see more such examples of international marketing strategy based on identification and exploitation of the product life cycle, regardless of location. Also, we may expect to see more firms establish production facilities in foreign countries at the outset of the product cycle, without going through a familiarization and development stage in their existing national locations. Initial national location will still play an important role, but there will be both greater capability and incentive to move into new national product-markets at an early stage of their development irrespective of their proximity to the firms existing facilities.

8
International Marketing Policies

The internationalization of industry and associated trends inevitably raise questions regarding the firm's international policies regarding its pricing, products, promotion, and other marketing decisions. The term *policy* is used here to refer to a predetermined decision guideline or procedure to be followed under specified conditions. For example, a company may have a policy to the effect that all employees will retire at sixty-five years of age. Decision rules of this type may be either explicit (written down in a policy manual) or simply a matter of company practice and tradition. Since policies are of a long-term nature, they will shape specific company decisions and strategies over time. This chapter examines a number of key policy areas likely to impinge on and form a part of the firm's regional/global marketing strategies.

International Product Policy

The success of the firm's international strategy turns about the acceptance of its products (including services) in different countries. The role of international headquarters in developing international product policies arises in the areas of product standardization, product development, and product safety and quality.

International Product Standardization

Products, such as industrial machine tools, that are expected to perform much the same task in different countries have long been associated with international standardization. It is understood that certain of these will be too expensive, complex, or otherwise less suited for some countries than others. But the firm that produces a stamping press found suitable for country A will usually also market the same press in country B with only minor modifications (of the type that adjust for differences in electrical current, climate, and so forth).

More surprising is the fact that international product standardization is also widely adopted in the case of consumer goods. In their research on marketing practice in leading European and U.S. multinational companies, Sorenson and Wiechmann found a high degree of international product standardization in consumer packaged goods.[1] Branding, packaging, as well as certain aspects of advertising and promotion also exhibited high standardization. In other words, these elements of the firm's marketing were not tailored to each country individually. The multinational firms investigated were found to be pursuing policies consistent with a high degree of international product standardization.[2]

These results should be interpreted with caution. Sorenson and Wiechmann's study did not include company practice in developing countries, where we might expect a greater discrepancy relative to developed countries in terms of taste, customs, income, and other characteristics. Furthermore, findings that indicate a high degree of product standardization do not mean that the products were identical; small product differences that may nevertheless be important are consistent with such results.

Product Development

Closely related to the issue of international product standardization is the question of product development: how should the firm go about developing products for international markets?

Figure 8–1 illustrates four policies regarding product development. The first option, national development, refers to a policy of developing a different product for each national market. This permits close adaptation of the product to the specific needs of individual national markets while incurring the costs associated with duplicate design and research facilities, as well as restricted economies of scale and volume.

Most companies pursue policies falling under the second and third policy options. The firm develops its products for a particular national market, which is usually the firm's home market. The product may then be transferred abroad without modification to another national market (option 2) or subsequently modified to adapt more closely to foreign market conditions (option 3). This has the obvious virtue of concentrating research and development, usually in a single national location. It also reduces risk in that the product is typically tried and tested in one country before being marketed abroad. An added advantage is that the product typically is launched first in a national territory, such as the firm's home country, in which the firm has had extensive experience. However, some firms, in pursuing the international product cycle, are launching products in less familiar countries that are in a more advanced stage of that cycle. As firms improve their ability to scan and interpret foreign markets, we may expect that all of the development options will be practiced in countries chosen more for their particular market and other strategic features and less on the basis of limitations imposed by the firm's present location and the accident of its home country origins.

1. National Development

Product developed
individually for each
national market.

2. Domestic Development

Product developed for a
specific national market
(typically the firms domestic
or "home" market) and
exported or produced
elsewhere without change.

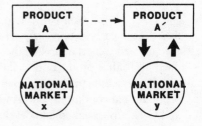

3. Sequential Development

Product developed to suit
one national market,
subsequently modified to
suit conditions in a foreign
market.

4. Multinational Development

Product developed from the
outset to fit conditions in
more than one national
market.

Figure 8–1. International Product Development Policies

The final option, multinational development, requires a high degree of co-ordinated market research and decision making across national borders. It also entails considerable risk. By attempting to develop a product that from the outset is designed and targeted toward customers in more than one country, it incurs the danger of pleasing no one. Peter Kraushar, a marketing expert in new product development, argues strongly against multinational development:

> In my experience it makes little sense to develop and launch new products inter-
> nationally. If the vital task in evaluating and launching a new product is to cut
> down the risks, it must follow that to cut down on possible negatives in a num-
> ber of different countries at once is either completely impossible or represents a
> sure recipe to introduce the lowest common denominator, i.e. a product which
> is so neutral that it will not attract any attention in any country.[3]

Despite the wisdom of these comments, there are indications that the international coordination of marketing programs and the development of products to
suit multiple national environments is spreading.

Companies competing in the more international industries cannot afford to
wait and see if the products they have developed for one country are acceptable
elsewhere. Electronics and pharmaceutical companies ascertain in advance the
government and customer requirements of their projected international markets.
Even small discrepancies between these and the products they have developed
may eliminate the latter from competition in major markets. Quite apart from
the expense, there is often not enough time to modify products, once they have
been launched in any part of the world, without incurring a high risk of competitive imitations.

The Ford Motor Company, at one time or another, utilized all four approaches. In the early export stage of its international expansion, the products
marketed abroad were the same as those developed for its domestic market. This
continued even after production facilities were established in Europe, but eventually Ford overseas plants were allowed to modify the U.S.-designed product to
suit local national conditions. Subsequently the major Ford subsidiaries in England and Germany designed and developed their own products, aimed mainly at
their respective national markets. More recently the company has adopted the
multinational mode of new product development. The Ford Fiesta was designed
primarily with five major European national markets in mind. Today many products and components are designed from the outset to meet regional and even
global requirements.

Product Safety and Quality

Questions of product quality and safety can affect the firm's reputation and credibility on an international scale. Central standards are widely used by multinational companies to ensure that minimal quality and safety requirements are met
throughout their international operations.

One major North American food producer espouses a high degree of independence for its national subsidiary operations except for those decisions bearing
on the safety and quality of its products. All new products, regardless of where
they have been developed, must first be submitted to its central laboratories for
rigorous testing and approval.

International Pricing Policy

International headquarters has four major options regarding international price policy.

Nationally Based Prices

Each national subsidiary is free to determine its own prices; there is no participation by international headquarters. Given the many differences from one country to another in terms of distance, conditions of production, and legislative constraints beyond the control of management, this has considerable appeal in that national prices are free to adjust to local conditions as interpreted by local management.

One major drawback is the possibility that different national prices arrived at in this manner may lead to intracompany price competition. The firm's products in country A may be transported by a third party to country B where they are sold at a price higher than that in A but less than the same company may be selling them for in country B. In other words, prices established by the firm's subsidiary in one country are undercut by its own products imported from another.

This practice is becoming increasingly widespread. Medicines and medical products sold by international pharmaceutical firms at low prices in Southeast Asia are reappearing in Western European markets where they are undercutting the firm's products in those countries. The practice is not confined to high value-to-weight products. The same practice has appeared in vegetable oil. The branded product of a well-known multinational food company has been purchased on the open market in one country and transported to another where the firm's national subsidiary has been selling the product at a higher price.

Standard Formula Pricing

The same formula is applied in each country to arrive at the price there. The cost-plus formula is the most often used. This begins with the production cost of the product and adds to that additional costs, such as transportation, local taxes, tariffs, distribution markup, and similar costs, plus the desired profit per unit, to arrive at the price for the product in that country.

While avoiding many of the inconsistencies that lead to intracompany price competition, standard formula pricing preempts the use of one of the most important strategic strengths of the multinational-international company. Bound by such formulas, the company does not have the freedom and flexibility required to vary price in a way that affects its profitability and market penetration in different national markets as part of a unified international strategy.

International Strategic Pricing

Prices are set by international headquarters as part of the firm's overall strategy. They may be varied internationally, from country to country, to take advantage of special opportunities without regard to the short-term cost and return situation associated with individual national territories.

This flexibility constitutes a major competitive tool. International headquarters determines national prices for the firm's product, which may vary from one country to another. In some countries, it may determine that the enterprise as a whole would benefit from exceptionally low prices aimed at gaining competitive advantage or penetrating new markets. In other parts of the world, prices may be geared toward high profitability. Or prices may be varied according to the different product life cycle stages.

Experience Curve Pricing

The essential feature of experience curve pricing is that price is set with reference to the firm's projected unit costs. These are expected to decline as accumulated volume produced increases. The downward sloping curve in figure 8–2 illustrates this relationship. The firm's unit costs for a particular product category decline as its accumulated volume (total units produced of that product) increases. The downward-sloping relationship between unit costs and volume produced is due to changes in production efficiency. As a matter of empirical observation, efficiency improves as volume accumulates.[4] In other words, the more the firm produces of a certain product, the lower will be its unit costs (calculated in real terms and excluding the effects of inflation).

Used as part of the firm's pricing strategy, experience curve pricing makes use of the relationship to gain competitive advantage. Initially prices are set below unit cost in the expectation that this will provide a price advantage over competitors. This will gain the firm a higher market share, further increasing its volume of production and hence increasing its efficiency and lowering unit costs still further. Eventually unit costs will be lower than price (even though the latter may have been reduced still further). Reductions in unit cost will outstrip reductions in price.

A successful experience curve pricing strategy will set the firm on a cycle of cost reductions, market share increases, and price reductions, as indicated in figure 8–3. Eventually unit costs will be much below those of competitors, enabling the firm to undercut their prices while still making a profit.

The implications for multinational companies are evident. If they can apply the method on an international scale to take advantage of the larger volumes associated with international markets, the firm may gain a decisive advantage, particularly over domestic competitors. Texas Instruments discovered that its unit costs fell 27 percent each time its production of semiconductors doubled. By

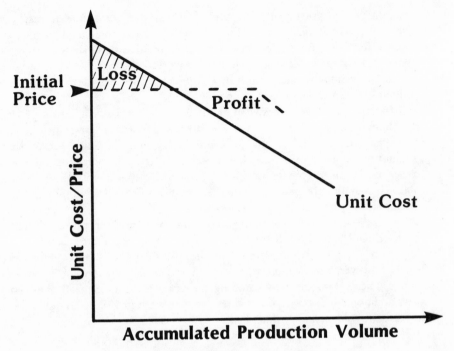

Figure 8–2. Experience Curve Pricing

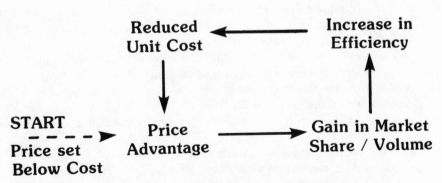

Figure 8–3. Experience Curve Pricing Strategy

using the type of pricing strategy outlined, it was able, for a time, to reap very high profits while pricing most of its competitors down to a small share of the market. Texas Instruments calculates the projected decline in costs that are expected to accompany increased volume on a worldwide basis. Demand and sales volume are estimated internationally, and prices are set accordingly. Price competition between subsidiaries is not permitted.[5]

The theory can be deceptive in that it assumes that the firm has the product distribution and other resources needed to make it work. Secondly, it presupposes that the firm will be able to secure the higher volume and market share without triggering a price war that cancels its price reduction. This requires a close calculation of competitor reaction, something that is not always predictable. There is an implicit assumption that either other firms will not use the same pricing strategy or that they will be less successful.

In 1982, the Timex Sinclair 1000 computer became the first home computer in the United States to sell for less than $100. The immediate reaction to the lower price initially was favorable, resulting in increased volume and market share; however, Commodore International and other producers of home computers quickly responded by lowering their prices. Timex Sinclair came back with additional reductions, but the net outcome left it in 1983 with reduced volume, market share, and profitability.[6]

International Distribution Policy

Distribution is probably the marketing area least susceptible to international headquarters policies since it often entails dealing with many independent or quasi-independent agencies. It may be expected that within each country, these will have developed their unique procedures and practices, influenced by different national industrial legislative acts, as well as the country's individual traditions and customs. Nevertheless, distribution plays such a key role and forms such an integral part of the firm's marketing strategy that some firms have developed policies aimed at achieving international uniformity and consistency in distribution procedures considered essential to their success.[7]

Avon's policy has been to replicate its door-to-door distribution methods in foreign markets. Canvassing of potential customers on their doorstep as developed by that company in the United States has been applied successfully in Latin America and Europe, though with important modifications that allow for differences in income levels in setting sales targets, as well as differences in national attitudes to house calls.

A major U.S. producer of consumer durables found on moving abroad that the distribution channels in some of its major foreign markets required that its product pass through multiple independent agencies before reaching the customer. After leaving the company, the products in question went to an import distributor, then a major wholesaler, and subsequently to a small wholesaler before passing to a retailer and finally the customer. The company decided that these multiple levels of distribution were inconsistent with its marketing strategy since they tended to insulate the firm from the final consumer.

Headquarters determined as a matter of policy that only one independent agency should intervene between itself and the customer. This change, to be implemented over a period of years, went against the accepted practice in some countries, including those comprising its major foreign markets. Several lawsuits were filed against the firm by agencies and distributors that felt that the proposed change went against accepted practice and violated their commercial rights. More important was a significant loss in goodwill because the proposed change was widely seen as an example of a foreign firm's taking advantage of local small businesses. Much of the conflict and friction could have been avoided by an early decision stipulating from the outset the company's distribution policy.

International Promotion Policies

All other things being equal, an advertising campaign specifically designed for a particular country will be superior to an international campaign adapted to suit multiple national situations. But all other things are far from equal. Even the largest multinational firms will find a wide discrepancy in the capability of their different national units to develop their own advertising and promotional campaigns. Inevitably there will be some very small subsidiaries, as well as sales branch offices and representatives. Management in these smaller units is generally too preoccupied with line duties to devote sufficient time to the development of appropriate promotion and advertising. These same units are often the ones with lower sales levels and advertising budgets.

In some multinationals, headquarters acts as a clearing-house for promotional ideas and campaigns generated by the various parts of the organization. In others, headquarters staff may be used to research, develop, and test advertising campaigns and themes that are then adopted on a regional or global basis. Usually such adaptation is done in close consultation with local subsidiary management, which fine tunes the advertising to local national conditions.[8]

Even more important is the development of the firm's international corporate image and reputation. With present-day improvements in communications, it is unrealistic to think that these can be kept in isolated national compartments. The firm's image and reputation developed in one part of the world is likely to spread to another. This also means that differences in nationally based promotional efforts may act to project an incoherent image, confusing to both governments and clients.

Company-wide policies governing the firm's promotional efforts include the following: (1) minimum national advertising budgets, either in absolute amounts or as a percentage of sales; (2) internationally standardized logo and trademarks (in companies such as Rolls Royce and Coca-Cola, the trademark is perhaps the most valuable part of the company); and (3) standards of truthfulness and openness in promotional claims.

The task of international headquarters is to arrive at policies in these and other areas that strike a balance between the discretion and flexibility to be allowed national operating units and the need for a degree of international consistency and coordination.

9

International Plant Location and Logistics

Multinational companies use three major logistics methods to transfer their operations across national borders: transfer of products (exporting and importing); transfer of technology by license, franchise, or other contractual arrangement; and transfer by investing in foreign-based plants and facilities.

By definition, multinational firms have a major stake in the last method. An integral part of multinational logistics strategy is direct investment in foreign-based facilities. This includes particularly investment in foreign plants (this term includes facilities devoted to the production of services and technology as well as physical goods). Where management decides to establish its plants will have a major impact on corporate risk, sales, and profits. This chapter presents a number of techniques for identifying plant and other location opportunities as part of the firm's regional/global logistics strategy.

Foreign Investment Decision Process

Given that company resources are limited, how does management assess different national locations for its plants and other facilities? A domestic company facing an analogous need to investigate plant location may be expected to lean heavily on financial analysis. Detailed estimates developed of projected costs and returns for alternative investment sites form the basis for estimates of future sales, costs and profits. Taken in conjunction with required capital investment, these data can be used to develop forecasts of future ROI. And ROI and associated financial methods can be used to develop a basis for systematic site selection derived from comparable estimates.

With some 150 countries to choose from, it is not realistic to expect financial analysis of each national alternative. Not even the largest multinational company can afford the resources, still less the time, required to identify and measure the many elements involved in arriving at estimates of cost, sales, profitability, and associated risk for even half the possible national locations for such investment.

In an investigation of the foreign investment decision process, Yair Aharoni concludes that "even the most cursory investigation of each one of more than 150 countries in the world is practically impossible."[1] The picture emerging from this and associated research into this area is one of decision making under conditions characterized by Igor Ansoff as "partial ignorance."[2] Decision making proceeds with less than full knowledge of all the parameters, but that does not imply that it is a random process.

The larger, more experienced companies (generally those with more at stake) use a number of screening methods with a view to reducing the potential sites to a more manageable figure—some four or five national sites—which are then subject to more orthodox financial and strategic analysis.[3]

Screening National Locations

Screening methods are used to facilitate a search that requires investigation of a large number of candidates. The success of a screen-based search depends on the existence of a close correlation between the screening criteria and the objective of the search, the cost-effectiveness of the screen (it should be more economical of time and effort than applying the more in-depth analysis directly), and its thoroughness (the screen does not overlook an unacceptable number of qualified candidates).

Single-Variable Screens

The simplest type of screen is based on a single characteristic, or variable. A company may wish to eliminate from further consideration all national markets that fail to meet specified minimum levels of per capita income or size of population or political stability or some other measure. Sometimes referred to as go–no go criteria, a number of these may be used in succession. Countries that go through the first single-variable screen pass on to be tested against the second and so forth.[4]

The chief danger of this screen is that the variables will be used to eliminate good national prospects from further consideration on superficial grounds. For example, some companies screen out national sites with low average national per capita income, but blind application of such criteria overlooks the potential of countries such as India and Brazil. In these cases, the average figure conceals a substantial population with high per capita income. Indeed its absolute size is larger than in many other countries with a much higher average income.

Rating Scales

A more comprehensive method incorporates several screening criteria into a rating scale. As illustrated in figure 9–1, each screening criterion receives a national

	National Rating (1–10)	X	Weight (1–10)	Combined Score
Screening Criteria				
Political stability	___		___	___
Government attitude to foreign companies	___		___	___
Repatriation of capital	___		___	___
Repatriation of earnings	___		___	___
Investment incentives	___		___	___
Tariff protection	___		___	___
Ownership restrictions	___		___	___
Controls on foreign managers	___		___	___
Taxation provisions	___		___	___
Exchange-rate stability	___		___	___
Per capita gross national product	___		___	___
Gross national product	___		___	___
Prospect for economic growth	___		___	___
Rate of inflation	___		___	___
Size of product market	___		___	___
Product market growth rate	___		___	___
Industry capacity utilization	___		___	___
Industry legislation	___		___	___
Distribution system	___		___	___
Competitor concentration	___		___	___
Buyer concentration	___		___	___
Industrial relations	___		___	___
Availability of necessary supplies	___		___	___
Industrial relations	___		___	___
Labor costs	___		___	___
Raw material costs	___		___	___
Total Combined Score				___

Figure 9–1. Rating Scale for Screening National Environments

rating along a scale of 1 to 10 points. A score of 9 for political stability would indicate a highly favorable outlook for political stability in that country; something in the 1 to 3 range would indicate just the opposite. Each national rating is also weighted according to its importance; the higher the weight, the greater the perceived importance of that criterion.[5] Firms comtemplating foreign direct investment generally assign a high weighting—in the 8–10 range—to political stability.

The national rating for each criterion is multiplied by the weight to arrive at its score. The individual scores are summed to arrive at a total score for the country being rated, and this score is compared to similar ratings for other countries. Those few countries with the highest total scores are selected as promising candidates for in-depth appraisal and investigation.

Rating scales are particularly effective in facilitating international comparisons in areas requiring a high degree of subjective judgment, such as government attitudes, prospects for changes in exchange rates, capital controls, and political stability.

As with any other device of this nature, it has certain drawbacks. In practice, the application of a system of weights is often considered useful but presents problems. For example, who does the weighting? There is no agreed formula for this; some firms use a consensus of informed managers. Others use a panel of experts in the area; government experts on foreign relations may be used to weight political variables, for instance.

The national rating awarded may also vary with the firm's strategy. For example, a logistics strategy that relies on imports into the national territory will interpret tariffs quite differently from one that anticipates the location of manufacturing facilities in that country. In the former situation, tariffs are a handicap, a country with high tariff barriers will be awarded a low rating. But if the strategy calls for establishing manufacturing facilities, the same national tariff barriers now represent protection against external competition, a potential asset that merits a high national rating. Multiple strategies may require multiple rating scales.

In some situations, it may not be appropriate to screen countries individually. Where tariffs and other national barriers have been drastically reduced or eliminated, as in a trade group, treating the countries in question as a single unit may be more suitable.

Above all, the use of such screens should not become overinvolved in their mechanics. If it does, simple points may be overlooked. One firm became so immersed in the detail of the rating scale calculations that it did not notice the fact that its own suppliers were expanding their overseas operations to a certain country. Much later, it identified that country as a major growth area and a desirable national location. In another instance a firm was searching for a new site on which to establish an assembly plant for steel components shipped from its British manufacturing base. A rating scale indicated that the West German market for its product was the largest, fastest growing, and most favorable of the candidates; however, it failed to point up the fact that steel prices in Germany were lower than those in Britain. A simple calculation, which also took transportation costs into account, showed clearly that the firm's product (40 percent of the cost accounted for by steel content) would be noncompetitive against similar products produced locally.

Portfolio Screening

There is a need to distinguish between national environments that are attractive in a general sense and the ability of the firm to compete successfully in those countries. These two quite distinct attributes are often confused. A country that appears to be very attractive may be completely unsuitable for a specific company.

In practice, rating scales tend to give a high weight to national characteristics associated with general attractiveness. The fact that a country has a large, rapidly growing product-market, with a favorable economic climate and political stability, may tip the balance in its favor almost irrespective of the firm's ability to compete there.

The usefulness of assessing these two dimensions (general attractiveness and ability to compete) separately prior to interpreting their implications for strategy has been recognized for some time. The Shell Company (also the General Electric Company and McKinsey and Co.) for some time has used a two-dimensional matrix to identify potential new business sectors.[6] Much the same approach may be applied to screen national locational opportunities. The idea is that countries that score high on both attractiveness and the firm's ability to compete are the most likely candidates for closer analysis for major international commitments.

This method can be particularly useful in the case of manufacturing and service companies seeking to establish facilities within foreign countries to service the national markets there (see figure 9–2). Countries are rated along two dimensions. Screening criteria are selected to rate each country in terms of its general attractiveness in a particular industry or product-market (the horizontal axis). Another set of screening criteria is used to rate the same countries in terms of each firm's ability to compete there. Not only new territories but also those countries where the firm has already established some form of operation may be included.

Countries that score high on both attractiveness and ability to compete are considered, subject to further investigation, the most promising areas for a major company commitment, such as new plant and other facilities. Those toward the middle part of figure 9–2 are identified as more suitable for a less intensive commitment of company resources, such as exports or licensing.

Questions are raised that might otherwise be overlooked. Is the firm adequately represented in the more attractive national territories? What is hampering its ability to compete in certain countries? Countries that rate as highly attractive but where a firm's own ability to compete is low merit special consideration. The firm should rethink its position in such territories with a view to improving its competitive stance.

A portfolio view of the firm's existing logistics locations and opportunities may also be used to highlight divestment possibilities. Although company facilities are usually established with a long-term national presence in mind, inevitably there will be situations where the attractiveness of a particular national location and/or the firm's ability to compete there are sufficiently adverse to consider divestment.

The measures of national attractiveness and ability to compete are derived from rating each country on two separate rating scales along the lines set forth in figure 9–1. Weights may be excluded in the interest of simplicity or where data are lacking.

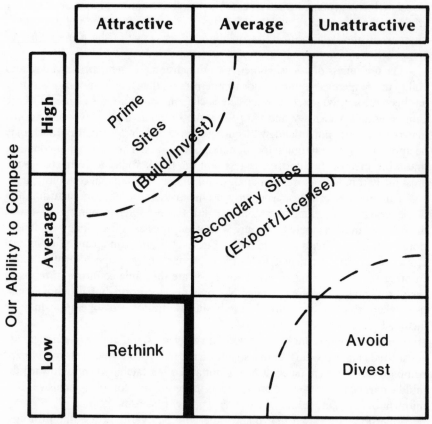

National Market Attractiveness

Attractive	Average	Unattractive

Our Ability to Compete

High / Average / Low

Prime Sites (Build/Invest)

Secondary Sites (Export/License)

Rethink

Avoid Divest

Source: Adapted with permission from S.J.Q. Robinson and D.P. Wade. "The Directional Policy Matrix—Tool for Strategic Planning," *Long Range Planning* 11 (June 1978), Pergamon Press Ltd.

Note: The national market may be defined as the national market for a given industry or, where that is too broad, as the national market for a specific product (the national product-market).

Figure 9–2. Portfolio Screening of National Location Opportunities

The national attractiveness rating is based primarily on screening criteria that are indicative of the general business potential in that country, including such factors as total size of product market, industrial relations climate, general political stability, per capita income level, repatriation of capital, exchange rate stability, and economic growth. The ability-to-compete rating is based on screening criteria that are more specifically related to the firm's ability to compete against other companies in that country. It may include criteria indicative of:

1. Capacity utilization. This refers to the percentage of national capacity currently utilized in the industry supplying this product-market. A low figure of capacity utilization, such as 50 to 60 percent, indicates that companies already there have both the resources and motivation to oppose new entry.
2. Competitor technology also has obvious relevance for competitiveness. Much of present-day investment in new plant investment abroad is triggered by the perception that the new entry enjoys some form of technological advantages.
3. The degree of industry concentration in a particular national territory will influence the firm's ability to carve out a place among established firms. In cases where a few major competitors dominate the industry (measured by the total cumulative market share held by the largest three competitors), new entry will be highly visible, and competitive response from established firms is likely to be coordinated.
4. Competitor market power may take a number of forms. Of particular interest in this context are close links between established local firms and government.
5. Buyer concentration. Domination of the national industry by a relatively few buyers raises the likelihood of a high degree of buyer power as well as closeness in existing supplier-buyer links. But it may also be indicative of an opportunity, particularly where the firm carrying out the screening is able to identify major buyers with which it does business in other parts of the world.

Other items, such as availability of distribution channels and supplies, may also be included. It should be noted that the screening criteria selected, as well as the interpretation of the resulting portfolio of national locations, will vary from one company to another, depending on individual circumstances, requirements, and strategy.

Plant Location and Regional/Global Logistics

Except for firms operated as international holding companies, the choice of plant site must consider how the new plant will fit into the firm's existing international logistics network. Although the international deployment of multinational production facilities provides access to multiple national markets and resources, it may also bring about a fragmentation of productive activity that sacrifices efficiencies of scale and volume.[7]

The more sophisticated multinationals are keenly aware of the potential competitive advantage to be gained from the following:

1. Efficiencies of scale: Greater efficiency (more output per unit of input) is obtained through increased size of the productive unit. Efficiencies of scale are

by no means limited to manufacturing. The Burger King Corporation, the fast-food restaurant group, attributed the poor profit performance of its European operations in 1983 to inadequate economies of scale.[8]

2. Learning curve effect: Greater efficiency is obtained through learning, itself a function of accumulated volume; the higher the total volume produced, the greater the learning and efficiency. The learning curve effect was first noted formally in 1925 when it was observed that the number of hours of labor required to produce an airplane declined with the number of aircraft produced.[9]

3. Experience curve effect: Like the learning curve effect, increased efficiency goes hand in hand with accumulated volume. But unlike the learning curve, the improvement is not limited to labor-associated costs nor is it due only to learning. The experience curve effect is more comprehensive, encompassing cost reduction due to learning, new improvements in design and processing, as well as efficiencies of scale. Its broader nature makes it difficult to separate and prove the separate contribution of all these factors. Perhaps more than anything else, it refers to the observed fact that unit costs appear to decline in many product areas as accumulated volume increases in a way that cannot be attributed to only learning or efficiencies of scale.[10]

Planning the International Logistics Network

Making maximum use of production efficiencies requires that plant location be viewed as part of an internationally related production system. To illustrate, we refer once more to the Ford expansion establishment of its plant in Spain. In the search for a new location to produce its new European small car, Ford took into account two broadly different sets of factors: those national site characteristics that affected its specific performance in Spain (country-specific factors) and those national site characteristics that affected the integration of the proposed new facilities with other parts of Ford's network of production facilities.

The first set of criteria takes into account the more familiar factors associated with evaluation of national environments on an individual country-by-country basis (the approach usually implicit in both rating scales and portfolio screening). Spain offered Ford access to the large and rapidly growing Spanish car market, otherwise inaccessible from the outside due to high tariffs. Spanish consumer reaction was tested and found to be favorable. Projections were made of Ford's anticipated sales in Spain and the implications of this in terms of revenue and profitability.[11]

Ford also had to consider those national conditions and characteristics that affected the integration of the proposed plant with other parts of Ford's regional and global logistics network. Ford's logistics strategy was geared toward achieving maximum European-wide economies of scale and volume. Its plants in the various countries specialized in producing parts and components at very high volumes, larger than those required by the national markets where they were located. These were then transshipped across national borders to be combined in the right proportions required to service national markets.

This type of logistics strategy depends on the ability of the firm to transfer products and components, as well as ideas and know-how, across national boundaries. In evaluating the Spanish site, Ford identified three potential obstacles to such cross-border transfer:[12]

1. Tariffs: Automobile components imported into Spain (from other Ford plants) were subject to a 30 percent tariff.
2. Local content requirements: Government regulations required that 95 percent of each car sold in Spain had to be produced locally.
3. Joint ownership: Spanish regulations at that time required joint ownership with local investors. No foreign company was permitted to own more than 50 percent of a Spanish company, posing a situation that some firms feel leads to a loss of control.

The effect of these regulations impinged on Ford's ability to coordinate and control the proposed Spanish facility with its other European plants. Only after negotiations with the government resolved these issues was the decision made to proceed. Ford committed itself to exporting two-thirds of its production; in exchange, the government allowed the company 100 percent ownership, tariffs on imported components were reduced to 5 percent, and required Spanish content on cars sold in Spain was reduced to 50 percent.[13]

Exchange rates provide an interesting problem in this context. According to the textbooks, the cross-border transfer of assets will expose the company to foreign exchange losses that should be carefully anticipated. No doubt, this was done as far as possible; however, given the long-term nature of new plant investment, with a time horizon of perhaps twenty years and beyond, together with the complexity of international asset flows both material and financial, it is doubtful that the full effect of exchange rate movements in this type of situation can be fully anticipated. More to the point was a feeling among some of Ford's top management that the diversity of the firm's plant locations in countries representing many different currencies would provide a rough hedge against exchange rate movements, with devaluations in some currencies compensated by complementary revaluations in others.[14]

Planning for the new Spanish facility had to take into account the impact of the new capacity on other parts of Ford's regional and global system. Projections of production in other Ford plants had to be recalculated and adjusted to reflect both the increased demand for the new car, as well as the increased flow of supplies from the new plant.

Final approval for the proposed site required evaluation of alternative national locations, including expansion of existing facilities. Deciding which plant would produce what parts also had to consider transportation costs. In some cases, components were produced in more than one plant to reduce transport costs, as in the case of heavy metal stampings, and to ensure against stoppage at any one plant, which could bring the entire system to a halt.[15]

Changing Patterns in Plant Location and Exports

The corporate resource commitment and logistics mode that is right for a given national territory may be expected to change with time. Companies typically begin their operations in other countries through exports. Where these succeed, the firm's commitment and eventual expansion grows incrementally, first through small-scale investment in facilities, such as a marketing branch or sales office, and subsequently into large-scale investment and the corresponding risk of locally based national production facilities.[16] There are, to be sure, variations on this pattern, but the overall message is clear: strategy requires that management look beyond current needs to anticipate future requirements. To what degree is this possible? Are there international change patterns that management can use to aid its ability to forecast future logistics requirements?

Raymond Vernon has forwarded a comprehensive interpretation of trade and international change based on the international product cycle. Vernon's theory presents an explanation of historical change in both plant location and exports. It is not in itself a strategy, though it clearly has considerable strategic significance.[17] According to Vernon, new products initially are produced in the more highly developed, economically advanced countries. The high per capita income in these countries may be expected to give rise first to a demand for new products, particularly in view of their initial high cost during the early development stage. Second, given that the market arises initially in a particular advanced country such as the United States, production facilities need to be located there during the early stages of new product introduction. At the new product stage of the cycle, the product is not standardized. Changes are usually required, hence, the theory goes, the need for facilities to be located near the customer in order to facilitate communication and feedback.

Eventually demand for the product will take hold in other parts of the world, beginning with other advanced (high per capita income) countries. Also, the product begins to become more standardized as the initial problems of product development are overcome, facilitating its transfer. Pressures arise to locate production facilities abroad, including the desire of governments to replace imports of the product (coming from the country of origin) with locally based production facilities providing employment and a better balance of trade. Production facilities are established in these countries, supplying local demand and also contributing toward exports.

Subsequently demand begins to expand in the less developed countries, giving rise to many of the same pressures to shift production location as well as providing access to labor at significantly lower wages. Production facilities are established in the less developed countries. These new facilities not only supply local demand but make use of lower labor costs to provide an increasing volume of exports. Some of these exports now supply the lead country, where the product originated and where it has now reached the mature stage.

Figure 9–3 presents a highly simplified illustration of the shift in plant location from the initial country producing and marketing the product (1), to the establishment of production sites in other highly developed countries (2), to the eventual establishment of plants in less developed countries (3).

There are a number of reservations concerning Vernon's international interpretation.[18] For example, some companies are developing a capability to separate production and marketing locations.[19] Nevertheless, experienced managers will recognize the considerable validity that still attaches to the international shifts in industrial location outlined. These are readily observable in the many product areas whose production has gravitated toward the less developed countries, to supply their markets as well as to export to other parts of the world. Included are textiles, steel production and fabrication, less sophisticated machine tools and telecommunications equipment, packaged foods, and certain pharmaceuticals. The impact of such change on the long-term logistics strategy of multinational companies is also evident.

The Singer Company, one of the first of the modern multinationals, was incorporated in the United States in 1863 as The Singer Sewing Machine Company, based on the patents of Isaac Merit Singer. Capitalizing on the early growth of demand for this product in the United States, Singer rapidly expanded abroad, becoming the world's leading producer of sewing machines. Production facilities subsequently were established in Europe to supply the growing demand there. As the product developed into maturity in the developed countries, production progressively shifted toward the developing countries. More recent plans call for concentration of worldwide sewing machine production in two manufacturing countries, Brazil and Taiwan.

Sourcing Options

Increasing international competition is placing considerable pressure on companies to consider a number of logistics options that may help them to make maximum use of their limited logistics resources. Sourcing decisions such as the following warrant careful consideration in formulating an international logistics strategy.

Offshore Plants. Much of the literature on plant location, including Vernon's international production cycle, assumes plant location is heavily, if not predominantly, influenced by the access it provides to national market opportunities. Most manufacturing expansion after World War II was, in fact, market seek-

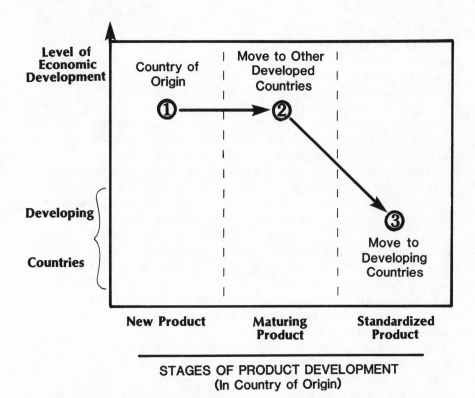

Figure 9–3. **International Change in Product Cycle and Plant Location**

ing—hence the often unstated assumption that plant location is part of the firm's international marketing strategy for penetrating foreign markets. However, many new plants are established abroad primarily as production centers from which to supply the multinational firms requirements in other parts of the world. Such offshore, or satellite, plants have little or no connection with any specific national market though they may play a crucial role in the firm's overall marketing strategy through opportunities in the country where they are located. Plant location in such cases is cost rather than market oriented. Plant sites may be located outside the national markets they are intended to serve (unlike those indicated in figure 9–2).

Second Sourcing. Second sourcing refers to the appointment of another firm to produce (usually through a licensing agreement) the firm's own product, offering potential customers another source of supply. Second sourcing has proved a valuable competitive tool, particularly in the fast-moving high technology industries. For example, in 1983, a major Japanese company offered both Philips and

Grundig the opportunity to produce its video tape recorders under license in Europe. This would have enabled the Japanese firm to avoid existing tariffs and other restrictions on imports of its video tape recorders and to service European markets without investment in new plants and facilities. From the standpoint of competitor strategy, this type of arrangement may turn a potential competitor into an ally and provide the basis for further exchange of technology between participants to such agreements. The licensee receives access to the new technology; the licensor receives a fee instead of the risks and benefits associated with equity investment in new plant.

Contract Production. Obtaining a local national firm to produce the firm's product under contract may provide many of the advantages of company-owned facilities. As the name implies, however, such production is made under contract provisions that are periodically renegotiated, when the contracting firm may decide to drop the contract altogether or (if the operations have been very successful and production alternatives few) substantially raise its price. Here, too, there is a risk that the know-how acquired by the local national firm may lay the foundations for the development of a potential competitor. Unless this possibility can be securely preempted, communications, information, and technology exchange between contractor and contractee will be impaired.

The Sinclair Company of Britain has become a major international competitor in computers while employing a staff of only fifty-five people. The production of its product is contracted out enabling Sinclair Research to concentrate on innovation and marketing decisions. It retains the flexibility to source its products with other contracting firms, perhaps located in different national territories, when the current contract expires.

Coproduction. This refers to an agreement between two or more organizations to share in the joint production of a good or service. It usually entails close cooperation between one or more foreign companies and domestic firms. For example, a major international supplier of aircraft, such as Boeing or General Dynamics, may agree to coproduce an aircraft in cooperation with locally based companies, thus saving the recipient country foreign exchange and providing local employment.

Conclusion

Strategy at the regional/global level is closely concerned with logistics strategy and particularly the siting of major productive facilities. Even within multinationals that conform to a holding company mode, central management will, through its allocation of company resources, have a major involvement with this aspect of decision making. The more integrative multinationals also have to assess the relationship of individual national sites to their overall logistics network, something not usually covered in screening methods that seek to identify the single best national location, which may be suboptimal for the network considered as a whole.

Part III
Strategy at the National Level

10
National Entry Strategy Appraisal

The multinational firm entering a new national environment arrives on the scene as part of an ongoing enterprise with operations in other parts of the world. Its situation is quite different from that of the domestic company. Strategy for the domestic firm is directed at a familiar national context. Even in cases where the firm has been recently established, management generally will have had considerable knowledge and contact with major national features, including political and financial institutions, markets, and the labor force. Furthermore, the resources necessary for the domestic firm's operations are already located within the country in question.

Strategy formulation for entering a new national environment initially will concentrate on gathering and evaluating information on the new environment and the firm's relationship to it. The main elements of strategic appraisal can be simply stated. First, some notion is required of the firm's objectives. Why is it going there in the first place and what does it hope to gain by such a move?

A major part of the appraisal will be directed at identifying the key attributes of the new national environment, including barriers to entry and business and market conditions. Initially the newcomer will be at a considerable disadvantage relative to established domestic competitors in terms of knowledge relating to national conditions of doing business in the new territory.

Another important aspect concerns the firm's own resources and capabilities. Although these may be known in terms of other national situations, their worth is purely relative. A strength in one country may be, and often is, a weakness in another. Research conducted on Sweden's Electrolux Corporation has shown that the relative strength of a particular product line may vary widely from one country to another.[1]

A further consideration is that certain resources may not be readily transferable to the new territory. A retail firm contemplating entry into the Dutch market discovered rather late in its planning that its main competitive strength lay in the large number of stores that it had in its existing national location. Given its financial limitations, this strength was not transferable to Holland. The proposed expansion was abandoned.

Appraisal should also look anew at the firm's overall company values, traditions, and philosophy because these will have an important bearing on evaluating the firm's strategic options in the new territory.

Figure 10–1 summarizes the characteristic elements of strategic appraisal. This chapter interprets and elaborates on their application to the special situation posed on entering a new national environment.

Strategic Appraisal—Objectives

Let us begin with the case of a firm contemplating international expansion. The firm in question, company X, produces a type of building material. Its analysis of international opportunities has established Nigeria as a potential area of expansion. Management wants to develop an entry strategy for Nigeria.

If the firm's investigation of Nigeria is to be systematic rather than random, it should have a firm notion of its objectives. But this familiar advice puts management in a chicken-and-egg situation since objectives that relate specifically to the Nigerian environment are difficult to pin down until management has had a chance to investigate the new territory. Fortunately the task is not completely circular. Management usually will have some notion of the new country, even if based only on fragmentary information and hearsay evidence. Moreover, it will have a good idea of the firm's general area of business interest, as well as certain objectives such as the following:

> We aim to achieve a minimum 15 percent return on investment within two years.

> Our sales target is 15,000 tons of building material the first year with a minimum increase of 15 percent annually in subsequent years.

Early objectives will tend to be in terms of minimum standards of performance, or threshold objectives. They will also reflect internal company aims rather than ones specific to any one country. Only after planning has progressed to the point where the firm has gained some familiarity with the new country will it be able to forward objectives specific to that environment, such as:

> We seek a 20 percent market share of the Nigerian building materials market supplied by importers.

> Our objective is to comply with Nigerian safety standards within the first year.

Objectives of this nature, environment-specific objectives, are important in focusing the firm's effort and resources, but until management has had a chance to

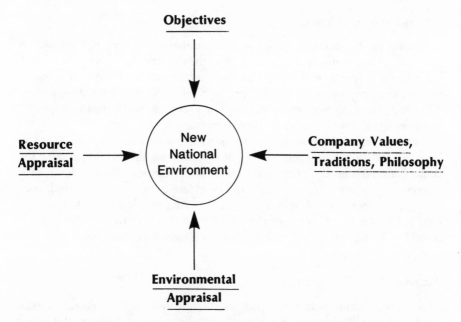

Figure 10–1. Entering a New National Environment: Areas of Strategic Appraisal

ascertain the size and nature of the market in Nigeria, who the leading competitors are as well as their capabilities, it will not be able to develop realistic objectives as to its future market share. Nor will it be able to state when it hopes to meet government requirements such as safety standards until it has had an opportunity to investigate national regulations and standards and what they require. In other words, strategy begins with and makes use of available data, however incomplete. Using this information as a basis for focusing further investigation, management improves its knowledge of the environment, as well as its perception of the firm's relationship to it. It is an incremental learning process with no built-in starting or stopping point.[2]

Environmental Appraisal

Most of the firm's search activity will be directed at gathering information on the new national environment, or what it needs to know about Nigeria to develop an entry strategy. Appraisal here needs to identify and interpret three sets of environmental features: national entry conditions, the national macroenvironment, and the national business environment.

National Entry Conditions

This refers to all aspects of legislation and national regulations that impinge on the firm's ability to move its resources into the country. The international firm hoping to do business in Nigeria must meet certain conditions to gain access to the business environment. Tariffs are one example; work permits and regulations on capital machinery imports are others. Not all of these will be restrictive; many countries have active incentive schemes to attract new companies.

The strategic significance of such border conditions is, first, that they will influence the firm's major logistics options for entering the country, notably the choice between transferring its product there in more or less complete form, such as exporting, or some form of local production facility or licensing. Second, since they apply only to cross-border transfers, they are much less likely to influence local national firms. This means they will have a strong bearing on the international firm's competitive posture relative to local national competitors.[3]

National Macroenvironment

This refers to national features, such as political institutions, culture, national laws, and overall economic conditions, that affect general business conditions and the investment climate. Within a domestic firm, much of this general knowledge is acquired in the course of day-to-day business. The domestic company may well be able to plan its strategy without an explicit assessment of its national institutions, culture, or political institutions. Over time, it assimilates an enormous amount of knowledge regarding these subjects that may (or may not) be adequate for its strategic planning needs. For the firm entering a new national territory, such macroenvironmental features will represent new and unfamiliar conditions requiring further investigation.

Much information will already have been gathered during the preliminary search. Management usually will have some idea of major national economic features and the general trends in the industry. The appraisal now becomes more selective and detailed. Certain features, such as those in the checklist shown in figure 10–2, will be singled out for on-the-spot investigation.

National Business Environment

If the firm wishes to develop an entry strategy for Nigeria, it will have to assess those conditions there that relate specifically to its business.

Identifying Major Product-Market Differences. The company entering a new national environment will be especially interested in identifying similarities and differences relative to its operations in other parts of the world. International comparisons are particularly useful toward the beginning of environmental appraisal,

Government

Stability of government
Form of government
Government role and participation in industry
Attitude toward private enterprise
Attitude and policies toward foreign investment
Industrial strategy and plans
Administrative procedures for dealing with foreign firms
Policies of major alternative governing groups

Economic

Domestic economic growth (historic and future outlook)
Per capita gross national product
Population growth
Income distribution
Record of inflation
Availability of local capital
Rate of interest

General Legislation

Legislation governing foreign investment
Restrictions on repatriation of capital, earnings, royalties, licence fees
Trade and investment treaties with other countries
Pollution and product legislation
Bookkeeping and records requirements
Corporate tax rates
Tax differences relative to domestic firms
Sales taxes, property taxes, local taxes, etc.
Tax treaties
Trade and investment treaties
Company contributions to national health, insurance, retirement schemes

Regulations and conditions of work

Regulations governing union rights and practices
Hours of work
Provisions for shift work
Severance pay and other requirements
Type of unions (e.g., craft, plan-wide)
Labor productivity record
Special skills
Work permits
Laws governing compensation of employees and managers
Regulations governing nationality of managers
Availability of special skills

Logistics

Availability and competence of suppliers and subcontractors
Raw materials, fuel
Transport system and costs
Insurance
Land (zoning requirements)
Communications (national and international)

Investment Incentives

National
Local

Cultural

Educational Level
Attitude to new products and techniques
Familiarity with industrial methods and practices
Technological sophistication

Living conditions (foreign personnel)

Education and health facilities
Housing
Sports and cultural
Personal taxation provisions
Cost of living

Figure 10–2. Checklist for General National Business Conditions and Investment Climate

pointing up features that will enable the company to shed light on the validity and transferability of methods and techniques used elsewhere. Figure 10–3 provides a framework for comparison between product-market characteristics the firm has experienced elsewhere (reference product-market) and those in the new national territory.

Characteristics in:

Item	Reference National Product-Market(s)	Proposed New National Product-Market(s)	Significant Differences
General Characteristics			
Product-market size			
Industry concentration			
Imports percentage			
Capacity utilization			
Legislation and safety standards			
Technical requirements			
Customer Profile			
Per capita income level			
Income distribution			
Demographic distribution			
Traditions			
Purchase patterns			
Shopping patterns			
Buying process			

Marketing Features
Average price
Price range
Product quality
Complementary products
Distribution channels
Average delivery time
Promotion

Competitors
Size
Special competences
Links to governmment
Supply sources
Technology
Industry agreements
Customer loyalty
Licensing agreements

Figure 10–3. Comparative Product-Market Analysis

Structural Characteristics. Appraisal should include a careful analysis of structural characteristics in the new environment. This refers to links and associations between certain customers and competitors, the channels of distribution and their relationship to particular supplier companies and industry groupings, and the degree of industry concentration.

Customer-Supplier Relationships. Established competitors in the country will have developed links with particular customers that the newcomer should be aware of. In some cases, these links may simply reflect a long-standing customer-supplier relationship between quite independent companies. In other situations, the relationships between established customers may be backed by more formal links, such as ownership ties between a producer company that has an equity interest in one or more of its customers.

In many national markets, legislation favors local national firms, particularly regarding purchases by government agencies. In countries with nationalized industries, the government is both a major customer as well as a competitor.[4]

Channels of Distribution. Distribution channels are the traditional weak point of the foreign firm. No matter how strong the company's product or how attractively priced, it will not succeed unless it has access to distribution services able to get it to prospective purchasers at the time and in the condition required. The problem for the newcomer is first of all identifying the particular channel structure.[5] This may vary in terms of the levels of distribution separating producers from the final customer, discounts and other rewards paid to the distributor for services, level of throughput per outlet, and other characteristics, all of which may affect the producer-distributor relationship.

Tied channels of distribution—those committed to particular producers—are probably the major threat to the foreign company since it may find that all or most of the channels considered appropriate for its product are already tied to established producers. The ties may be informal, as in the case of a long-established and mutually profitable relationship that links a distributor exclusively to a particular producing company. Such informal ties can prove very effective, particularly in the developing countries where there is generally a scarcity of qualified distributors.

Distribution channels may also be linked to particular national producers through outright ownership or formal agreement. In Britain, breweries typically extend substantial loans to those who sell their products. The distributor depends on these loans for financing his business operations, effectively tieing his services to the lender company. In other cases, the distribution outlet may be owned outright by the brewery.

Appraisal requires the identification of such links between local national companies and available distribution outlets, an estimate of their probable strength, and, if necessary, identification of new, nontied channels of distribution.

Industry Concentration. National borders and the different environmental conditions they represent can make for great disparities in the degree of concentration within the same industry. In oligopolistic situations, where a few major firms supply the bulk of the demand for the company's product, there is likely to be great sensitivity and awareness of any new foreign intruder. The competitors, being few in number, are able to monitor the entry of new companies easily. Also, being few in number, they may more easily have arrived at some arrangement for allocating certain portions of the business among themselves. This is in contrast to highly fragmented industries where the sheer number of firms makes early identification of a new entry more difficult (depending on the size of the entering firm) and any form of concerted opposition less probable.[6]

Collusive Agreements. Agreements and informal associations among established competitors can be a formidable barrier to new companies. These are not entirely or even primarily a matter of management decision. Other factors, such as the historic development of the industry, technological influences, and, above all, the attitudes of government, will play a major role.

At one extreme, the United States takes a militant stance against such agreements, as reflected in its antitrust legislation. More recently, Japan, Germany, and a number of other industrial countries have also adopted legislation to discourage collusive agreements among competing firms. Nevertheless, there remains considerable scope for legal and informal collusive agreements.

Competitor Analysis. An essential feature of any appraisal of the national business environment is the analysis of prospective competitors.

International Competition. In industries that are highly international in scope, competing firms will have had occasion to observe each other in a number of countries. Over time, management is able to piece together a picture of general competitor capabilities that can prove useful in a new territory where these same international firms are present. For example, a firm with a certain technological capability in one country probably will demonstrate the same proficiency in another. Companies like Unilever, Sony, Hewlett-Packard, and Electrolux implement world standards of quality and performance that facilitate interpretation of their capabilities from one country to another.

Major Competitor Characteristics. The main analysis of competitors will be based on their behavior and characteristics within the country that is the subject of the appraisal.[7] It is important to arrive at an understanding of the competiton rather than a statistical portrait. Appraisal will focus on competitor strengths and weaknesses, as well as the nature and likelihood of response by competition to a new entry from abroad. A number of key features must be considered.

Size is an important feature. How big are the national competitors in terms of sales and assets? The ability of established firms to mount a response to a new entry is dependent on their size to some degree. This refers not only to the size of the firm within the national territory in question but, in the case of international companies, also likely support that may be available from units of the firm in other countries.

Both the disposition and the ability of competitors to mount opposition to new entry will be related to present capacity utilization in the industry. Firms producing bulk chemicals, for example, have had a history of substantial over-capacity in most of the industrialized countries. New firms entering these countries in direct competition with such companies may expect vigorous opposition. Given the ready availability of idle capacity, a new entering company may expect competitors to have a ready supply of products. Pricing at less than full cost is a distinct possibility.

It is important to note, however, that some excess capacity is a normal feature of most industries. Even when operating at the practical limits of capacity utilization, there will usually be outmoded plant and machinery lying idle. Those experienced in the industry will have little difficulty in distinguishing between this type of normal underutilization and depressed conditions.

Competitors in the new territory may be expected to have developed certain characteristic strengths and weaknesses atuned to local national conditions. For example, producers of office equipment find that some of their Japanese competitors experienced initial difficulties in developing typewriters and word processors because this machinery proved cumbersome and difficult to adapt to the Japanese Kanji alphabet consisting of more than 10,000 characters. Without the stimulus of the home market, development lagged.

The same situation motivated Japanese firms to develop particular strengths in the production and marketing of facsimile machines that had no need of keyboards. Although subsequent developments have overcome many of the early problems associated with the Japanese alphabet, the initial handicap of Japanese firms in this area provided a competitive advantage for foreign firms.

Competitor Performance. The performance of the example firm's prospective competitors in Nigeria is crucial to an understanding of their competitive strengths and their capacity to mount a successful response to a new company. Three performance indicators are particularly relevant.

First, an analysis of national market share is essential in identifying the leaders in the industry and, when tracked over time, changes in industry leadership. Analysis of shifts in national market share, say over the past five years, can provide valuable insight into changes in industry leadership.[8]

Particularly relevant in this context is the performance of established foreign companies. Changes in their market share position can provide useful indications of the changing role and position of foreign companies in that country, particularly if they can be linked to particular strategies, such as reliance on imports versus local production.

Closely linked to market share performance will be growth in company sales. An analysis of individual firm performance should focus on intercompany differences in three areas. First is stability of company sales. Some firms invariably will exhibit a more stable sales pattern than others, even within the same industry in the same country. Differences in sales pattern can provide valuable clues to a new entry, reflecting as they do important distinctions within the industry regarding choice of end markets, technology, product design, inventory policy, and other decision variables. Second is sales specialization. Over time there is a tendency for firms to specialize in some sections of the market. Since the newcomer will lack data on competitors' internal strategy and objectives, these may have to be inferred from specialization in particular segments of the product-market. Third is geographic concentration.

Some measure of competitor profitability is desirable for assessing the general attractiveness of the industry and the competitor's capacity for response to new entry. In the international context, this may be complicated by differences in national accounting practices and regulations regarding the treatment of depreciation allowances, adjustments for inflation, and interest payments. In short, the definition of profit is subject to change from one country to another, making meaningful comparisons difficult.

In countries where company financial information is available, one approach is to start with the company financial information and make the necessary adjustments to arrive at some comparable notion of profit. Another approach is to arrive at a proxy measure of profit. One such method developed by R. Hodgson and H. Uyterhoeven specifically for making international comparisons uses value-added to derive an estimate that provides considerable information on the firm's financial performance while avoiding the problems posed by national differences in accounting practice.[9] The term *value-added* refers to the difference between what the firm receives for its products and what it pays out for materials and services purchased from other firms. A virtue of this approach is that the costs of such external materials and services can be readily ascertained for most countries. Together with an estimate of the price the firm expects to receive for its own products, they can be used to arrive at an estimate of value-added.

Potential Target Markets. The appraisal should move toward an identification of potential target market segments—that is, which segments within the national market the firm is aiming for. The temptation will be to apply segmentation schemes that have been used successfully in other national markets. These may prove useful as a first approximation, but ultimately they can prove misleading, particularly when it comes to making the more subtle distinction between one group of potential customers and another, which is the basis for a successful scheme of segmentation. The market research techniques which apply to domestic situations are valid here, in principle. Putting them into practice may offer difficulties in implementation.

One group of market researchers found that in certain African developing countries, questionnaire methods employed in Western industrial markets had to be considerably modified.[10] For example, in Cameroon where the language spoken is pidgin English, Western opinion measurement scales (allowing for five to seven differences of opinion) were found to be untranslatable because the language could not match the subtlety of so many distinctions. Therefore they reduced the measurement scales used in the questionnaire from five points to three. Sophisticated Western market methods may not only be difficult to apply; they can also be misleading if not adapted to local conditions.

Mapping can prove useful at this early stage when very little is known about the market. Figure 10–4 illustrates one such map, segmenting the market by price and the technical sophistication of the product. The map here shows that sales and competition are concentrated in the low-product-sophistication, low-price segments of the market. That is by no means necessarily synonymous with the area of major market potential for the firm. It helps to identify the current situation and to provide a reference framework for positioning the firm's own product offerings in the new market versus its competitors.

Identifying and Interpreting Change and Trends in the Environment. An essential part of the appraisal is to identify and interpret changes in the environment. Strategy is essentially concerned with future events and hence requires estimates and judgments as to the likely direction of future change. Projections of key trends will be required. In making these projections, the firm crossing national boundaries may employ any of the various tools for making economic and market projections normally used to forecast future change. In addition, frequently it is able to draw on international change patterns and relationships between countries (such as various interpretations of international lead-lag patterns and the international applications of the product life cycle concept) in a particular business.[11]

The appraisal should yield an explanation of why some firms within the national industry are doing better than others. Inevitably there will be winners and losers. The former are typically companies that have identified and associated themselves with emerging trends and turned them to their advantage.

National Success Factors. In every business, it is possible to identify a number of factors required for success. Producers of certain industrial goods may find sales of their product dominated by only two or three major purchasers whose orders are necessary to succeed. Or success may depend on the ability to develop a network of suppliers that deliver on time and to specification or the ability to provide a twenty-four-hour repair service or to meet certain government regulations. The criteria for success may not be the same for all firms in the industry. Often

Sales of Major Competitors by Price and Degree of Product Sophistication

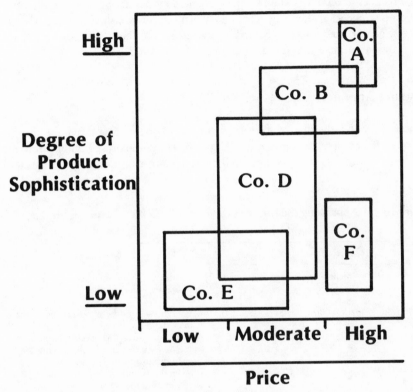

Note: Area of squares proportional to competitor sales

Figure 10–4. Mapping

the factor or combination of factors valid for the smaller company is quite different from that required of the major firm or firms dominating the market.

Success factors differ from country to country. Appraisal of the national business environment should identify the key factors associated with success in the country in question. These will probably refer in the first instance to the present situation, factors required for success in the existing national business environment. Although they are highly relevant, it should not be assumed that today's success factors will be unchanging. A foreign firm, bringing with it a different set of competences and experiences developed in a different environmental context, may be able to change the traditional requirements for success.

Banking is one of the most traditional of industries. The competitive rules of the game are further reinforced by government regulations and financial controls. Yet international banks frequently have based success on overturning established practice. In Western Europe, branches of U.S. banks have introduced new practices in retail banking, such as so-called money shops, credit cards, and interest payments on checking accounts, which have established new factors for success. Major points to be covered in appraising the business environment in new national product-markets are outlined in figure 10–5.

Resource Appraisal

In order to match the firm to the new environment, management requires a firm notion of the company resources at its disposal. The company expanding abroad will find resource appraisal complicated by two major considerations. First is the

Figure 10–5. Appraising the Business Environment in New National Product-Markets

Topic of Appraisal	Items to Be Considered
Product-market dimensions	How big is the product-market in terms of unit size and sales volume?
Major product-market "differences"	What are the major differences relative to the firm's experience elsewhere, in terms of customer profiles, price levels, national purchase patterns, and product technology? How will these differences effect the transferability and effectiveness of company capabilities to the new business environment?
Structural characteristics of the national product-market	What links and associations exist between potential customers and established national competitors currently supplying these customers? Identify the major channels of distribution (discount structure, ties to present producers, levels of distribution separating producers from final customers, links between wholesalers, links between wholesalers and retailers, finance, role of government). Identify links between established producers and their suppliers. Industry concentration and collusive agreements.

(continued on next page)

(Figure 10–5 continued)

Topic of Appraisal	Items to Be Considered
Competitor analysis	Major competitor characteristics (size, capacity utilization, strengths and weaknesses, technology, supply sources, preferential market arrangements, and relations with government). Competitor performance in terms of market share, sales growth, and profit margins.
Potential target markets	Characteristics of major product-market segments. Segments which are potential targets upon entry.
Relevant trends (historic and projected)	Changes in total size of product-market (short-, medium-, and long-term). Changes in competitor performance (market share, sales, and profits). Nature of competition (e.g., national and international). Changes in market structure.
Explanation of change	Why are some firms gaining and others losing? Are foreign firms already operating here gaining or losing? Is there some general explanation of observed change, for example product life cycle, change in overall business activity, and shift in nature of demand? What is the future outlook?
Success factors	What are the key factors behind success in this business environment, the pressure points which can shift market share from one company to another? How are these different from those we have experienced in other countries? How do these success factors relate to our company?
Strategic options	What elements emerge from the above analysis which point to possible strategies for this country? What additional information is required to identify our options more precisely?

question of transferability. Questions of family, such as children in school, and other personal impediments may prevent international shifts. In some cases, the country of citizenship and even the manager's religion can block transferability.

National laws in the proposed target country such as antitrust and monopolies legislation and patent and licensing regulations may prohibit the transfer of certain assets that the company considers strengths. International pharmaceutical firms have discovered national differences in drug legislation that prevent the transfer of certain medical products from country A to country B.

In sum, certain corporate resources and the capabilities these represent may be country specific. A simple inventory of company resources that does not take into account their transferability across national boundaries can prove deceptive. Moreover, the strategic worth of a resource is relative and may change from one country to another. Nothing provides a better recipe for failure abroad than the blind assumption that what works well in country A will necessarily prove effective in country B. A particular manager, piece of equipment, or technology that is a corporate strength in one country may be a weakness in another. It can also work the other way around; a weakness in one national location may prove a source of strength elsewhere. One European firm has found that its capability for producing simple agricultural tools is an effective strength in Brazil and in a number of developing countries in Africa. The same capability is considered obsolescent in its home market.

Resource appraisal for the purpose of expanding company operation into another national territory should answer the following questions:

1. What is the general magnitude of resources available for this venture?
2. How transferable are specific company resources that are potentially available for expansion into this territory?
3. How effective will such resources be in the new environment?

Company Values, Tradition, and Philosophy

Crossing national boundaries may be expected to challenge the firm's current beliefs. These, usually developed in the country of origin and suited to conditions there, may prove unsuitable in a different national location. For example, a company that has always required 100 percent ownership of its operating facilities will find that many countries, particularly developing countries such as Nigeria, have legislation strongly encouraging investors toward joint ventures with local shareholders.

National differences in culture, customer attitudes, worker legislation and practices, and managerial backgrounds cannot always be reconciled with existing corporate values, traditions, and philosophy.[12] Although the company's core of basic beliefs probably will remain intact, operations in different national environments will pose new conditions that make a much greater degree of flexibility desirable. The international firm must be prepared to examine management values and beliefs. Initiated and shaped under different cultural and institutional conditions, they may have to be altered to match a new national context.

11
National Entry Strategy Decisions and Options

I n the early stages of planning an entry strategy, management's knowledge of the new national territory will reflect a large measure of intuition. Toward the latter stages, several visits will probably have been made to the country in question. Detailed knowledge of potential competitors, markets, and national institutions will have been obtained and assimilated. As the investigation progresses, management will address a number of key entry decisions:

Is the project feasible?

What are the firm's major strategic options?

Which logistics method should be used? Exports have certain advantages over foreign direct investment, and vice-versa. Also, there are other possibilities, such as licensing and contract production, to be considered.

How should the various strategic alternatives be evaluated?

This chapter focuses on these and associated elements of entry strategy.

Planning Entry Strategy

The planner's perception of the various elements of entry strategy will change as planning progresses and data accumulate. During the first part of the process, the firm has only a vague idea of many of the planning variables. Managing the planning processes during this stage requires a high tolerance for ambiguity and the ability to muddle through. Relatively early in its investigation, the company may wish to implement a feasibility study. The study does not seek precise estimates of expected results; rather its focus is on whether the project can be executed in the light of already known constraints identifiable in the early stages of the planning process. It deals with threshold requirements and potential bottlenecks, addressing such questions as:

Will necessary government permission be forthcoming?

Are the required supplies and personnel available in the new territory?

Does our product conform to industrial specifications?

Can we expect the national market to achieve a certain minimum level of demand? /

The feasibility study represents a preliminary evaluation that yields a decision either to stop the investigation or proceed.

Generic Entry Strategies

As management becomes more familiar with the new national environment, a number of strategic options will begin to emerge. In their detail, these entry strategies will differ from company to company, reflecting individual needs and circumstances; however, at a high level of abstraction, they can be grouped into four generic strategies, as outlined in figure 11–1.

Skim Strategy

The objective here is one of a high rate of return consistent with a low level of resource commitment. The thrust of the firm's operations will be directed at picking off the more readily and easily available targets of opportunity while minimizing risk and investment. The preferred logistics method usually will be some form of exporting or licensing. In the case of exporting through independent agencies, the success or failure of the strategy will turn on the choice of agents and distributors. Once signed on, these middlemen take responsibility for distribution and marketing. Product development to adjust the firm's offerings to suit national market characteristics will be minimal. Prices will be geared to high margins.

Penetration Strategy

A penetration strategy takes a long-term view of national opportunities and profitability. The company is prepared to eventually back its entry with a heavy commitment of resources and personnel in pursuit of long-term market penetration and profitability. For the multinational firm, this means that the country in question is probably considered sufficiently important to warrant direct investment in local facilities. Establishing the firm's name and reputation plays a key role. Contacts of a long-term nature are cultivated with customers, government, and associated firms such as suppliers and distribution outlets. Pricing is set with a view

Strategy	Objective	Features
Skim strategy	High rate of return consistent with low commitment of corporate resources	Aims to exploit limited and readily accessible segments of the market at minimum cost to the firm. Usually implemented through exports (or licensing) with extensive use of agents and other middlemen.
Penetration strategy	A significant and increasing share of the national market	Implies a major commitment of company resources, including capital and management. Prices and other aspects of marketing strategy are set with a view to a long-term presence as major competitor.
Dump strategy	Generate new sales to reduce inventories and improve capacity utilization.	Uses price competition to secure short-term sales. Usually implemented through exporting.
Explore strategy	Establish national presence to gain experience and contacts with view to possible future expansion	Low-level company presence providing maximum exposure and contact with national market trends, customers, suppliers and competitors.

Figure 11–1. Four Generic National Market Entry Strategies

to sales growth, even if at the expense of near-term profits. A major effort is made to tailor the firm's products and marketing decisions to local requirements. A penetration strategy anticipates the possibility of head-on competition with already established competitors.

Within this general category, a further distinction may be made between those penetration strategies aiming for a major national market share and those directed at particular niches in the national market.

Dump Strategy

Few firms have not at one time or another been faced with problems of overcapacity and excess production. Use of foreign markets to reduce the burden of overcapacity is not only widely used but legitimate as long as it does not contravene rules against illegal dumping (defined by GATT as selling products below the price in the market where they are produced after allowing for transportation, local taxes and other costs).

A dump strategy takes a short-term view of national market opportunities. The aim is to generate the maximum sales with minimum effort and involvement. Profitability is secondary and may be sacrificed. Distribution is carried out through independent agents. Promotion is minimal, and use of the company name is often avoided. It is common in such cases for firms to resort to large volume sales to independent middlemen using their own labels.

This strategy requires that the firm be able to enter the market and begin operations quickly, while retaining freedom of exit with minimum entanglement from contractual obligations and other constraints. The firm's marketing efforts typically stress price competition; hence, the application of this strategy to the more standardized products and those commodities with high price sensitivity, such as standard steel forms, certain types of plastics and chemicals, and agricultural products. There are also signs that this application is spreading to more sophisticated and less standardized products, such as pharmaceuticals.

A basic underlying assumption is that products subject to a dump strategy will not be shipped from the target national market to other countries where (due to their lower price) they may be used to undercut the firm's marketing operations in those countries. This type of strategy should not be used in markets that the firm might choose to enter in the foreseeable future on a more permanent basis.

Explore Strategy

An explore strategy seeks to establish a company presence within a particular national market with a view to acquiring direct experience, establishing local contacts, and observing national market features at close range. Market share, sales, and profitability are not primary objectives. Priority is placed on activities and associations that will put the firm in direct contact with major customers, competitors, government, and other institutions that may be useful should the firm decide to enter this market on a larger scale in the future. Essentially it is a learning and contacts type of strategy offering the firm a low-cost method of keeping in close touch with national situations that could develop into major future opportunities.

During the early years of the European Community, a number of major banks established listening posts in Brussels. Personnel assigned to these branches provided financial advice to a small, limited number of customers, usually referred to them from their branches in other markets. Their primary function, however, was to explore the future possibilities of the new situation brought about by European regional integration. This information would enable them to advise their parent regarding future decisions on whether the bank should enter the market at some future date on a major scale and what specific form this entry should take.

Logistics Methods for Market Entry

The choice of logistics methods is often the most important decision determining the choice of entry strategy. Empirical studies show that companies initially enter a new country through exports. In cases where the firm finds the opportunities sufficiently attractive, the next step is usually the establishment of a sales office and, finally, in selected national sites, direct investment in production facilities.[1] This incremental approach makes sense in that risks, both commercial and political, are minimized during the early stages of national investment when company knowledge and experience in the territory are minimal. There are indications, however, that competitive pressures and the need for rapid penetration of certain markets are motivating some firms to bypass the export stage. Also, in some parts of the world, national tariffs and other trade barriers rule out entry through exports. There are several major logistics options.

Entry through Exports

Entry through exports offers the prospect of low asset exposure to foreign political risk and stability.[2] The company also retains the flexibility of switching the geographic direction of its operations with minimal disruption. In the Nigerian example, if the Nigerian market does not live up to expectations, the company can shift its efforts to other countries unhampered by the commitment of its assets to a Nigerian location. The penalties associated with exporting through independent, locally based agencies (agents and/or distributors) are those of high transport costs, entry barriers (tariffs, quotas, and so on except within free trade areas), and low level of control due to the fact that such independent agencies are not employed directly by the firm. They frequently have commitments to multiple exporters, providing a potential for conflict of interest and diluting the focus of their attention and response to individual company needs. However, the firm that pays close attention to the selection and motivation of these middlemen is often able to change this picture for the better. Another penalty may be inadequate feedback from the independent agencies.[3]

The last two disadvantages can be alleviated through the use of more direct company representation in the target market. Many industrial firms use their own sales force, based in the exporting country, to provide a direct link between themselves and the market. Obviously the use of direct sales exporting requires considerable travel on the part of company personnel. It is usually practicable only for such high-value items as machine tools, aircraft, and construction projects.

Sales Branch

The establishment of a local national sales branch supplied by company exports from its production centers provides a significant improvement in feedback and control while eliminating the travel associated with direct sales.[4] The disadvantages of high transport costs, including susceptibility to delivery delays, and tariff barriers remain. There is a moderate amount of investment (though this can be reduced to a very low level through renting and leasing).

License and Franchise

Sale of company technology and know-how through licensing and franchising agreements offers a low-risk method of market entry free from transport costs, tariffs, and other border barriers such as quotas. Control is variable; typically it is better in situations where the technology and know-how is relatively scarce. The license contract may provide for some form of monitoring by the licensor.[5] Where the licensor provides a product or service essential to the success of the licensee, this can be used to exert some control.

The Pilkington Company, a major European manufacturer of glass products, makes extensive use of licensing. Given the high transport costs associated with transporting glass products, exporting is not a realistic option for many parts of the world. Glassmaking is also a well-established industry in most countries, with entrenched, well-developed competitors that can be expected to respond vigorously to new entry in the form of exports or direct investment, the latter requiring substantial capital outlays to reach minimum efficient size. Licensing offers a quick way of penetrating foreign markets, generating a return from Pilkington's advanced glass technology. It also gives the national licensee a vested interest in defending Pilkington patents against infringement by other local firms.

A major drawback of this method is the technological foothold it provides to potential future competitors.

Investment in Foreign-Based Facilities

Establishment of local production facilities provides the company with shorter lines of communication between production and marketing and avoids (or reduces) exposure to transport costs and national entry barriers. It also establishes the firm as a local producer in the eyes of the customer and, to a variable degree, in the eyes of government. As such, it has important advantages, not the least of which is the leverage it provides with governments for preferential treatment relative to importers, as well as government support in the form of investment incentives.[6]

On the minus side, it reduces the geographic flexibility of the company to shift its operations to other parts of the world (as in the switching of exports from one country to another) and exposes company assets to foreign political risk.

Some of the major advantages and disadvantages associated with this method are not readily quantifiable. Political risk is one of these, though progress has been made in this direction. Another is the crucial matter of control. In principle, the development of modern means of communications should enable the company to communicate and exercise whatever degree of control is deemed appropriate at either short or long distances. In practice, geographic distance does make a difference. The shorter lines of communications between production and marketing, where these are located in the same country, significantly improve feedback and control between these two functions, leading to prompter deliveries and a better adjustment to local markets.[7]

Low-Equity Foreign-Based Operations

The general advantage of company-owned facilities in another country is the local company presence and control they provide; however, few, if any, companies have the resources required to establish their own facilities in all countries where this advantage may comprise a desirable aspect of the firm's strategy. Even if they did, the risk might prove excessive. Multinationals have developed a number of methods for reducing the equity investment required while maintaining a degree of operational control over foreign-based facilities.

Joint Ventures

Joint ventures represent a major option for reducing capital investment and risk associated with local facilities. They offer the further substantial benefits (where the joint venture partners are nationals of the country where the facility is located) of intimate knowledge of local conditions and government. An associated potential disadvantage is the fragmentation of control often associated with joint ownership. The close coordination of logistics flows from one country to another may be hampered if, for example, one of the partners, decides to block a proposed investment in new equipment.[8]

A number of measures exist for minimizing disagreement of this nature:

1. One party controls more than 50 percent of the voting rights. This will normally give formal control; however, even a minority opposing view can carry considerable influence, particularly if it is seen that the differences of opinion reflect different nationalities (that is, the foreign directors are opposing views held by local citizens).

2. Only one of the parties to the joint venture is responsible for the actual management of the operation. This may be complemented by a buy-out clause in the contract that provides that in case of fundamental disagreement among the equity holders, one will purchase the equity of the others.
3. Control of input and/or output. If one of the parties to the joint venture controls either the input (supply) or output (marketing) of the product, significant control can be exerted over joint venture decisions quite apart from ownership rights.[9]

Nonequity Management

Nonequity management of foreign-based operations is a promising development, offering the possibility of avoiding the emotive entanglements and conflict often associated with foreign ownership.

Service contracts are becoming more widely used in the oil industry. The oil company does not take title land or mineral rights; instead, it is awarded a service contract that provides compensation for its services in the form of a fee paid according to the number of barrels of oil produced.

Management contracts are similar conceptually. The firm is paid only for services provided in managing a foreign-based facility. Equity ownership resides in the country where the facility is located.[10] This avoids asset exposure to local political risk, while eliminating the problems of transport costs and entry barriers. It is analogous to licensing and franchising in that a fee is paid for management know-how, which in this case involves the physical presence of company managers.

Despite its apparent advantages, this method is not widely used, perhaps reflecting the fact that internationally mobile management is a very scarce resource. As with any other contractual arrangement, commitment is limited to the time period involved. Since management contracts involve no other commitment of company resources, the fixed time period may result in a situation where management progressively loses interest in the project as the date of expiry approaches. Perhaps more fundamental is the fact that most companies do not perceive their business as one of providing only management services. A company is a combination of services and equipment, ideas, and technological and other resources. It is the combination, or package, that is typically the source of the potential high returns that motivate entrepreneurs to initiate such enterprises in the first instance.

Strategy Evaluation and Selection

The various options generated in planning the firm's entry strategy will require comparison and evaluation to select which, if any, shall be adopted.

Financial Analysis

The great advantage of financial analysis is its ability to interpret the many diverse components comprising a given strategy in terms of a single dimension, financial performance.[11]

Payback Period. This rather crude measure is in the form of an estimate regarding the period of time required to return the firm's original investment (original investment divided by the annual cash flow available for repatriation).[12] Used by itself, this method gives no indication of the degree of profitability or even whether the project being evaluated will be profitable at all. Nevertheless, it is frequently used to give management a simple measure of the time period over which the firm's original investment will be at risk.

Return on Investment. Where capital investment is involved, most firms will resort to one of the more systematic financial estimates of return on capital. ROI is based on forecasts of future financial returns from the proposed strategy, expressed as a percentage of the required investment. Other financial criteria include discounted cash flow, net present value, contribution to earnings per share, and internal rate of return.

Return on investment may be calculated on a narrow project basis—for example, ROI associated with the firm's return and investment in a particular country— or it may be calculated on a wider systems basis, encompassing any and all of the firm's operations, including those in other countries, that may be affected.[13]

For holding-company-type multinationals, the narrower interpretation of treating each project as a separate national entity may prove satisfactory; however, most entry strategies will entail certain cross-border flows that extend beyond the specific country and project in question. The firm's entry into, say, Nigeria may involve exports and licensing sales to Nigeria that are incidental to the main project and accrue to parts of the firm's operations not located in that country, imports from Nigeria, such as certain supplies made available through the firm's entry into that country, which again affect financial performance in other (non-Nigerian) parts of the system, and synergy between the firm's projected operations in Nigeria and its operations elsewhere, such as access to greater efficiencies of scale or a better portfolio balance.

For multinational companies pursuing a more integrative approach, these returns to the wider system may well be dominant. Financial analysis in such cases will include estimates based on the incremental costs and returns to the wider international system rather than a particular project or national segment viewed in isolation.[14] It is also worth keeping in mind the differences in the international headquarters' perception of return on investment and that at the national level due to the influence of exchange rates, government restrictions on repatriation, and other factors.

Sensitivity Analysis. Sensitivity analysis may be used to subject the different components that enter into financial calculations to systematic variation, with a view to measuring the effect of such variation on financial results. For example, suppose the firm's sales to a particular segment of the national market fall 10 percent below expectation. What will be the impact on ROI? Or suppose sales to this segment exceed the expected result by 10 percent. The same procedure may be applied to any number of combinations or number of variables or combinations of them to test the sensitivity of the financial results to such systematic variation. Sensitivity analysis will give management some idea of the likely range of variation it may expect in its predicted results. The analysis also enables it to identify the most sensitive variables within the strategy and to focus action on these points. For example, if it found that a drop in sales to a particular segment of the market had a particularly large and adverse impact on expected ROI, it might want to bolster its marketing efforts to that segment, perhaps by launching a special promotional campaign directed at that segment, directing its best personnel there, or improving distribution facilities serving that part of the market.

Premium for Risk. Where potential investment associated with new market entry is judged to entail extra risk, a risk premium may be required in the form of a higher target return. Let us suppose that management in our firm normally requires a minimum of 15 percent from any new investment. If the proposed venture in Nigeria is judged to be particularly risky, management may decide to add a 5 percent premium for risk, requiring a 20 percent minimum ROI. The 5 percent premium represents a quantified estimate of the risk attached to a particular investment. According to a French survey of political risk estimates, "flair or intuition" appears to be the main source of inspiration for the estimate.[15]

Risk Analysis. Expressions of expected financial returns necessarily refer to a probability that such expectations will in fact be fulfilled. Risk analysis extends the consideration of the probability of success or failure beyond the usual single point estimate (the probability that attaches to a single outcome) to take explicit consideration of the probabilities of a wide range of possible outcomes. This analysis provides considerably more information as to the risk involved; however, the information required to make such estimates is very extensive, particularly in the case of international investments. Given the difficulty of projecting such factors as future exchange rates and government behavior, there is danger of spurious accuracy; nevertheless, some firms do use this technique.[16]

Switching Analysis

While financial analysis is able to compare the expected financial results of proposed strategies, it is not able to test their underlying assumptions. It is possible to become so involved with the financial calculations that one loses sight of the

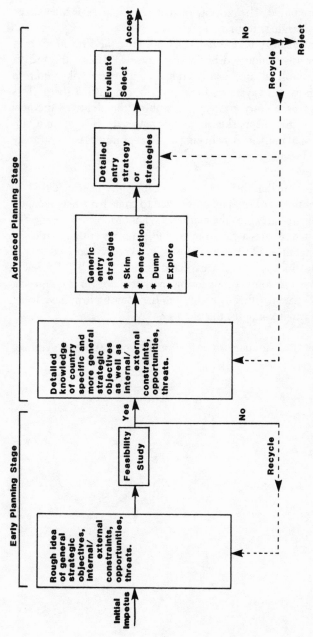

Figure 11–2. Entry Strategy Planning Process

reality on which they are based. The purpose of switching analysis is to evaluate and review the proposed strategy from a different perspective.

By definition, entry strategy is directed at establishing the firm in an area where it has not previously conducted business operations. Unless the firm is entering through acquisition of an existing company, its entry will require a switch of purchasing power away from firms already established there. This means that the success of the entry strategy turns about the ability of the new firm to switch customers, and the market share they represent, away from established firms in that national market. A switching analysis examines entry strategy in the light of the following questions:

1. What is the market share that the firm hopes to gain with this strategy?
2. What proportion of this market share is expected to come from new demand (generated by the firm's entry into the market)? What proportion is expected to come from a switch of sales away from established firms in that market?
3. Which specific competitors in the new national market are expected to lose market share? How much is each firm expected to lose?
4. Considering each of the competitor's losing market share (to the entering firm) individually, what specific advantage will the entering firm have using this strategy which can account for this change?

Figure 11–2 provides a summary overview of the entry strategy planning process.

12
National New Product Introduction

The firm's products and services are at the core of its business strategy. Any initial competitive advantage it enjoyed on first entering a particular national market will usually have been based on products imported into that country from its operations in other parts of the world. With time, these may be expected to reach maturity, raising the need for new product introduction. This chapter looks at strategy from the standpoint of management in the national subsidiary engaged in new product introduction.

Within the larger national subsidiaries, a number of new products may be developed on a purely local national basis, much like any other domestic company. In other cases, product development will be part of an internationally coordinated product development strategy. But a high proportion of new products will have been marketed elsewhere previously. The word *new* is used here with reference to geography. Products that have not previously been introduced into a particular national market are considered to be new there, though they may have been marketed for many years in other parts of the world.

Strategic planning in this situation turns about identifying which product or products in other parts of the world may be suited to the firm's needs, objectives, and resources within the proposed target market and developing a plan for introducing the new product(s) into that market.

In most such instances, management at the national level will look first at products already marketed by their firm in other parts of the world. The advantages of such intercompany transfers have already been outlined in this book; however, it is worth emphasizing that part of the potential gain in these cases is the advantage from transferring associated prior experience with the product.

Provided adjustment can be made for the inevitable differences among national markets, previous marketing experience may provide valuable lessons and clues for managers charged with developing a market strategy for these same products in another country. The decision process associated with such new product introduction is best illustrated in terms of a case study.

New Product Introduction at Kellogg's

Kellogg's, the U.S.-based breakfast manufacturer, first expanded internationally into the Canadian market.[1] A British subsidiary, Kellogg's of Great Britain, was established in 1924. Initial new product introduction in Britain was based largely on products the company had sold in the United States and Canada. The first of these was the famous Kellogg's Corn Flakes. Since then a wide variety of breakfast food products have been introduced to the British market, including in recent years a growing number of products developed nationally within the British subsidiary. However, Kellogg's of Great Britain continues to draw on the firm's worldwide product portfolio as a major source of prospective new products. A watchful eye is kept on promising product developments in other parts of the Kellogg's organization that might be transferred to the British market. ·,

Information about Rise and Shine, a new orange drink, first came to the attention of Kellogg's of Great Britain through information disseminated by the parent company. At the time, Kellogg's of Great Britain was systematically searching for new product ideas. The parent company distributed a monthly bulletin, *Opportunity Booklet*, aimed at keeping the firm's various overseas operations informed about product developments throughout the company's worldwide network.

News was circulated in this manner of a new company acquisition in Canada. Among the products that this acquisition brought into the corporate fold was a powdered orange drink, Rise and Shine, that had been marketed successfully in Canada and the United States.

The newly acquired orange drink appeared promising to Kellogg's management in Britain. It fit neatly with the British affiliate's product development and marketing objectives. Management had already established the desirability of future product diversification, and resources were available for this purpose. The Canadian drink was also in line with the subsidiary's policy of focusing new product development on breakfast foods.

Preliminary Analysis

The fact that Rise and Shine had done well in the Canadian market undoubtedly was an influential factor. There is a certain rough comparability between Britain and Canada in terms of consumer incomes, distribution channels, mass media, and consumer tastes. And a number of products had been transferred from there successfully to the British affiliate. But management was also aware that such comparisons could be deceptive. A few years earlier, another product that had been successful in North America had proved an expensive failure on the British market.

The hope was that the new orange drink from Canada could duplicate its success in Britain, but even at an early stage of analysis, there were a number of obvious problems. The British public bought extensive quantities of cheaper, artificially flavored orange drinks known locally as squashes but had not acquired the orange juice breakfast habit. Powdered foods had acquired an unfavorable image, left over from World War II when they had become associated with substitute products. And British legal requirements on products that included the word *orange* indicated that substantial changes in the product's original formula would be required.

Consumer Testing

Samples of the product, together with details of its formulation, were transferred from the Canadian acquisition with the assistance of the U.S. parent company. These samples were used to carry out a consumer panel test using disguised white box packaging. The results of these panel tests for flavor and general acceptability were favorable though indicating a number of possible changes. For example, the product was altered in both color and sweetness when it became evident that British tastes differed from Canadian on these items.

Product Tailoring

The product formula was revised substantially in the light of consumer tests and to conform to British legal requirements on the use of the word *orange*. Legislation required that this word could be applied only to products that contain a proportion of real fruit. Kellogg's executives noted that the product was completely rebuilt. The resulting new version incorporated substantial product improvements, which were subsequently transferred back to the parent company.

Early Market Strategy

Competitive factors played a major role in developing market strategy for the new product. There was no direct competition from similar fruit drinks. The nearest competition came from the cheaper orange-flavored drinks that dominated the market. The decision was made to position the new orange drink in the British market so as to avoid confusion with these less expensive nonfruit orange products.

A detailed marketing strategy was drawn up featuring the conscious positioning of Rise and Shine as a real fruit type of product. Accordingly, the price was set higher than that of artificially flavored drinks. Promotion and advertising were designed to emphasize the new product's real fruit content. Kellogg's distribution managers went to extra lengths to secure supermarket shelf space alongside fruit juices, well away from artificially flavored drinks.

Product Sourcing

Management decided to produce the product in Britain. Importing the product would reduce initial investment, but it could also have the effect of increasing costs in the long term and reducing national control over product supply and specifications.

The parent firm, acting as intermediary, provided the technical details of production and product formulation from the Canadian acquisition. Kellogg's of Great Britain subsequently undertook the major revisions in the product formula.

Associated Transfer

Assistance was received from the U.S. parent in the form of sample television commercials and other promotional material used in North America, together with audience ratings. Print advertisements and packaging used in the U.S. and Canadian markets were also examined. These provided useful starting points; however, the final advertisements and television commercials were designed nationally to fit British tastes and to support the product positioning chosen for that country.

Test Marketing

The new product was first marketed within a limited geographic area representing 15 percent of national households with a mix of both rural and urban consumers. During the twelve-month test market period, particular attention was given to market penetration performance and repeat purchase patterns. Favorable ratings during this phase supported the decision to launch the product nationally.

Resource Allocation

Where new product introduction requires substantial outlay, the subsidiary may have to secure investment approval and/or additional funds from higher authority. Kellogg's of Great Britain received approval from the U.S. parent company after providing detailed estimates of projected sales, profits, expenditures, advertising and promotion, and market penetration, together with plans for test marketing, timing of the national launch (if any) and an indication of when the product was expected to become profitable to its capital expenditure committee.

A major consideration in such cases is product quality. Rise and Shine had to meet high quality standards before receiving the approval of the parent company's international product review committee for use of the Kellogg's name.

National Launch

No matter how thorough the previous testing and analysis, questions and doubts will remain. One Kellogg's executive observed that such preliminary work seldom yields black and white answers, just various shades of grey. The decision was eventually made to launch Rise and Shine nationally. It caught on and, as with most other successful products, was soon emulated; however, the fact that it was the first of the real fruit drinks on the British market gave it a valuable lead.

Tracking the Product

Once the product is launched on the market, close watch is kept on market reaction to it. Market penetration and performance relative to competition are carefully monitored. All products are subject to scrutiny for possible modification. Either the product itself, the product range offered, or some aspect of the market mix may be altered. A major decline in sales or profitability may even require that the product be dropped. The introduction complete, the product begins to assume a national identity.

Figure 12–1 summarizes the interaction of the British subsidiary of Kellogg's with other parts of the organization in launching Rise and Shine.

Comparative Market Analysis

An important feature of the Kellogg's decision to introduce its new product into Britain was the fact that it had been successful in Canada. In effect, Kellogg's used Canada as a reference market, noting certain similarities between the two markets, such as per capita income, distribution and promotional facilities, and the recipient market. Also considered were major differences in consumer attitudes, product legislation, and competitive products.

Some firms have reservations about the validity of international market comparisons, pointing out that the virtually infinite number of differences between one national market and another render them meaningless.[2] The frequent failures encountered by firms attempting to transfer products from one country to another underline these differences. Even as successful a firm as Procter and Gamble has encountered a high proportion of product failures in transferring products across national borders.[3] Nevertheless, many companies have used international comparisons to good effect.

A company producing synthetic fibers found that consumption patterns for a particular item of clothing in Argentina were related to those in the Italian market with a lag of several years.[4] A firm producing a consumer durable good discovered that significant international similarities existed in size and other product characteristics demanded by consumers for its product at similar per capita income levels. This information enabled the firm to project changes in consumer product preference. Product characteristics demanded in the higher-income countries were used to anticipate the nature of product changes forthcoming in national markets with somewhat lower levels of income, enabling the firm to implement such changes ahead of its competitors.

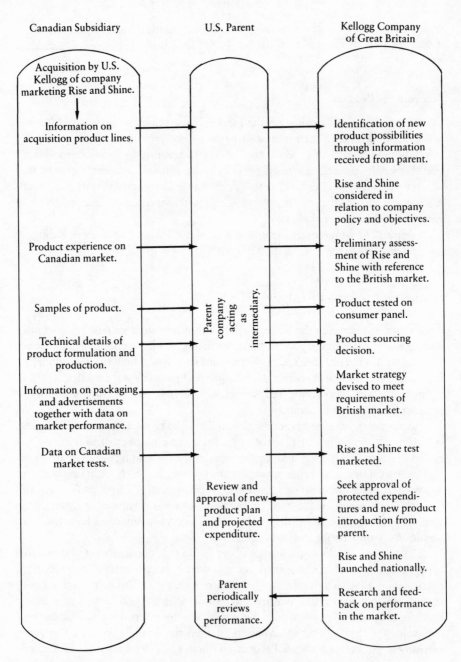

Figure 12–1. Marketing Interaction and Transfer in a Multinational

Comparative Analysis for Product Transfer

Comparative analysis for purposes of international product transfer begins with the question, What are the factors that have made this product a success (or failure) in other national markets, and how do these factors compare with the situation in the new target market? The question is uncomplicated, but in practice such comparisons encounter a number of obstacles.

Management perceptions are often colored by the pressures and constraints of the business situation at the time. For example, the company's urgent need for a new product may tempt an analyst to see opportunities that are not there, or the fact that the product was "not invented here" may bias the local management's perceptions about its prospects.[5] The complement to the latter point is the tendency of some managers to see and interpret all national markets in terms of their own national territory. If the product was a success there, then, the reasoning goes, it is bound to succeed elsewhere.

Another hurdle is the plethora of differences and similarities thrown up by such comparisons. Selecting the relatively few essential items that can be isolated, measured, and compared calls for a high degree of discretion and selectivity.

In dealing with a product that has been particularly successful, there is a tendency to assume that all environmental differences (relative to those in the country where the product was successful) are bound to have a negative influence. Clearly this is not true.

Implementing International Comparison

One way to minimize mistakes and unconscious bias is to make international comparisons systematic and explicit. Figure 12–2 illustrates key aspects of a country-to-country comparison for purposes of product transfer. Initially the comparison will focus on similarities and differences in national environmental characteristics. As market strategies and product modifications are suggested, they will also be included, to arrive at an overall assessment of transferability (see also figure 10–3).

Given the usual limitations of time and resources, the investigation will have to focus on those that are most relevant. At the most basic level, these may include such environmental characteristics, often taken for granted by the domestic company, as climate and national geographic features. Robert Buzzell notes that climate and topography can affect the demand for some products indirectly through the effect on population density, transportation, and distribution patterns.[6]

The priority attached to specific items of comparison will alter from one product category to another. A company dealing in consumer goods may be expected to focus on economic characteristics, such as consumer income and income distribution, associated with consumer purchase patterns. For firms inter-

Reference National Market   New National Market

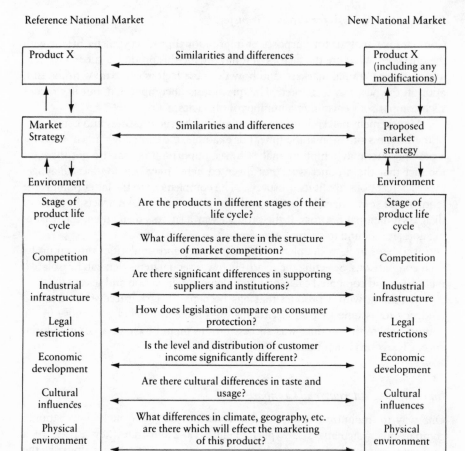

Figure 12–2. **International Comparison for New Product Introduction**

ested in industrial machinery and equipment, important points of comparison would be relative wage levels (particularly as they relate to the price of such equipment), productivity, and growth in industrial production.

Strategy-to-Strategy Comparison

Insofar as comparative analysis is meant to shed light on future market strategy in the new territory, it eventually will require a comparison of the latter (proposed market strategy in the new territory) with the firm's prior market strategy in the reference market. A good starting point for such strategy-to-strategy comparisons is product positioning, the relationship of the new product to competitive products as perceived by the customer. Often this relationship is quite loosely defined—for example, "We make a practice of positioning our products 'upmarket,'" or "The product is positioned as a luxury product."[7]

In introducing Rise and Shine, Kellogg's was careful to position it away from the artificial orange drinks that dominated the market in Britain. The product's physical position in distribution outlets, its promotional material, and its price all aimed at depicting Rise and Shine as a real fruit drink, as it had been in Canada.

This does not mean that the positioning of the product in the new national market will necessarily duplicate that in previous markets. In Ireland, Guinness beer represents a widely available traditional drink within the established dark beer part of the market. When Guinness was contemplating entry into the formidable West German beer market, it was noted that the situation there was quite different; dark beers were relatively unknown. Further, market research indicated that there was a potential niche in the market for a beer that was different. Guinness market strategy capitalized on this difference, adopting a positioning that stressed the product's uniqueness.[8]

International comparisons are particularly useful in pointing out unexpected similarities and differences. The comparison should look for positive features—such as new favorable environmental features, including higher rates of industry and sales growth, high levels of consumption, and more favorable prices—and negative features—imperfections and problem areas in the new business environment, such as complex and difficult product legislation, adverse transport facilities, inefficient suppliers, and a lack of modern machinery. Even negative environmental features, particularly as they hamper local competitors, may prove to be a potential source of opportunity. For example, a new company that can provide modern machines, meet industry regulations, and establish an efficient supply network will have a competitive advantage over any established firms that cannot do so. Many of the most successful international firms have based their strategy on overcoming apparently negative national features.

In making such comparisons, particular note should be made of those areas in the reference market where the firm has displayed special competence. Are the conditions for the transfer of this competence to the new business situation present? Will it prove effective in the new environment? If not, what are the strategic implications?

Time Shift Comparisons

Since different national markets are frequently at different stages of development it may sometimes be more appropriate to compare them at different points of time. In the example cited earlier, Argentina was compared with the Italian market of *several years earlier*, when incomes in Italy were more nearly in line with those in Argentina at the time of the comparison. Such time shifts not only permit closer comparison but may be used as a basis for projecting market patterns; for example, since Italian market trends are apparently leading those in Argentina by several years, they may be used as a basis for forecasting the latter.[9] In other words, discrepancies thought to be primarily a question of time may be used to identify possible future trends.

Special Situations in Developing Countries

Transferring products from the more affluent developed countries to the developing countries poses special problems.

Purchasing Power Differences

Since incomes in the developing countries are, on average, much lower than those in the developed countries, much of the population may be excluded from the effective market due to lack of purchasing power. Products that may have enjoyed a mass market in the wealthier developed countries may be accessible to only a small part of the population living in what is sometimes described as the supermarket economy.

Research shows that products that are purchased by the great majority of households in the advanced industrial countries may be purchased by only 2 to 3 percent of the households in developing countries. This elite segment of the population typically is found in cities rather than in rural areas. They are well educated and in many respects little different from the customers that the firm has encountered in the more developed countries.[10]

There are certain product categories, including some pharmaceuticals, patent medicines, a number of food products, and toiletries, that may appeal to major portions of the population (mass markets) in both developed and developing countries. But although the product may be essentially the same, major changes are often required in product positioning and marketing.

Cocoa malt drinks are often drunk at bedtime in Sweden, Britain, Australia, and other countries of the Western world where they are considered conducive to sleep. Advertising reinforces this image by showing someone drinking a cup of cocoa before falling asleep. The product is positioned as a nighttime drink. In many developing countries, however, there is a higher premium on nutrition, and such products are valued primarily as sources of health and vigor. There, cocoa and sugar content is valued for its energy. In Nigeria and India, advertising for such products is based on the appeal of the energy content of these ingredients. Cocoa malt drinks are positioned as health and energy foods.[11]

Adaptation

The fact that the firm's products fall within the purchasing power of only a small segment of the population rather than a mass market requires an adjustment in marketing strategy. Management has to think in terms of a smaller, more concentrated market. Mass media methods of promotion and distribution have to be tailored to this situation. For example, billboard advertising may replace television commercials. Distribution may be concentrated in urban areas. Inventory and stocking have to be adjusted for the lower-volume, higher carrying charges, and a general shortage of capital.[12]

To counter such limitations, a number of firms have developed products specifically for developing countries. One well-known firm has produced a smaller washing machine for use in developing countries. Indications are that product development to suit the special needs of these countries is still not widespread. Many firms find the costs and risks of such product tailoring to be prohibitive. This may turn out to be shortsighted considering that these countries account for the bulk of the world's population.

Government Regulations

Many developing countries have difficulties with their balance of payments. During times of extreme shortage of foreign exchange, it is not unusual for the government to curtail the import of certain products and components considered to be nonessential. At such times, success or failure of the firm's marketing strategy may have less to do with consumers than with the government's view of just how essential its products are to national economic welfare and, particularly, their contribution to the balance of payments.

Governments in developing countries tend to take a more directly interventionist role in business. They encourage some types of new products while discouraging others. Taiwan is aggressively seeking to attract products that will increase the value-added content of local production, particularly in more sophisticated electronic products. At the other extreme, the Indian government has taken steps to encourage the introduction of hand looms as opposed to more automated weaving equipment to encourage more intensive use of available labor.[13]

Measures at the disposal of government to influence new product introduction include tariffs that may be adjusted to discourage certain products, local content programs that specify the proportion of the product (by weight or value) required to be produced locally, incentives of various sorts, usually in connection with investment in national production facilities, preferential treatment in government-related purchasing, and government constraints on competition.

Summary

Within the multinational company, new product introduction is often associated with the transfer of products from one country to another. Where successful, this has a number of advantages, not the least of which is the ability of the firm to profit from experience on an international scale.

There is also considerable risk attached since there will inevitably be major international differences to take into account. Undoubtedly most managers involved in such international product transfers do make international comparisons, if only on an informal and intuitive basis. Making such comparisons explicit can help to pinpoint relevant similarities and differences and reduce unconscious bias.

Once such product transfers are extended to include exchanges between developed and less developed countries, the greater differences introduced increase the need for a high degree of product and marketing adaptation.

13
Anticipating and Managing Political Risk

All corporate strategic planning depends on certain assumptions regarding national political conditions. Through its legislative power, government is able to influence and change the national business environment, including regulations affecting the firm's ability to compete and even the ownership of company assets.

Politics and government are particularly significant to the strategy of multinational companies. Because such companies operate within the jurisdiction of more than one government, the probability that their plans will be affected by some form of government initiative is increased. Their international mobility means that they have a certain degree of choice regarding their political environment. Unlike the domestic firm whose operations are limited to its country of origin, the strategic choice open to multinational firms includes national location and hence government. The political environment itself becomes a variable, part of management's strategic decision making. The foreign ownership links of the multinational enterprise place it in a special category in the eyes of host governments. Even though it may be incorporated under local national laws, it is classed as a foreign firm, and this often means that it is subject to special regulations and government actions not applied to domestic firms.

The practical result of these characteristics is reflected in the high priority that most multinationals place on their relations with government, and with good reason. History has shown that even the smaller nation-states, such as Chile, Cuba, Zambia, and Bolivia, are able to assert major influence and expropriate the assets of some of the world's largest multinational firms. Although such takeovers are the exception rather than the rule, they serve to underline the distinction between economic and political power. All companies derive their authority from and are dependent on government. Recognition of this fact does not imply that they are without resources in managing their relationships with government.

This chapter considers methods of anticipating national political risk. Since strategy is essentially concerned with the firm's future direction, familiarity with existing government and political conditions is not enough. Farsighted managers will attempt to anticipate political changes and what that may mean in terms of the firm's exposure to political risk. Another aim here is to consider strategies and alternatives open to the firm for dealing with political risk. Although the ability of the firm to influence national political events is very limited, there are measures it can take to avoid or mitigate the effects of adverse political actions.

Political Risk: A Definition

In its broadest sense, political risk refers to government-associated change that might adversely affect the firm's operations or assets. The term *risk* stems from the fact that such predictions are probability statements, estimates as to the likelihood of certain events, based on available evidence.

Although readily defined in principle, in practice there may be differences of opinion on the dividing line between events that constitute risk and those that do not. All firms, both domestic and those with foreign operations, are routinely involved with government actions and change that affect their business. Changes in taxation, industry regulations on safety and pollution, company law, and manufacturing standards may affect some firms adversely, but they are so much a part of the normal business of government that as long as their impact is minor and they are not directed at foreign firms, management tends to think of them as part of the firm's normal business activity. At the other extreme are certain events, such as nationalization and expropriation of company assets, that clearly qualify as potential political risks.[1]

In practice, political risk is defined more narrowly to refer to government-associated hazards of doing business in foreign countries. Figure 13–1 presents a typology of such political risk. Category 1 contains those events that, being less visible and less associated with threat or force, are not always identified under the heading of political risk. Nevertheless, they merit close attention since they may have a major impact on the firm. These include special taxes falling on the products, profits, or assets of foreign firms and discrimination in government sales or purchases. Price controls have been imposed by some governments on certain products of multinational firms, particularly drugs and medicines. Quite a few multinationals have found that excessive bureaucratic requirements or "red tape" represent a major obstacle to their international operations. Indigenization of management refers to government programs aimed at increasing the proportion of local nationals in the management of the firm's operations in that country.

Indigenization of capital refers to government pressure on the multinational to award an ownership stake in its operations (within the country in question) to local national investors. Finally, there are the more obvious risks associated with the loss of company assets. Note that the ordering of the risks indicated in figure 13–1 does not necessarily indicate their importance or impact on the firm. Certain types of tax discrimination or price control may have a greater impact and

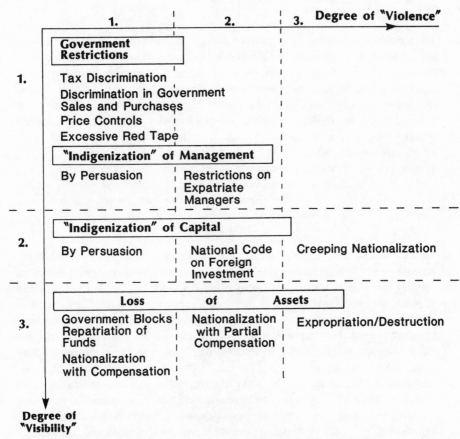

Source: Adapted from Bernard Marois, *Comment Gérer le Risque Politique lié à vos Operations Internationales*, Collection L'Exportateur, C.F.C.E., Paris, 1981. Reprinted with permission.

Figure 13–1. Typology of Political Risk

be considered far more important than, for example, indigenization of capital or restrictions on repatriation of funds.

Forecasting Political Risk

The purpose of political risk forecasting is to anticipate the likelihood of future events. Political risk forecasts fall into two distinct categories: predictions about evolutionary change, which unfolds with only minor deviation within the existing political system, and forecasts aimed at predicting major discontinuities in the political system itself.

Evolutionary Political Change

The emphasis here is on understanding and interpreting the existing political system, its likely future actions and directions of change. Valuable assistance toward this end may be obtained through the use of outside experts. Former political figures, diplomats, and specialized consulting firms are used by multinational companies to supplement their own efforts. However, many of the most important judgments are those that require internal knowledge of the firm, its specific circumstances and future plans, and how these may be expected to interact with future government actions. Ultimately political forecasts of this type will rely heavily on the ability of the company's own management to interpret future change in three areas: the firm's political leverage with the host government, the relationship of the firm relative to the host government's objectives and strategy, and internal change within the host government.

Firm's Political Leverage. The basis of the agreement between the firm and the host government begins to change as soon as the company commits itself to the country in question. Once the investment is made and the company's facilities are in place, the firm's original bargaining position is sharply altered. Its chief bargaining lever, the freedom to commit its resources to another part of the world, has disappeared. Host governments are not unaware of this fact. The original agreement between firm and government has been aptly characterized by Raymond Vernon as an "obsolescing bargain."[2] Unless the firm is able to forward additional contributions, in the form of prospective new investment or future contributions in the way of new technology, there will be a tendency toward progressive weakening in the firm's bargaining position. Supporting evidence is readily observable though not easily quantifiable. An exception is to be found in the statistics on the host government share of the pretax profits of foreign investors in Chilean copper. In 1930, the host government took a modest 16 percent of pretax profits. Over the years, this percentage has increased to nearly 70 percent, reflecting the progressive weakening of the copper investors' bargaining position in Chile.[3] Much the same trend can be traced in the share of pretax profits going to the oil companies. Once the firm has lost the discretionary power to remove its contribution (the investment has been made and the oil discovered), its political bargaining power is reduced. The firm's political leverage derives from its perceived future contribution. Sustained political leverage depends on the ability of the firm to offer the host government a continual prospect of future exports, new investment, employment, new technology, or other valued contributions, preferably of a type not readily duplicated by domestic firms.

One firm that manufactures containers constantly upgraded the complexity of its operations to keep a jump ahead of the capability of domestic firms. The company started its operations by producing simple cork-lined bottle caps in the host country. Subsequently it shifted to more complex plastic-lined caps, then to metal cans, and currently to aerosol cans. Continual upgrading has kept host government intervention to an extremely low level.[4] The same phenomenon is observable in the extractive industries. In the case of oil exploration, preferential treatment is accorded companies working the more difficult, less easily duplicated areas. Offshore drilling generally is given preferential treatment compared to land-based exploration.

The government's perception of the contribution is important. Research shows that firms that initiated frequent contact with the host government, keeping it fully informed of their contribution, have significantly less government intervention in their affairs than those that do not.[5]

Relationship of the Firm to Host Government Objectives and Strategy. Most governments, particularly in the developing countries, are often actively engaged in setting objectives for the national economy. Multinational companies that are seen to contribute toward those objectives are generally welcome. Thus, Morocco welcomes firms that are able to contribute toward its objectives of increasing the country's exports. Singapore is interested in attracting companies that can improve the country's technological base.

In recent years, government attitudes toward multinational firms have become more sophisticated and pro-active. With few exceptions, they are ready to encourage investment by those firms that fit in with their own plans. In many respects, governments are thinking and planning very much like the companies themselves; they have developed strategies for attracting and managing multinational companies.

Identifying and understanding the host government's strategy is an important aid in forecasting its actions. Although no two countries will have precisely the same strategy toward foreign direct investment, it is possible to describe a number of national groups that have certain similarities in their general strategic approach toward multinationals.

Indigenous Industrialization. A large number of developing countries are primarily interested in the contribution that multinational firms can make to the development of domestic companies and industries. India and Mexico fall into this group. Government policies are developed to ensure that foreign direct investment is largely owned and managed by nationals of the host country. A high priority is placed on the transfer of technology to national firms.

Leapfrog. Countries such as Singapore, Taiwan, Hong Kong, South Korea, and others aggressively seek international foreign direct investment to achieve a level of industrialization associated with the more advanced industrial countries. Favorable tax and other incentives (including production facilities in tariff-free zones) are provided for foreign investors, particularly companies that can contribute to the development of the country's technological and management skills.

Singapore recently opened a science park industrial site, providing incentives to multinational company investors engaged in the production of precision machinery and electronics to establish facilities there. Government pressure to shift the ownership and management of multinational subsidiaries is absent or minimal.

Infant Industries. Japan is the prime example of this strategy, directed primarily at sheltering domestic companies from competition against foreign investors until they are judged able to complete effectively. Until relatively recently, incoming foreign investment was subject to severe restrictions. Only a few select firms, generally in high technology areas, were allowed into the country on the basis of 100 percent ownership. Most foreign companies that were permitted to invest did so on the basis of minority joint ventures, under the watchful eye of the government. Since the early 1970s, there has been a gradual lifting of such restrictions. They were formally terminated in 1980, though the government continues to influence the foreign investment climate.

Open Door. Foreign investors are offered equal treatment with national firms, but there is no particular drive by the central government to encourage or prohibit such investment. The United States is one of the few countries falling into this category, perhaps because foreign direct investment was a relatively minor segment of the economy until recently. (It should be noted that individual states actively seek foreign direct investment.)

Systematic Screening. Most countries today are selective about the type of firms that are encouraged or discouraged from establishing themselves within their boundaries. Australia and Canada are examples of two nations that, perhaps due to the large percentage of their domestic industry accounted for by foreign firms, have developed highly systematic procedures for selecting and monitoring such companies. Based on far-reaching investigations of the impact of foreign investment on the national economy, both countries screen potential candidates to select those companies with attributes considered desirable and in the national interest. The screening criteria are subject to change in line with the government's economic objectives. For example, the changing energy picture brought about extensive Canadian incentives for oil firms with a minimum of 50 percent Canadian control.

Change within the Host Government. Evolutionary political change within the present system of government becomes a certainty with the passage of time. Political parties and the members comprising the national government will alter as a result of elections or other provisions for succession. Political attitudes and policies also will change in response to economic and other developments.

Japan at one time exercised stringent control over foreign investors entering that country. Industries open to foreign firms and the degree of foreign ownership were controlled in line with government strategy. Over time the country's economic situation has improved so dramatically that most of these restrictions have gradually been lifted. In other cases, the reverse happened. The 1983 fall in oil prices forced Nigeria to take measures to curtail imports and import-intensive industries.

Forecasting internal evolutionary political change requires a close knowledge of the political pressures for change shaping the course of the current government and its likely successors. Inevitably the analysis will extend beyond the purely political. It will include cultural, economic, and institutional considerations and their influence on political events. There is no substitute for close, preferably personal, knowledge and on-the-spot contact with political trends, leaders, and institutions.

Discontinuous Change in the Political System

Major change in the political system, such as the overthrow of the established government through revolution, is viewed by some as the major source of political risk. This type of change strikes at the very foundations of the assumptions underlying all of the firm's plans and poses a threat to its continued existence in that country.

There is, admittedly, an element of irrationality in viewing all such change as inevitably negative. It may be argued that every major change is bound to benefit some, even if adversely affecting others. Nevertheless, it is understandable that management would seek advance notice of impending political discontinuity and also that it would perceive such change as introducing the possibility of major adverse political events. Perhaps it would be more accurate to describe such forecasts as concerned with predicting the stability of political systems and the probability that the present rules of the game might be changed. In making such forecasts, companies rely on both subjective and quantitative assessments.

Expert Opinion. The traditional method of forecasting political change relies on expert opinion. The firm may seek the subjective judgment of people who are well informed on the national political situation, but there are obvious hazards in this approach. Experts have been proved wrong before (few anticipated the overthrow of the shah of Iran). More to the point is conscious or unconscious bias. For example, if the expert is a member of, or closely associated with, the national government, he or she may have personal reasons for wanting to encourage foreign direct investment to help stabilize and improve the national economy. Similarly, the company's own managers will not be without individual biases. Line managers, with everything to gain from new expansion within their own jurisdiction, are known for their optimism.

Nevertheless, this approach can be effective, especially where the government structure is more a matter of personalities than established constitutional practice, as in the Middle East. Rummel and Heenan advise that this "old hands" approach can be useful in appraising the objectives and personalities of the country's current leadership, the strengths and weaknesses of competing political groups, and the likelihood of new legislation.[6]

Checklists, as shown in figure 13–2, are used to assist in the interpretation of political systems and potential change. Expert opinion can also be sampled on a large scale, such as with the use of Delphi techniques. A number of consulting firms that advise on political events employ a panel of experts to assess political stability. The Delphi method of using a panel of experts in successive iterations is supposed to move opinion toward a consensus view that is superior to individual estimates.

Quantitative Methods. More recently, there has been a growing emphasis on quantitative methods to forecast discontinuous political change. Although they must be considered promising (and their use growing), they are still considered somewhat experimental.

In principle, the employment of such methods is not unlike the use of leading business indicators used to forecast economic change. In forecasting discontinuous political change, the objective is to arrive at a probability estimate of political upheaval through the use of certain measurable events that act as lead indicators. The variables selected are usually those thought to be causally related with drastic political change. The reasoning here is that measurable change in these variables will precede discontinuous political change.[7]

Hans Schollhammer has developed a quantitative model that uses measures of certain causal factors to forecast political change (defined as government executive transfers and executive adjustments). The causal factors are of two types. Political causal factors include quantitative estimates of national riots, armed attacks, deaths from domestic violence, government sanctions, defense expenditures and fractionalization among political parties. Another set of measures has reference to economic causal factors, such as average per capita income, national income distribution, capital formation (as a percentage of GNP), per capita education expenditures, and available food supply measured in terms of calories per capita. Quantitative measures for these factors over time were assembled for sixty countries and adjusted for differences in population size. A statistically significant relationship was found between these factors and political change.[8]

Integrating Subjective and Quantitative Assessments. Both methods have weaknesses. The more mechanical approach of the quantitative techniques is unlikely to capture unique characteristics and subtle changes in mood that may shed light on particular national situations. The expert opinion approach is subject to the problems already noted together with the fact that it is unlikely to be consistent across different national territories where assessment includes more than one country. Inevitably there will be numerous cases where the decision is not clear-

Political Environment	*Foreign Pressures*
Form of government	Threat of war
History of government stability	Military related violence
Party fractionalization	Diplomatic crises
Party political platforms	Trade disputes
Volatility of electorate '	External threat to supplies
Popular support of ruling party	Alliances
Role of military	
Attitude to foreign companies	*Economic Pressures*
Legal system	
Treaties on tax and investment	Per capita income
State companies	Economic crises
Religious or ethnic splits	Balance of payments
	Inflation rate
Internal Stability	Exchange rate volatility
	Controls on repatriation of capital
Riots	National debt
Public demonstrations	Income distribution
Political strikes	Wealth distribution
Purges	
Assassinations	
Government crisis	
History of military coups	

Figure 13–2. Checklist of Political Risk Indicators

cut. In these marginal cases, it may make sense to use both methods. In the words of one executive, "What bothers us most are the borderline cases. . . . It's with investment in these countries that we see the advantage of the combined approach."[9]

Rummel and Heenan conclude that political change is influenced by domestic instability, foreign conflict, political climate, and economic climate.[10] In assessing these headings, they advocate an integrated approach combining quantitative analysis and expert qualitative judgments.

Managing Political Risk

Although there is little a firm can do to influence national political change, this is far from suggesting that management has no power to mitigate or otherwise manage the effects of political change, whether evolutionary or discontinuous.

One method is the premium for risk approach, a form of self-insurance that the firm implements by requiring a higher rate of return in countries considered exceptionally risky.[11] Although this is one of the best-known and most widely used methods, there are a number of hedging strategies that are often more effective. These are discussed in two categories: hedging strategies that the firm can take prior to investment in a given country and those available to it after investment. These categories are subdivided into measures internal to the firm and those that depend on passing the risk to external agencies. Figure 13–3 summarizes these methods.

Before Investing

Minimizing Local Equity. An obvious way to hedge against loss is to minimize the firm's equity investment in the country. Local borrowing not only limits the company investment subject to political risk, it has the important further benefit of creating allies, local lenders who have a vested interest in the success of the firm. Furthermore, it reduces the firm's exposure to foreign exchange risk since locally generated earnings can be used to repay local capital and interest payments denominated in the same currency.

Minimizing the company's equity stake can also be achieved through local equity participation—that is, forming a joint venture with local shareholders. Participation of local shareholders will also help to build links with the local community and provide the benefit of local management advice and knowledge. Where there are local indigenization programs in effect, such as those in Mexico, India, and other developing countries, participation of local equity shareholders is a prerequisite rather than an option.

Equity risk may be eliminated altogether through a management contract that compensates the firm for management services provided. No company investment in ownership of facilities is involved.

International Integration. If the company established in the foreign territory is dependent on raw materials, technical skills, machinery, management, or other inputs from abroad, the government will have to think seriously before taking any measures that jeopardize the flow of such supplies. A strategy of international integration builds interdependence between the company facility in question and links with facilities in other countries. Peru's Velasco regime omitted Chrysler from its extensive program of foreign company takeovers. The Peruvian plant manufactured only some 50 percent of the Chrysler product; the remainder was imported from Chrysler plants in Detroit, Brazil, and Argentina.[12] The Peru plant could not be operated without cooperation from Chrysler plants in these countries. Integrating production internationally with supplier plants in other countries effectively preempted a successful takeover.[13]

The protective effect of international integration can also be achieved through control of corporate output, such as markets for the firm's products. For many years, the international oil companies operating in the Middle East were relatively immune from government takeovers because of their control over the market for petroleum products. Nationalization of the oil wells was of limited use unless the government also had the means to dispose of their production profitably.

Before Investing

Internal hedging

Minimization of local equity

Local borrowing
Local equity (joint ventures)
Management contract

International integration

Production integration
Marketing integration
International supply sourcing

External hedging

Government insurance (OPIC in USA, BFCE-Coface in France, ECGD in England)

Private insurance (Lloyd's)

Host government guarantees

After Investing

Internal hedging

Good citizen policy
Increase in technical contribution
Negotiation and arbitration

External hedging

Private insurance (Lloyd's)
International investment codes
Divestment

Source: Bernard Marois, "Comment Gérer le Risque Politique lie à vos Operations Internationales," Collection L'Exportateur, C.F.C.E., Paris, 1981. Reprinted with permission.

Figure 13–3. Hedging Strategies

Another form of international integration on the output side can be implemented through the use of international trademarks and brand names. Increasingly companies are able to register their international brand names under protective legislation in a wide number of countries. Should a government expropriate the national production facilities of such a firm, the company in question is still in a position to refuse to allow the government the right to use its brand names in other countries. This would significantly reduce the value of such assets to the expropriating government. Perhaps with this in mind, the Mexican government passed a law in 1976 that required manufacturing firms to use a local trademark in all advertising and packaging.[14]

External Hedging. In his research into the hedging strategies of French multinationals, Bernard Marois found that the risk-reducing strategy preferred by most firms was to try to shift political risk to an external agency.[15] Several means are available for this type of hedging.

Government and Private Insurance. Many governments in the industrial countries provide various forms of insurance for companies that invest abroad, particularly if the investment is made in the developing countries. Private insurance provided by such firms as Lloyds of London is also available to cover certain types of political risk. In both cases, whether the insurance is public or private, there are insurance premiums. The insurance covers only some portion of the assets lost by the firm in the country in question. It does not cover opportunity cost.

Host Government Guarantees. Another frequently used method is the use of host government guarantees, agreements arrived at between the firm and the host government prior to investment (when the firm's bargaining power is highest) guaranteeing certain provisions in writing. These may cover tax concessions, provisions for compensation in the event of expropriation, and other contingencies. They serve as an additional protective measure, though management will be aware that the governing power of the country will, at any time, have both the power and the authority to repudiate such agreements. This does not mean that they are without value. Many governments with an eye to the future credibility of their statements will not take such action lightly.

After Investing

After the firm has committed itself to a particular national territory, its bargaining power is usually diminished, but is is by no means without measures to influence government actions that might be against its interests.

Good Citizen Policy. Corporate behavior conforming to what is usually referred to as a good citizen policy is one of the most popular prescriptions for avoiding adverse political initiatives. A good citizen policy as applied to the behavior of a foreign firm refers to corporate initiatives such as the following:

1. Prompt response to both the letter and spirit of host government requests. These may not always be a matter of legal requirement. Governments frequently will exhort companies to embark on various measures judged to be in the national interest on a voluntary basis, such as hiring handicapped workers, purchasing goods and components from national suppliers, and setting high standards of safety.
2. Contribution to national goals. In all countries, there will be certain recognized national goals that the government hopes to forward. These may include increased exports, building up the national technological base, and de-

veloping new products. Identifying where and to what degree the company can contribute toward such goals without sacrificing its own interests is a matter of management discretion.

3. Contribution to national welfare. This refers to company support of educational institutions, hospitals, and other programs that contribute to the general national welfare.

4. Developing a corporate image. A company that seeks to be recognized as a good citizen will be interested in projecting an acceptable corporate image. This is as much a matter of what it does not do as much as anything else. It is possible for any foreign firm to accentuate its international links to the point where they irritate and aggravate public relations. Especially in the developing countries, a low profile is frequently an important part of being ‚a good citizen. Nevertheless, many firms that have qualified as good citizens have been the subject of government takeovers.

Increase in Technical Contribution. The strategy of systematic and planned increase in the firm's contribution to national technological capability is closely related to the previous point. The increased importance of technology and its near universal pursuit by government, together with the perception of the multinational as a technology transfer agent, means that the firm that can present itself in this light to the host government is in a powerful bargaining position.[16]

Negotiation and Arbitration. For the multinational firm, entry into the host country in most cases will have been the subject of negotiations with the host government. Particularly in cases involving large-scale foreign investment or investment in sensitive areas, such as those related to national defense, communications, and natural resources, normally there will have been detailed discussions between the firm and the host government in arriving at the complex arrangements and commitments that comprise the final agreement governing the conditions of entry. In the developing countries, negotiations between the investing company and the host government will apply to virtually all cases of foreign investment.

Both the company and the host government will have a degree of flexibility in terms of the entry conditions that are considered acceptable. The final agreement reflects an area where the interests of the two parties overlap, that is, an area of mutually acceptable terms and conditions of entry.

In the case of major political change, the firm's position in the country and its relationship with the new government may have to be renegotiated. In the event of such change, prudent management will seek to establish whether such new negotiations are called for. Negotiations with the new government regarding proposed initiatives that threaten the firm can prove effective in minimizing or avoiding loss. The multinational firm inevitably will have certain bargaining counters, such as possible new investment, continued licensing of technology and the use of trade names, and provision of overseas outlets. Presented to government tactfully and effectively, these can significantly improve the company's position.

Where such negotiations fail, third-party arbitration is a possibility. Although relatively rare, the greater involvement of international agencies in developing codes of conduct for both companies and host governments offers the hope that this will become a more realistic option in the future.

Private Insurance. Even after the firm has committed its resources, it can resort to private insurance schemes to hedge against future loss. The insurance premium will be proportional to the threat of asset loss.

Investment Codes. An increasing number of international organizations are attempting to promulgate international codes providing reciprocal guarantees between multinational companies and host governments. Organizations involved in such efforts include the United Nations, the International Monetary Fund, and the OECD. As yet such codes have had limited validity; however, there is hope and even expectation that in the future they may provide for international investment the sort of regulatory framework and grievance procedures currently provided for international trade by the GATT.

Divestment. Voluntary divestment of national assets can prove a valuable device in reducing the damage caused by government takeovers that are inevitable. Planned well in advance, divestment can be effective in extricating the firm from a situation that is no longer tenable with a minimum of damage.

Conclusion

The firm's abillity to adjust to the constraints and conditions imposed by national government depend on its ability to anticipate and interpret political change. This refers to change within the existing political system as well as change in the system itself. Even where political developments appear to be moving against the firm, a number of hedging strategies are available that can prove effective in reducing or eliminating loss.

Outside expert opinion and forecasts may assist management in its projection and interpretation of political change. But in the final analysis, the objective will be to determine the impact of such change on the firm's own particular situation and prospects (generalizations about sweeping national political change are only a means to this end). This indicates that many of the key decisions concerning such change and the firm's reaction to it will require the judgment of internal company management.

Part IV
Coordinating Strategy across National Borders

14
Strategic Planning Systems and Other Coordinative Mechanisms

One way that large-scale organizations manage complexity is by decentralizing responsibility to business subunits, but even the most decentralized companies require some subunit coordination. This is illustrated vividly in Alfred P. Sloan's account of his experiences as chairman of General Motors during the early days of that organization.[1]

Sloan points out that GM's corporate headquarters initially lacked both information and control over the financial assets in the hands of the firm's powerful divisions. The corporate treasurer had to guess how much cash each division had and then try to persuade each to part with a portion of it, something they were quite loath to do, with the result that some divisions had excess cash while others were short of necessary funds. This and the lack of any systematic procedure for allocating capital among the divisions eventually led to a situation that jeopardized the survival of the company. Only after corporate headquarters obtained some control over division funds (by ensuring that all revenue from division sales was deposited in the name of the corporation) was Sloan able to implement his scheme for a decentralized structure.

Within the multinational company, the relationship between headquarters and the subunits is complicated by distance, national boundaries, culture, and national allegiance. The multinational firm's foreign-based subsidiaries are in a particularly strong position to resist instructions and influence from headquarters. Greater distance and national differences also mean that international headquarters often has little first-hand knowledge of events at the national level. It is not surprising that relations between international headquarters and its national subsidiaries are sometimes strained and difficult.[2]

Research reveals a widespread view among many managers at the national level to the effect that "international headquarters is not qualified to participate effectively in the process of setting objectives and goals."[3] Another study on multinationals draws attention to the fact that there is considerable alienation between these two levels of the corporate hierarchy.[4]

First-hand contact with managers at both levels reveals a high degree of sensitivity to headquarters' requests for more information on which to base its decisions. These tend to be seen by subsidiaries as more red tape at best and at worst as unwarranted incursions into their area of responsibility. In these circumstances, how does management bridge the gap between strategic thinking at international headquarters and that in its geographically dispersed subsidiaries? This chapter discusses a number of methods, including the use of planning routines that mesh company strategy and strategic planning at the two levels.

Annual Planning Cycle

A growing number of companies are structuring their planning activity around a planning cycle. Planning at different levels of the multinational firm's hierarchy covers progressively larger geographic segments of the firm's business. The final corporate global plan incorporates information and is consistent with plans at the national and regional levels (figure 14–1).

The timing of the annual planning process is synchronized so that lower-level plans feed into higher headquarters planning early enough to have their results incorporated into the plans formulated at that level. For example, some companies require that the national planning cycle should be sufficiently advanced to make an input (in the form of a preliminary plan) to the planning process at regional headquarters by June. Regional plans should be sufficiently advanced to feed their preliminary plans into the global headquarters planning cycle by October so that the final global plan may be completed by December. The term *cycle* has reference to the repetitive, annual nature of this process.

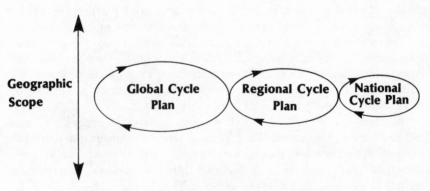

Figure 14–1. Planning Cycles in a Multinational

Formal and Informal Planning

Why formalize planning into a system? Strategic planning essentially is a creative process. The latest strategic thinking in any company is unlikely to be in written form and in many cases is not sufficiently advanced to be put in writing. It exists in the first instance as an idea or set of ideas.

The great danger of any planning system is that it becomes an academic exercise, performed largely for the benefit of the planners. But there are also benefits. Incorporating the firm's strategic thinking into a standardized planning process repeated annually has a number of advantages. First, it provides a forum that annually probes and challenges current thinking and raises fundamental questions about corporate directions and objectives. Second, it makes explicit company thinking that may exist in various parts of the organization but that no one has yet formulated in any systematic fashion. A planning routine that makes ideas more explicit contributes to their wider dissemination internally, facilitating critical examination and association with other strands of strategic thinking. Third, it stimulates new strategic thinking by setting aside time during which managers preoccupied with putting out fires are able to spend time considering new ideas and possibilities. Fourth, it encourages wider participation in the strategy formulation process by making provision for contributions by various specialists and managers that might be otherwise excluded. Fifth, by increasing management participation, it helps to widen the consensus within the firm on future strategy. Finally, it facilitates communication among operating units within the organization, encouraging direct communication as well as the use of a common language, such as common definitions of frequently used concepts as profit, loss, sales, and market share.

Resource Allocation: Capital Budget Planning

The fact that company resources are limited, together with top management's ultimate responsibility to shareholders for the financial health of the company, ensures that most large firms have developed a planning system for making capital budgeting decisions.[5] Up to a certain point, management at the national level has the power to make its own spending decisions. The upper limit of such discretionary spending power provides an interesting insight into the degree of company decentralization. This will vary from one firm to another, but in virtually all cases, major items of capital expenditure, such as new plant and equipment or product development, will require a formal capital appropriation request. These requests may be part of the annual cycle plan (for example, the national subsidiary will forward a request to regional or global headquarters), or it may be forwarded in connection with a particular project.

In most companies, application for new capital is a bottom-up process. The business unit making the request usually prepares its case in writing, setting out the reasons for the proposal behind the proposed capital expenditure together with detailed financial analysis, and forwards it to international headquarters for approval. However, it is a rare case where the proposal has not been discussed beforehand. Even within the more decentralized organizations, such requests will have been preceded by visits between the headquarters staff and that of the initiating unit. At that stage, there is an informal exchange of views and opinions, which may encourage or discourage the request for capital.

At international headquarters, requests for capital are subjected to preliminary screening against minimum acceptable financial criteria, or threshold objectives. There may also be constraints and limitations to consider at this point regarding new capital investment in parts of the world judged to represent an unacceptable degree of risk in particular product areas and technologies.

For capital requests that pass the initial screening, the process moves on to a personal presentation. The managing director of the business unit submitting a request for capital will make a formal presentation to management at the firm's regional or global headquarters. Figure 14–2 provides a format for this type of presentation. After an initial statement of purpose and a brief outline of the project for which the appropriation is requested, there is an exposition of the macroeconomic and political factors regarding the national site of the proposed investment. Particular emphasis will be placed on the future outlook, with special reference to projected political and commercial risk and how this may affect the proposed expenditure. A strategic analysis of the current national business situation facing management in that country follows, culminating in a projection of the initiating unit's future prospects if the request is granted and if the request is not granted. Finally, the proposed strategy that includes the new investment is interpreted in terms of its expected financial results, including forecasts of future revenue, cash flow, new capital investment, and ROI.

The presentation is made before a capital appropriation review committee. The committee's task is to probe the objectives as well as the analysis and projections behind the capital requests. The face-to-face meeting with managers who are planning national-level strategy offers the opportunity to go beyond the written document, raising questions regarding the individual merits and hazards of the proposed investment. Is the timing right? What alternatives and contingencies have been considered? Is there any way to reduce risk still further? The presentation will also provide a fresh look at international opportunities for the firm and threats to it. Within a relatively short space of time (ten to twenty such presentations in a single day is not unusual), management at international headquarters is exposed to an enormous amount of information covering different countries. Even allowing for the fact that not all of the material presented is assimilated, the process provides an effective method for acquiring in-depth information of multiple national environments. Much of the material will be specific

General purpose and objectives.

Brief outline of project and nature of appropriation requested.

National economic and political climate in country or countries where capital is to be invested.

Firm's present situation there (if company has existing operations within national territory in question).

Strategic appraisal of the business environment at the proposed national site(s). Resume of firm's external threats and opportunities.

Specific changes expected in firm's position there if (1) capital request granted and (2) if rejected.

Identification of key conditions necessary for success.

Financial projections of costs and revenues (1) related directly to the specific project being proposed and (2) associated with the wider system of company operations which will be affected by the project (where appropriate).

Examine sensitivity of expected results.

Figure 14–2. Format for Capital Appropriation Request

to individual countries, but there will also generally be information on competitive and market trends that may be reflected in several presentations, offering insight into international patterns of change and competition.

The committee will relate and interpret the various requests for new investment in terms of the firm's regional/global portfolio strategy. The exposure to requests from a wide number of the firm's operations in different countries provides an opportunity for headquarters management to make interunit comparisons essential to portfolio strategy. These inputs may have to be supplemented by additional information, particularly regarding investment opportunities in countries and businesses that were not represented in the review process.

It is the responsibility of the review committee to see that the funds required to meet the needs of the approved projects are consistent with the resources at the disposal of the company and to ensure that the allocation of such capital is consistent with the firm's portfolio objectives in terms of growth, risk, return, market share, and technology.

The procedure enables the reviewing body to communicate to management at the national level possible changes in their mission and/or objectives contingent on the approval (or rejection) of the request under review. It provides management at headquarters a unique opportunity to express to the firm's managers working in different parts of the world headquarters' view of where their operations fit into the overall corporate strategy. This is an essential task from the purely informational standpoint and also with reference to management morale and overall corporate cohesiveness.

An important part of this procedure is to fix responsibility. It is obvious that management at international headquarters can have only limited knowledge regarding the details of the various capital project proposals reviewed. Even allowing for the fact that headquarters' staff will have had prior access to the written proposals and time to review the backup data supporting the proposal, knowledge of the political, economic, and business conditions in so many countries is, at best, partial and incomplete. The process depends on the fact that such proposals also assign responsibility. This is especially evident where the review committee has expressed serious doubts and reservations about a particular proposal for new investment. Consistent with the bottom-up nature of the process, it is unlikely that a determined request from a manager, firmly convinced of the worth of his or her project, will be turned down. Most companies will defer to strongly held beliefs from managers regarding their own areas of responsibility, as in the following quotation:

> If one division feels strongly enough about a project that's outside the traditional areas of the corporation you let them do it. For example, one division wanted to go into a new product. They proposed it, it came up for the first time and we turned it down. Six months later they brought it up again. Again we turned it down. The third time they finally convinced us that we just had to go in. I'm not sure that we agreed with them but I think we felt that they believed they were right and felt strongly that they should have a chance to try their idea.[6]

Although the project may be approved, the manager forwarding the proposal will be made aware of any major reservations. In continuing to press the request, he or she is unequivocally putting his or her judgment on record. Responsibility for the success of the project is made highly visible.

Beyond Capital Budgeting

For some firms, the capital budgeting system is all that is required to meet company needs. In other situations, this is not the case. Company needs and requirements are constantly changing, and international planning has to change with them, as in the case described next.

In 1976, two senior managers from Cadbury Schweppes, the multinational food company, made a tour of the firm's overseas subsidiaries. They were surprised by some of the differences they found.[7] Cadbury Schweppes marketed many of the same products in its various national locations, but these were promoted, packaged, and branded differently, reflecting major discrepancies in marketing methods and standards in different countries. For example, the media expenditure to sales ratios varied widely to a degree that appeared illogical, from 1.5 percent in some countries to 5 percent in others. The managers from the firm's international headquarters were also surprised to find that costly research in which the company had invested heavily was not being used, there was considerable duplication, and the final result was not always in line with company standards. This first-hand look at the firm's international operations also disclosed undue delay in introducing some of the firm's new products abroad, with the result that competitors were sometimes able to establish their own versions of these products in direct competition against Cadbury Schweppes in foreign markets.

Cadbury management concluded, "We had no international marketing objectives, policy, strategy or tactics but rather a series of domestic or local ones." Another conclusion was that the local autonomy of the subsidiaries should work within a framework of international policy and procedures to achieve international corporate objectives. Furthermore, such changes were not to be imposed by orders from headquarters but through mutual agreement and acceptance by the national subsidiaries.[8]

Discretionary Coordination

The Cadbury Schweppes situation is by no means exceptional. International competition and other strategic considerations require some firms to exert a greater degree of international coordination. At the same time, there is considerable reluctance to resort to measures that infringe on the autonomy and decentralized authority of the firm's international subsidiaries. The search for a solution has led multinational firms to develop a number of coordinative devices that leave final decisions on international coordination to the discretion of management at the national business level.

A number of companies (including Cadbury Schweppes) hold regular meetings of their international executives to provide a forum for the exchange of ideas and experience. A particularly effective device at such meetings is the product smorgasbord. New products are placed in a central area with brief details of their introduction and performance. A management presentation may be provided at the meeting for products considered to be particularly promising. A manager of a subsidiary who feels that the product might be of value in his or her particular national location will consult with the company unit (or units) that have had prior experience with the product to obtain further information concerning its attributes, consumer response, and supporting marketing programs such as media and servicing. Such meetings also provide an opportunity for discussion of possible regional global strategies and programs. Headquarters management has the opportunity to set out its ideas and to discuss these with the various national managers.

Another approach is the appointment of certain units, usually the firm's larger subsidiaries, as competence centers. These are typically the subsidiaries with the best performance record and/or experience in a particular field (for example, marketing a specific product). Other units may contact such competence centers to obtain detailed information.[9] Hence, a subsidiary planning to launch a new product with which it has had little or no prior experience may contact a competence center to identify best practice. In some firms, best practice is assembled and communicated in written form, drawing on the more successful experiences of the firms operations around the world. The final result may combine experience and developments from several subsidiaries. A variation of this approach is the practice of developing experience books. Each national subsidiary is required to record, using a standard format, its experience in marketing its product. This record is made available to other units within the firm.

Another method uses outside companies as coordinators. An example is the appointment of a single international advertising agency to coordinate the firm's advertising efforts around the world. Advertising agencies with international branch networks are particularly useful in this regard. The multinational client company works closely with the advertising agency to develop an international advertising campaign. Subsidiaries of the client firm in various parts of the world are able to contact a branch of the advertising company, often located in their own geographic area, to find out about the program and work with the agency to adapt it to their own special needs.

A particularly effective coordinating device is the use of cross-national membership on boards of directors. Managers from the firm's national subsidiaries may be represented on the board of the international headquarters company (both registered as separate companies, each with its own board of directors), or vice-versa. Also, subsidiaries in the same or different countries may be linked together through overlapping memberships in each other's boards. Even with no other formal mechanism, coordination in such cases can be very effective and sometimes less discretionary than might appear. For example, in one company noted for its autonomous subsidiaries, the chairman of the parent company's board of directors also serves as chairman of each of the subsidiary boards.

Some companies promote coordination through the use of joint staffs and special committees. One major multinational encourages staff from the national subsidiaries to communicate directly with staff from international headquarters working in the same field. For example, national-level planners involved with making projections of the market for the firm's products meet with staff managers from international headquarters addressing the same issue to arrive at agreed projections on future market demand.

One of the most frequently used coordinative devices is the project team. Uniroyal uses a task force approach when engaged in special projects such as entering a new market or introducing a new product.[10] Managers comprising the task force team are drawn from both the domestic and international operations of the company and from various functions to develop a basic strategy. The strategy subsequently is implemented through regional and country managers.

International Policy

The discretionary procedures are aimed at encouraging international coordination on a voluntary basis. Where this is not enough because more central control is required, they may be supplemented with international company policies. The term *policy* refers to a decision rule that is automatically applied under given circumstances; examples are, "Our policy is to promote from within the firm" or, "Our policy is to produce only products that satisfy the highest national standards."

International policies can be effective for establishing a degree of uniformity, but they can also prove inflexible. A policy to the effect that media expenditure would be equal in all countries to 2 percent of sales would eliminate the sort of inconsistencies encountered by Cadbury Schweppes but at the cost of rigidity that could be counterproductive. Some companies that require close, flexible coordination of their national business units have resorted to strategic planning systems of the sort described next.

Strategic Planning in a Highly Integrated Multinational

Company X is a multinational producer of consumer durables.[11] Its regional headquarters in Europe is responsible for a network of national subsidiaries. Until a few years ago, strategic planning at regional headquarters was confined to capital budgeting and product planning, supplemented by special conferences and executive visits. More recently, a strategic planning system was introduced, partly at the instigation of the parent company. There was also a growing feeling among some managers at regional headquarters that the increased complexity of the firm's operations called for a more systematic planning procedure.

Initiating the Strategic Planning System

Initial implementation of the strategic planning system in the firm's European headquarters encountered a number of problems. Staff responsible for initiating the new system found considerable difficulty in getting some of the participants to think about strategy. Priority tended to be placed on more immediate problems. Staff were surprised to discover how few managers had a view of the firm's overall situation in Europe. Matters were not helped by initial efforts to develop a strategic plan that attempted to describe in great detail the firm's European strategy and environment over the next ten years. This generated a mass of data and a tendency to get bogged down in detail. Subsequent efforts paid less attention to detailed projections and greater attention to strategic thinking that explored and emphasized the unpredictability of the firm's future environment.

Strategic Planning at Regional Headquarters

The new strategic planning system formed the core of the headquarters annual cycle plan. The cycle begins in the spring with an open-ended inquiry into what businesses the company is in and how it defines its strategic business units. The plan establishes the firm's mission, goals, and objectives, though all are subject to change as the process develops. Goals differ from objectives in that they are less specific and have no time limit—for example, "Our goal is to produce the highest quality products in our industry." Objectives are more precise and measurable over time, such as, "We want to increase our sales by 40 percent within the next three years."

External Analysis. This focuses on analysis of the firm's regional environment, including industry business trends and macroenvironmental factors relating to national economic and political conditions. Particular attention is paid to areas of uncertainty that could affect the company's future. In general, the external analysis brings managers from different parts of the company together to develop a regional view of the firm's European environment, beginning with an analysis of the current situation before attempting to identify, project, and interpret future trends, events, and issues.

Internal Analysis. Participating managers are asked to look inside the regional organization and to assess current and future areas of strength and weakness. The analysis is carried out on a regional basis, with the heads of the major functions examining their own areas of responsibility. For example, the regional chief of manufacturing is responsible for analyzing and interpreting the firm's manufacturing strengths and weaknesses, first on a country-by-country basis by examining the situation in each of the firm's operating units before bringing the data together into a Europe-wide analysis. A regional perspective is thus developed for each of the major functional areas and fed into the overall analysis of the region. Special studies may be undertaken in areas of particular sensitivity and uncertainty.

Results of Analyses. The results of the internal-external analyses raise specific issues relating to competition, regional markets, political considerations, and other factors that are then examined. The discussion in this type of exercise leads to an airing of views and opinions, many of which may be expected to diverge from what has heretofore been the conventional wisdom. Consensus on certain points will begin to emerge, though the aim of the exercise is not to eliminate differences of opinion. On the contrary, scenarios are developed reflecting alternative assumptions about future events that could disrupt the strategy. The most likely of these are used as the basis for the development of contingency plans, available for implementation on short notice.

The purpose of the strategic planning system is to organize and facilitate this decision-making process. It produces, first, an overall ten-year strategic plan for the region as a whole together with strategic subplans for each of the major functions. These are used to develop a five-year financial plan for the region and for each of the major functions (again on a regional basis).

Global Headquarters

Once regional headquarters has approved the strategic plan for Europe, it is forwarded to the firm's global headquarters. At this level, the plans from all of the regional organizations are reviewed and incorporated into the overall global strategic plan. Global headquarters will offer suggestions and probe the various regional headquarters regarding their strategic plans and associated requests for capital.

Global headquarters maintains a federal relationship with the regional units, offering advice and support. Close integration of the firm's various international operations is left largely to regional-level coordination.

Regional Headquarters and National Units

Information and advice flow bottom up from the national operating units to regional headquarters at the beginning of the cycle, with the various national functional heads advising their regional counterparts on the situation within their own country. This national advice is reflected in the contributions made by the regional heads of department into the regional strategic plan.

Subsequently, when they are equipped with their respective regional strategic and financial plans, the various regional chiefs are in a position to meet with their functional counterparts in the national operating units to develop national business plans consistent with regional strategy.

There is a distinct top-down flavor about this stage of the process. Although the emphasis is on negotiation, the heads of the various functional areas at the regional level have the authority to issue directives covering capital investment, product development, research, and other major decisions to national managers to ensure that plans are coordinated within the regional plan.

Costs and Benefits

The strategic planning system has helped to achieve a high degree of international coordination, but national boundaries have lost much of their significance. They are still relevant as environmental units of analysis, since national sales, profits, and market share are still broken out by national territory; however, the major functions within the national operating units are now controlled from regional headquarters, which has direct authority and responsibility for them.

This more centralized approach is in line with the company's strategy of reducing unit costs through international integration of manufacturing, marketing and product development. While the new strategic planning system has helped this company to attain this objective, management recognizes the system described entails associated costs.

Administrative Costs. At the time the new strategic planning system was introduced, the company was in the midst of an all-out drive to reduce administrative costs. There was particular concern at meeting Japanese competition, which was known to have a far lower administrative cost-to-sales ratio. The new system made further demands on regional headquarters staff in terms of additional information and information processing, which ran counter to this aim.

National Image. In common with many other multinational companies, management aimed to capitalize on the geographic distribution of the firm's facilities to project an image as a national producer within those countries where such facilities were located. This is important from both the standpoint of customer relations and relations with host governments. To some extent, the close coordination and integration brought about by the new system undermined the firm's national identity, presenting it as an international rather than a national producer.

Management Authority and Accountability. At one time, the firm's national functions were coordinated by and responsible to a single national managing director. This had the advantage of clearly fixing management authority and accountability within a smaller, more readily coordinated management structure.

Management Development and Motivation. Small, autonomous operating units with clearly defined areas of responsibility also provide a good training ground for future managers, who are clearly accountable for both their failures and successes. Motivation is high since individual management performance is clearly identifiable. This tends to be weakened once systems that create interdependence between the various units are introduced.

Friction. Formal planning systems can prove to be a source of organizational tension and friction between headquarters and its associated operating units, as well as among operating units themselves. By their nature, such systems attempt to introduce common international goals and objectives, which often require that some units suboptimize their individual situation for the good of the overall enterprise.

Progress toward Improved Understanding

We may expect that with the passage of time, there will be improved understanding of the workings of international organizations. Geert Hofstede points out that thinking on headquarters-subsidiary relationships traditionally has turned about the issue of control. Much less attention has been paid to support from headquarters in the form of advice and expert assistance that will enable subsidiaries to perform more effectively. Research shows that headquarters' support to subsidiaries helps to reduce alienation within the organization.[12]

Developing a Multinational Company Culture

In no small part, the difficulties of implementing international coordination may be traced to the inherent problem of developing a company culture within the multinational organization. Even the most sophisticated planning system depends on goodwill and the ability of individual managers to work together.

The usual lines of demarcation that impede interpersonal relationships in domestic companies are reinforced in multinational companies by geography and differences in national background. These additional barriers to intercompany communication make it difficult to develop the shared beliefs, philosophy, and values that contribute to the development of a common ground or culture within the firm.[13]

The tendency is to develop national subcultures, each national business unit looking inward and concentrating on its own national environment, reflecting nationally focused beliefs and loyalties. To counter this, a growing number of multinational firms are pursuing programs designed to encourage their managers to view themselves as part of a wider, international organization.

International Career Paths

Management careers that are nationally limited to progression within a specific national organization contribute to the development of a national identity, reinforcing a national mentality and a "we-they" relationships with other parts of the company. An alternative approach stresses international career paths.[14] Management promotion is planned to include systematic international job changes. Managers are rotated to different parts of the organization on an international basis, receiving experience in different countries, as well as different parts of the corporate hierarchy. The manager of one of the firm's operations in country A will move to a position in the firm's regional headquarters in country B before rotation to a subsidiary in country C. Experience in different parts of the world, different units, and different task situations is part of a planned succession path designed to produce managers capable of interpreting conditions and associating with people in widely different national settings.

Training Courses

International career paths may be supplemented by company training, bringing together managers from the company's international business units. Exposure to similar techniques and methods helps to promote a corporate identity. An important part of such training courses is the informal contact among managers after the regular training sessions. Personal relationships that are formed facilitate communication and coordination between participating managers after they return to their respective units.

Reward Systems

The reward system exerts an important influence within any organization. Reward schemes (usually in the form of bonus payments) that compensate managers strictly according to the performance of their own particular national business unit are bound to reinforce a national mentality and view of the business. For that reason, many companies now include an international element in their scheme for executive compensation. Part of the executive bonus payment is geared to the firm's regional/global performance. This international element tends to increase with promotion.

Management Recruitment

Developing a cadre of internationally oriented managers starts with management selection and recruitment. The nationality and other characteristics of the firm's pool of managers will have an important bearing on the firm's internal environment.[15] At one extreme are those companies that draw their top management from the firm's home country. The higher levels of the corporate hierarchy are occupied almost entirely by managers with a common citizenship. Foreign nationals are limited to promotion within their respective national organizations. The management pool is, in effect, divided into two groups, those whose citizenship qualifies them for higher managerial positions and the rest.

For some time, the more progressive multinationals have implemented personnel programs designed to break down these barriers. Potential candidates for higher managerial positions are recruited from diverse national backgrounds. Selection, training, job assignments, and reward systems are structured to develop a pool of multinational managers representing diverse nationalities.

Information Systems

The ability of management to identify with the aims of the corporation as a whole will depend on the nature and scope of information available. In those cases where the flow of information from the multinational company's national operating units is mainly one-way (information provided to international headquarters with little or no corresponding return flow from either international headquarters or other units of the company in other countries), management at the national level will find it difficult to identify with any but local company operations and objectives.

Many multinationals are now going to considerable lengths to supply their various national units with information on the firm's worldwide activities. Since such information is costly in terms of both its direct cost and management time, its dissemination has to be highly selective. But modern means of information processing and telecommunications now make practicable information systems designed to keep management in the firm's subsidiaries and other operating units in touch with international plans and operations, enabling management at the national level to take a more proactive role in formulating regional/global strategy.

15
Changing the Organizational Structure

T he pressure for organizational change is nowhere more evident than in multinational companies. Initially, the organization of the firm's foreign operations may come about more as a matter of expediency than by design. As and when such operations continue to expand, management has to consider how these will be related to the other parts of the organization. The purpose of this chapter is to identify the major organizational options open to such companies and to explore their various attributes. Much of the discussion focuses about the dynamics of organization change.

Export Organizations

The incremental nature of international expansion tells quite a bit about certain changes in organizational structure. As we have already noted, companies typically begin their international operations through exporting.[1] Export activity begins within the existing organization of an ongoing enterprise serving domestic markets and structured accordingly. The major question is how to fit the personnel and resources devoted to exports within an existing, domestically oriented structure. One solution is to attach the new export unit to one of the existing major parts of the organization. In companies organized along functional lines, as in figure 15–1, exporting frequently is attached to the sales division. In its early growth stage, it may simply be labeled as International Sales and no more important than any other sales department.

In firms operating a divisionalized product structure, the major divisions of the company corresponding to different products or product groups, the export department is often appended to the product division whose exports it handles. Thus, one or all of the major product divisions may have its own export department. As exports expand, companies organized in this fashion will contemplate amalgamating the various export departments into a single unit serving the entire company.

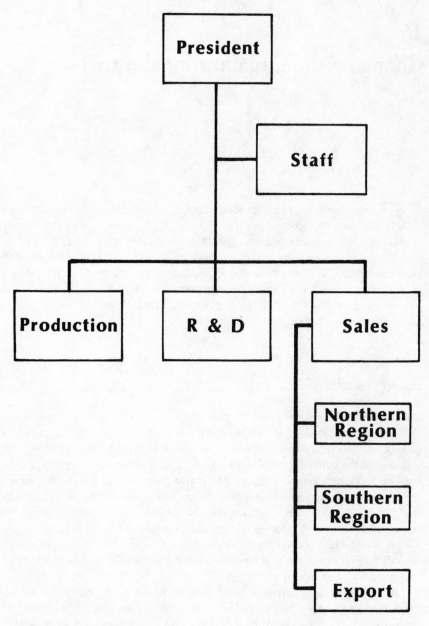

Figure 15–1. Domestic Functional Organization with Export Department

The pros and cons of changing from one structure to another were experienced recently by a small producer of textile products. The firm carried a highly diverse product line of several hundred textiles. An export department was attached to each of its domestic product divisions, each division producing a different line of textile products. Experiencing a rapid expansion of the firm's exports, management's attention was drawn to the increasing waste involved in duplicate sales trips. This became particularly obvious with reference to trips made by sales staff representing the firm's various product divisions, many of them to the same customers. To reduce such duplication, the company decided to centralize its export activities within a single department. Under the new organization, a single company sales representative presented the firm's entire product line to each customer. Duplicate sales trips were eliminated. But the company soon discovered that no single sales representative was able to answer the numerous technical inquiries by customers concerning its entire product range. Furthermore, the close relationship that previously had existed between the product divisions and their individual export departments was broken. The new, larger export department had difficulty communicating with the divisions. Export orders tended to receive lower priority, delivery dates were missed, and orders canceled. Eventually the firm was forced to revert to its earlier organization. Other firms with less-diverse product lines have found the move toward a central export department has improved their performance.

Japanese trading companies represent a major departure from the organizational structures and the pattern of international expansion that occupies most of the discussion in this chapter. For the typical Western firm, international expansion is producer led; that is, the initiative, management, and strategy for international expansion are provided by the company producing the product or service in question.

Producers whose exports are handled by a trading company play a more passive role. The initiative, management, and strategy of their export activities are provided by the trading company. In its role as a middleman, the trading company brings together international customers and producers.[2] A major advantage of the trading company type of organization is its flexibility to choose among various producers, finding those best suited to particular national markets. The fact that such trading groups typically have a special relationship with a bank helps to overcome a familiar problem encountered by many exporters.

The initial core competences of the trading company are marketing and distribution, the most critical problem areas for novice exporters. Producers exporting their products through trading companies need have little or no knowledge of either the mechanics or marketing expertise usually required of exporters in the West.

Since trading companies handle the products of many producers, they are able to achieve economies of large-scale international distribution that enable them to support formidable international intelligence systems beyond the reach of all but the very largest Western firms. The fact that they deal in trade both to and from any country where they have established facilities adds to this volume.

Japanese trading companies have certain significant advantages over Western alternatives, particularly in the early stages of international operations when the Western producer is likely to be inexperienced and of a small size. They also have advantages in less developed countries where small, complex markets require considerable expertise while offering relatively low-volume market opportunities.

The fact that trading companies service many producers also has drawbacks. It may detract from the trading firm's ability to give individual attention to any one product. Since the trading company does not control the producer, this may also limit its ability to influence the producer's strategy in a way calculated to take advantage of international possibilities. The strategic focus of the trading company is international, while that of the producer may remain largely concentrated on domestic opportunities—hence, the need for the type of close, informal coordination that Japanese firms are famous for.

Where the products of a particular producer do find a ready market abroad and the company attains large-scale international sales, the advantages of the trading company diminish. The successful exporting producer becomes better able to provide its own finance, marketing intelligence, and distribution. At the same time, customers ordering large volumes often prefer to deal directly with the producer.

There is a tendency for such successful exporters to establish their own sales subsidiaries abroad, significantly reducing their dependence on trading companies.[3] Furthermore, trading companies themselves are now investing heavily in foreign and domestic production facilities, becoming, at least in part, multinational companies.

The Hitachi company relied heavily on Japanese trading companies to carry its product abroad during the early stages of its international development. As its volume of business abroad expanded, it gradually relied less on trading companies and more on its own management of foreign operations, including joint ventures and wholly owned subsidiaries.[4]

Early Multinational Organizations

Once the firm has established its own operating units abroad, the organizational issues change substantially from those in the export stage. Foreign-based subsidiaries have a potential for operating independently under their own management and productive resources as quasi-independent units. Questions of organization now turn about the relationship of these units to the overall corporate structure.

European Multinationals

In the early stages of development, European multinational organizations tend to be very informal. An analysis of their development by Larry Franko shows that the typical European multinational begins as a domestic company organized in functional departments.[5] As national subsidiaries are established abroad, the chief executive deals with them on an individual basis. This highly personalized relationship, with the chief executive officer of the parent firm on one side and the managing director of the firm's various foreign-based national operating subsidiaries on the other, has come to be known as the mother-daughter type of organization (figure 15–2). Its roots no doubt trace back to the days when the firm's various operating units were staffed largely by relatives of the founder, and the company itself was a family affair.[6] That, together with the close geographic proximity of European markets, helped to support an organization that allowed considerable discretion to the managing directors of the firm's national operating units and where control from the center was exercised mainly through personal visits by the chief executive to the various managing directors.

The fact that these managers were drawn from much the same ethnic and even family background helped to ensure a similarity in management philosophy, values, and points of view. The high tariff barriers between the European countries at that time helped to restrict each national operating unit within its own borders, minimizing both the need for and the possibility of cross-national coordination. Given the lack of staff and the highly short-term nature of the chief executive's visits, surveillance and direction from the parent focused largely on financial performance.

The mother-daughter structure is most effective within a relatively small enterprise adopting a holding company mode of control over closely situated national operating units. Once multinational companies began to expand geographically and in other ways, the limitations of this structure became readily apparent. In companies with fifty or sixty subsidiaries located in twenty-five to thirty countries, the mechanism of personal control and relationships depending on visits becomes physically difficult to maintain. The chief executive's personal knowledge of countries as diverse as those in Asia, Africa, and the Middle East is necessarily superficial. Hopping from one country to another means that there is little opportunity to get any in-depth understanding of the background and assumptions that support the subsidiaries' financial calculations.

Major advantages of this structural form are its leaness in terms of supporting staff and the direct contact provided. The fact that the chief executive meets directly with the managing directors in the field lends an immediacy and directness to information obtained in this manner that is all too often missing in more elaborate organizations. The relative autonomy of the various subsidiaries carries with it the usual advantages of decentralization, such as the freedom and flexibility to respond to local national conditions and the fixing of authority and responsibility within an unambiguous and uncomplicated organizational structure.

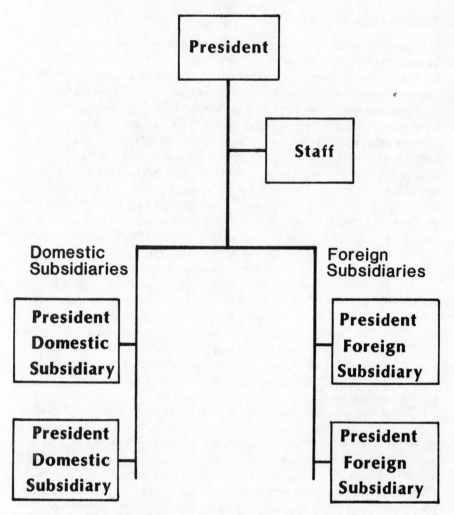

Figure 15–2. Mother-Daughter Structure

Perhaps for these reasons, some European firms retained their mother-daughter structures long after their size and geographic spread pointed toward the need for an alternative approach. Significantly, the larger and more successful European multinationals, such as Philips, Ciba-Geigy and Nestlé, led the move away from the mother-daughter organization toward more global structures.[7]

U.S. Multinationals

U.S. multinational companies have followed a different route. The expansion of operations abroad and the establishment of subsidiaries raised the need for organizational change. Since many of these firms were already organized along divisional lines (product or functional), it was natural that the initial response in most cases took the form of an international division, added on to the existing structure.

The international division, unlike the mother-daughter structure, has its own staff and chief executive. Usually it encompasses all units whose primary activity is directed toward countries outside the home country of the parent firm.

The main operating subunits within the international division are comprised of the firm's various foreign-based operations, defined by national territory (national subsidiaries), as in figure 15–3. However, operations in certain foreign countries because of tradition or convenience may also be grouped under a domestic division, as in the case of many U.S. firms that group their Canadian operations within their domestic division structures.

A number of advantages attach to the international division structure. It provides a central focus within the firm for strategy directed at the firm's international opportunities. The grouping together of the various units within a single international division gives them more weight within the organizational hierarchy. There is a tendency in many companies to neglect the often different requirements associated with international customers and production requirements in favor of the more familiar needs of the domestic divisions. For example, the needs of the export department may be accorded such a low priority by domestic production managers that delivery dates are not met.

Unlike the mother-daughter structure, the international division lends itself more readily to the establishment of formal reporting procedures and a less personal form of control. Grouping together the firm's international operations facilitates the training and development of a core of international managers. Moreover, the considerable autonomy that the managing directors of the various national subsidiaries typically enjoy within their national sphere clearly fixes responsibility and accountability for results while leaving them free to respond to local conditions.

This structure has proved to be very flexible. Its basic structure can be readily supplemented with special project teams and international committees to accommodate, within limits, the need for a greater degree of international coordination.

The international division system also has disadvantages. The fact that it focuses a significant proportion of the firm's management toward international operations sets up frictions, which may take the form of a cultural split between international managers working abroad and domestic managers oriented toward the national context of the firm's home country and prone to see much of the world through that, as if through a prism.

The above dichotomy may be exacerbated through differences in the training and background of staff supporting the domestic and international divisions. Another problem is that by grouping its foreign-based operations on a national basis, the division may discourage cross-national expertise and coordination. For

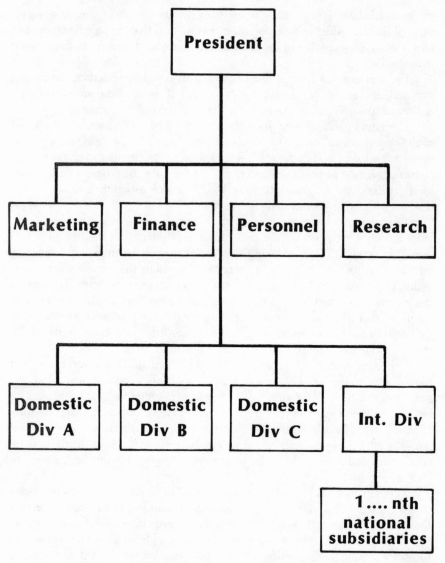

Figure 15–3. Divisional Structure

example, it is not uncommon to find that though many of the managers are international in the sense that they are accustomed to working abroad; they have spent their entire careers within a single national territory. Rotating managers from one country to another may yield a management group with experience in several countries but little or no experience with international coordination, i.e. managing operations in more than one country at the same time.

Finally, the international division still remains one of several divisions. The other domestic divisions, taken together, carry much more weight in the overall decision-making structure. This lopsidedness in favor of domestic operations may prove a disadvantage for firms with a high commitment to international business. Such companies will tend to move toward one of the more global organizational structures described next.

Global Structures

Global Product Structures

Global product structures assign primary responsibility to international product managers with a worldwide mandate for specific product groups (figure 15–4). Each manager in charge of an international product group is assisted by a staff equipped to scan the international environment on a global scale. He or she has both the necessary information and the authority to mobilize the firm's international resources behind global strategies.[8]

Compared with the international division, the global product structure shifts authority away from managers managing national subsidiaries and places it in the hands of executives with worldwide product responsibility. The aim is to achieve better international coordination within specific product groups. Hoped-for benefits include a more global view of competition and the firm's strategic opportunities, as well as better cross-border coordination of product-related activities, which may include manufacturing marketing and technology transfer. Technology transfer is particularly important for firms with sizable investment in R&D that has to be defused globally within a relatively short period. For example, the Corning company cites technology transfer as a major reason for its adoption of a global product structure: "Dissolving the international division will remove a major barrier to the transfer of technology from our domestic product divisions to our markets abroad."[9]

In practice, the hoped-for benefits are not always achieved. In a study of fifty-seven multinational companies, it was found that the international transfer of technology occurred more slowly and less frequently within firms organized along global product lines. Also there was a greater tendency toward licensing the firm's technology to other companies. Furthermore, duplication was not always reduced overall since the division of the company into product groups operating with a high degree of independence from each other, even within the same country, led to other and different forms of duplication.[10] A possible explanation for this somewhat surprising result may lie in the background, training, and outlook of the managers chosen to assume positions of leadership in newly adopted global product structures. Particularly in those companies (including most U.S. firms) where the domestic market has been dominant prior to adopting the global form, it may be expected that a high proportion of the most senior posts

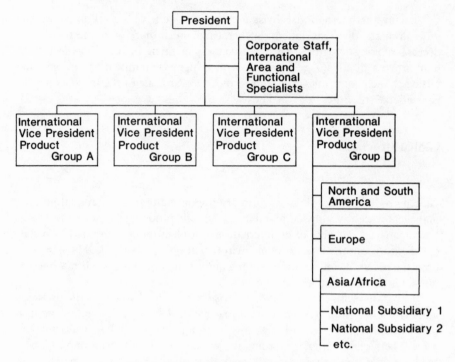

Figure 15–4. Global Product Structure

in the new organization will be occupied by managers whose experience and background have been mainly within the firm's domestic operations. Managers from the international division generally will be in the minority and occupy a relatively small proportion of the new senior management positions. Hence, whatever the merits and objectives of the new structure, the end result may be a more domestically biased company.

Within the global product structure, national-level coordination plays a secondary role. This is sometimes assigned to national directors responsible for coordinating the activities of the various product groups within a given national territory. This national role may include collective representation of their interests to government, presenting a coherent company-wide view rather than making multiple and separate representation on behalf of each product group. It may also include provision of a common administrative umbrella of facilities such as offices and secretarial help.

The emphasis that the global product structure places on cross-border rationalization of marketing and productive activities does appear to have the very important benefit of improving cost efficiency.[11] The fact that so many of the more experienced multinationals have continued to use this structure indicates that potential problems are manageable, particularly if its adoption goes beyond formal structural change to the development of a corps of senior managers with an international outlook and experience.

Global Area Structures

Global area structures segment the firm's operations geographically into several regions of the world, each the responsibility of an area (regional) headquarters, as in figure 15–5. In some multinational companies, the global area structure evolves from regional managers and their staff who may have been established initially within an international division to improve communications between division headquarters and the national operating units. There are several subcategories of this type of organization:

1. Global area–product structures. The next reporting level, below area headquarters, is organized by product group.
2. Global area–functional. The next level below area headquarters is organized by function.
3. Global area–national. The next level below area, which is to say regional headquarters, is organized by national geographic units, for example, the firms various national subsidiaries, as in figure 15–5.

Global Functional Structures

In a functional form, the firm is organized internationally along functional lines, each function coordinated from a global headquarters. This system can lead to

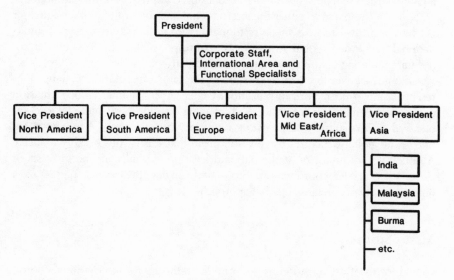

Figure 15–5. Global Area Structure

highly integrated manufacturing operations, making maximum use of the global efficiencies of scale and volume; however, the split among major functions may result in lack of communication and feedback, as between manufacturing and marketing.

Common Features of Global Structures

The following are features that all global structures (product, functional, and area) have in common:

Multiple international headquarters and staffs. Unlike the international division or mother-daughter organizations, global structures are characterized by multiple international headquarters with global or regional responsibility.

Absence of any inherent distinction between the domestic and foreign. The major segments of the firm are organized by product, function, or area, avoiding the split between domestic and foreign operations that particularly characterizes the international division.

International power balance. A complement of the previous point is that the firm's domestic operations do not hold a special position of power within the organization (as in the case of the international division and the mother-daughter structures).

Seen from the very highest levels of the corporate hierarchy, the move toward a global structure represents a more decentralized approach to international operations, as compared to either the international division or the mother-daughter organization. Instead of a single headquarters exercising control over all international operations, global structures spread responsibility for cross-border coordination among multiple international headquarters.

From the lower levels of the hierarchy, the same organizational change represents a higher degree of centralization. Under either the international division or the mother-daughter structure, the managing director at the national level (of one of the firm's subsidiaries) will enjoy considerable autonomy. A move toward one of the global structures usually will mean that this is considerably reduced. Autonomy and authority at the national level are curtailed in the interests of closer cross-border coordination. From both angles, the change represents a higher priority on a regional/global approach.

Matrix Structures

Global forms of organization assign primary authority for international coordination to a single control dimension, either product group, region, or function.

In doing so, they orient the firm's international coordination along one or other of these dimensions, a trade-off that may be costly. For example, by vesting authority in global product managers, the global product structure may facilitate certain types of product-related coordination while sacrificing the benefits of a global area structure with its greater emphasis on the needs and opportunities within a given region.

Matrix structures attempt to get the best of all worlds by assigning equal authority and responsibility along at least two dimensions. Figure 15–6 illustrates a matrix structure organized by product and region. Its various product groups are coordinated globally, each by its own vice-president. The firm's operations are also coordinated by area, with authority for this type of control vested in regional vice-presidents. The aim is to get the best product and area-centered coordination. Potential problems stem from the abandonment of the traditional unity-of-control principle, which calls for a single line of authority-responsibility. In figure 15–6 the president of the national subsidiary is directly responsible to the vice-president of the Latin American region. The product groups within his subsidiary and under his direction also report to their respective product group vice-presidents. The national managers of product groups X and Y are responsible to both the president of their national subsidiary and the vice-presidents of their respective product groups.

Despite its apparent inconsistencies, many of the world's leading multinationals have adopted the matrix structure type of organization. Not surprisingly,

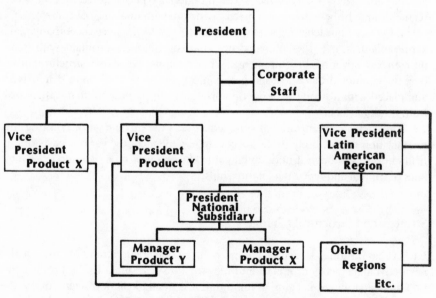

Figure 15–6. Matrix Structure

a number of firms have encountered problems in managing dual reporting relationships.

ISS (International Service Systems) is a Danish multinational marketing a number of services internationally, including leasing, energy control, and building maintenance. ISS adopted a product country matrix, giving equal authority to both national managers and product group managers. The firm's annual report states that the aim was "to provide fruitful interplay between local market know how and product expertise."[12] The result, however, was a reduced capability for strategic planning, crossed lines of authority, and a consequent slowing down of decision making. The new matrix structure was eventually abandoned in favor of an organization more along the lines of a global product organization.

Hybrid Structures

In an effort to minimize some of the problems of matrix structures, a number of firms are adopting hybrid forms of organization. In particular, diversified companies recognize that the type and direction of control that may be most appropriate and relevant for one type of product may not be suitable for another. Such firms may choose to combine several organizational forms. Certain operating units whose situation and needs call for a high degree of international product-related control might be organized as in a global product structure. Other parts with quite different characteristics, perhaps requiring close coordination by geographic area, may be organized under a regional type of structure. Still other segments may be best suited to a matrix structure with dual lines of control.

J. Quincy Hunsicker cites the example of a matrix-organized company marketing toiletries, over-the-counter drugs, and confectionery products with quite different organizational requirements. While retaining the matrix structure for its over-the-counter drugs and toiletries, confectionery products were dematrixed and placed within strong national organizations subject only to financial control from headquarters.[13]

This lack of organizational symmetry offers the advantage of tailoring the organization more closely to the specific requirements of the various parts of the firm's business, though it undoubtedly introduces a new type of complexity into lines of control and reporting relationships.

Strategy and Structural Change

Each organizational structure has its own characteristic strengths and weaknesses. Management's task is to find the structure best suited to the firm's situation and capabilities, keeping in mind that it is in all likelihood a temporary solution, part of an evolutionary process of change. Certain key variables that influence this change, such as size, technology, and strategy, have been identified, but there is no model as yet that can bring all the various factors together and tell us which structure is best suited for a specific company.

For our purposes, the influence of the firm's strategy on its organizational structure has obvious and special relevance. Chandler's classic analysis, to the effect that organizational structure follows strategy, provides the conceptual starting point. The precise linkage referred to in this statement may sometimes appear arguable; for example, it is possible to hold that a certain organizational structure, by providing a particular scanning and data-gathering capability, may identify strategic possibilities that might otherwise have escaped attention and thus lead to a different strategy. Nevertheless, few would doubt that there is a close association between the two. Building on this insight, data collected by John Stopford on U.S. multinationals point to a significant relationship between certain aspects of international strategy and multinational organizational structure.[14]

Figure 15–7 provides a conceptual view of this strategy-structure relationship. Those firms whose strategy is characterized by a low foreign product diversity and a relatively low proportion of sales abroad tend to have an international division structure. Multinationals whose strategy calls for a high degree of for-

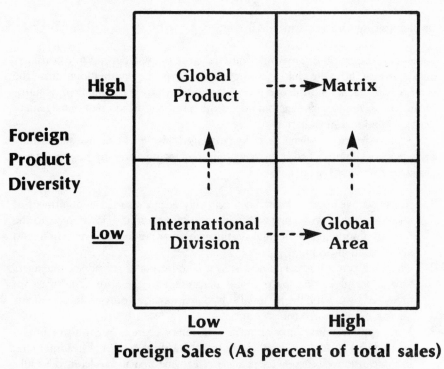

Figure 15–7. Multinational Company Strategy and Structure

eign product diversification with a relatively low proportion of sales abroad tend to be organized as global product organizations. Those with a strategy of low foreign product diversity and a high proportion of total sales abroad are generally found to adopt global area structures. Firms with a strategy calling for both high foreign product diversity and a high proportion of their sales abroad fall into the matrix structure category.

By omitting all of the other factors affecting the choice of organizational structure, figure 15–7 presents a highly simplified picture. It should be interpreted as a tendency; that is, there is a tendency for the organizational structure of U.S. multinational firms to conform to the relationships indicated. There are bound to be significant exceptions.

The arrows in figure 15–7 indicate two paths of organizational change suggested by the data. Beginning with an international division, those companies expanding abroad with a high degree of foreign product diversification will tend to adopt global product structures first. As sales abroad increase, they will move toward a matrix form of organization. Companies with a low degree of foreign product diversification will tend to go from the international division to a global area structure. With the introduction of new products, they too will move toward the matrix type of organization.

Implementing Organizational Change

Successful adaptation of any organizational structure will depend to a considerable degree on how the change is implemented. For the multinational firm, the most sensitive area, and the one probably most frequently encountered, is introducing organizational change that affects the status and freedom of management within its national subsidiaries.

An investigation of firms that have managed this type of change successfully finds that they approached it incrementally, employing a step-by-step procedure along the following lines:[15]

1. Key executive appointment. They generally began with the appointment of a key executive, who enjoyed a high level of respect and acceptance, to the task of improving performance through international coordination and avoiding duplication.
2. Changing perceptions. The next step was to introduce subsidiary managers to a more global perspective and perception of the firm. This was approached by placing the national subsidiary managers on various coordinating committees and business teams.
3. Minor power shifts. After about a year, minor changes began to be implemented that shifted a degree of control toward international headquarters. In some instances, these were changes already desired and welcomed by sub-

sidiary managers, such as export coordination and technology transfer arrangements.

4. Major changes. Only after such familiarization and preparation were major changes, such as those involving status and career paths, introduced.

International Coordination: The Broader Context

Organization structure plays a major role in coordinating strategy across national borders. It is a chief tool in helping management adjust to the more inter-

Coordination Mechanism	Low Coordination Profile	High Coordination Profile
Formal organization structure	Mother–daughter/ international division	Global/matrix
Strategic planning system	Limited to capital budgeting and portfolio strategy	Comprehensive system for developing regional/global strategic plans
International policies	Cover only financial reporting and procedures	Policies set standards and procedures in various functions and activities
Management reward system	Based on national company performance only	Has reference to international as well as national performance of firm
Management career paths	Nationally limited	International rotation and job opportunities
Information system	International information provided to national units only on a "need-to-know basis."	Information on firms' international activities and plans made available to national units as a matter of routine
Management recruitment and promotion	Nationally based	Provides for recruitment and promotion across national boundaries
Management training	Develops national management skills	Develops international management skills
Other coordination mechanisms	Executive visits	Executive visits International meetings International project teams Competence centers Overlapping membership in boards of directors

Figure 15–8. International Coordination Mechanisms

national business environment, but it must be seen in the context of the total company, its resources, and particularly its international strategy. Change in formal organization structure implemented in isolation of other considerations may have little positive impact. Indeed such change may severely disrupt the effectiveness of existing coordination and intrafirm relationships.

Looking toward the future we may expect that more multinational companies will be caught up in the move toward internationalized industries and their associated pressures for greater international coordination. At the same time, increased competition will place a premium on avoiding the rigidities and costs associated with top-heavy bureaucratic procedures. The key question regarding headquarters–subsidiary relationships will be, "How do we achieve the degree of coordination required by our regional/global strategy while keeping down headquarters' costs and intervention in the affairs of our subsidiaries?"

Arriving at the right balance between central coordination across national boundaries and the advantages of decentralized operations will depend to a large degree on the combination of organization structure with other mechanisms for international coordination. To illustrate, figure 15–8 sets out two quite different profiles or combinations of coordination mechanisms. On the left-hand side, under "low coordination profile," are the organization structure and specific features of other coordination mechanisms appropriate for a multinational whose strategy requires a low degree of international coordination; that is, a holding company mode.

The profile on the right illustrates a combination of such features more suitable for a company whose strategy requires a high degree of international coordination, such as characteristic of an integrative mode multinational.

Notes

Chapter 1

1. Organization for Economic Cooperation and Development, *Gaps in Technology—General Report* (Paris: OECD, 1968), p. 41.

Chapter 2

1. A.D. Chandler and F. Redlich, "Recent Developments in American Business Administration and Their Conceptualization," *Business History Review* (Spring 1967): 6.
2. Ibid., p. 8
3. Ibid.
4. See especially C.W. Hofer and D. Schendel, *Strategy Formulation: Analytical Concepts* (St. Paul: West Publishing Company, 1978), chap. 3. See also P. Lorange, *Corporate Planning, An Executive Viewpoint* (Englewood Cliffs, N.J.: Prentice-Hall, 1980), pp. 21–28. G. Hamel and C.K. Prahaled, "Managing Strategic Responsibility in the MNC," *Strategic Management Journal* (October–December 1983): 341–351. Milton Leontiades, "A Diagnostic Framework for Planning," *Strategic Management Journal* (January–March 1983): 11–26.
5. *Financial Times*, November 8, 1982, p. 12.
6. E. Sciberras, *Multinational Electronic Companies and National Economic Policies* (Greenwich, Conn.: JAI Press, 1977), pp. 77–94.

Chapter 3

1. M. Wilkins and F.E. Hill, *American Business Abroad: Ford on Six Continents* (Detroit: Wayne State University Press, 1924), p. 226.
2. I am indebted to the many managers at Ford of Europe who provided much of the material in this chapter.
3. R.M. Cyert and J.G. March, *A Behavioral Theory of the Firm* (Englewood Cliffs: Prentice-Hall, 1963), pp. 27–43.
4. Ford Company, *Ford Facts—History of Ford Sales in Europe*.

5. D. Hackett, *The Big Idea* (Nottingham: Thomas Forman and Sons Ltd., 1978), p. 29.

6. Ford, *Ford Facts*

7. G. Turner, *Cars* (London: Hodder and Stoughton, 1965), pp. 18, 19.

8. *The Times*, London, March 17, 1969, p. 17.

9. Ford interview, November 3, 1981.

10. Ford interview, August 2, 1978.

11. E. Seidler, *Let's Call It Fiesta* (Cambridge: Patrick Stephens, 1976), pp. 164, 165.

12. Ibid., p. 88.

13. G. Maxcy, *The Multinational Motor Industry* (London: Croom Helm Ltd., 1981), pp. 200–202.

14. *Financial Times*, January 11, 1984.

15. For example, see Maxcy, *Multinational Motor Industry*, pp. 146–154.

16. A.D. Chandler, *Strategy and Structure* (Garden City: N.Y.: Anchor Books, 1962).

17. Ford interview. November 3, 1981.

Chapter 4

1. H.I. Ansoff and J. Leontiades "Strategic Portfolio Management," *Journal of General Management* (Autumn 1976): 13–29.

2. P. Haspeslagh, "Portfolio Planning, Uses and Limits," *Harvard Business Review* (January–February 1982): 59.

3. *Lonrho Limited, Report and Accounts* (annual report) (1981), p. 8.

4. R. Cushman, "Norton's Top-Down, Bottom-Up Planning Process." *Planning Review* (November 1979): 7.

5. *International Management* (October 1982): 59–61. See also *Financial Times*, April 10, 1984.

6. *Financial Times*, November 2, 1983. See also J.J. Boddewyn, "Foreign Divestment: Magnitude and Factors," *Journal of International Business Studies* (Spring–Summer 1979): 21–27.

7. For portfolio risk reduction in multinationals, see A.M. Rugman, "Risk Reduction by International Diversification," *Journal of International Business Studies* (Fall–Winter 1976): 75–80.

8. I. Ayal and J. Zif, "Market Expansion Strategies in Multinational Marketing," *Journal of Marketing* (Spring 1979): 84–91.

9. Y. Aharoni, *The Foreign Investment Decision Process* (Boston: Division of Research, Harvard Business School, 1966), pp. 93, 96.

10. M.E. Wicks Kelly and G.C. Philippatos, "Comparative Analysis of Foreign Investment Evaluation Practices by U.S. Based Manufacturing Multinational Companies," *Journal of International Business Studies* (Winter 1982): 23.

11. H. Gernon, "The Effects of Translation on Multinational Corporations Internal Performance Evaluation," *Journal of International Business Studies* (Spring–Summer 1983): 103–112.

12. F.W. Gluck, *McKinsey Quarterly* (Winter 1980): 21.

Chapter 5

1. T. Hout, M. Porter, and E. Rudden, "How Global Companies Win Out," *Harvard Business Review* (September–October 1982): 98–108.

2. W.V. Rapp, "Strategy Formulation and International Competition," *Columbia Journal of World Business* (Summer 1973): 105, 106.

3. E. Sciberras, *Multinational Electronic Companies and National Economic Policies* (Greenwich, Conn.: JAL Press, 1977), pp. 182–183.

4. Ibid., pp. 146–182.

5. A.E. Scaperlanda and L.J. Mauer, "The Determinants of US Direct Investment in the EEC," *American Economic Review* 59 (September 1969): 566–567; R.T. Green and W.H. Cunningham "The Determinants of US Foreign Investment: An Empirical Examination," *Management International Review* 15 (1975): 113–120; R.S. Basi, *Determinants of US Private Investment in Foreign Countries* (Kent, Ohio: Kent State University, 1963); Y. Aharoni, *The Foreign Investment Decision Process* (Boston: Division of Research, Harvard Business School, 1966), p. 100. For association of market size with other factors, see W.H. Davidson, "Location of FDI Activity: Country Characteristics and Experience Effects," *Journal of International Business Studies* (Fall 1980): 13.

Chapter 6

1. D. Channon, *The Strategy and Structure of British Enterprise* (Boston: Division of Research, Harvard Business School, 1973), p. 125.

2. *Economist*, January 16, 1982, p. 18.

3. IBM, *Annual Report* (1982), p. 40.

4. See, for example, *Economist*, July 4, 1981, p. 75.

5. Ibid., November 21, 1981, p. 34.

6. ICL, Proposal for Rights Issue and Summary of the Audited Results for the Year Ended 30 September, 1982, p. 5.

7. *Economist*, October 10, 1981, p. 79.

8. *Wall Street Journal* (European ed.), June 23, 1983, p. 1.

9. *Scotsman*, June 21, 1982.

10. See, for example, S. Schoeffler, R. Buzzell, and D. Heany, "Impact of Strategic Planning on Profit Performance," *Harvard Business Review* (March–April 1974). See also R. Buzzell, B. Gale, and R. Sultan, "Market Share—a Key to Profitability," *Harvard Business Review* (January–February 1975): 97–106, and R. Buzzell, "Are There Natural Market Structures?" *Journal of Marketing* (Winter 1981): 42–51.

11. J. Leontiades, "Market Share and Corporate Strategy in International Industries," *Journal of Business Strategy* (Summer 1984): 30–37. D.F. Hefler, "Global Sourcing: Offshore Investment Strategy for the 1980's," *Journal of Business Strategy* (Summer 1981): 7–12.

12. J. Leontiades, "International Sourcing in the LDC's," *Columbia Journal of World Business* (November–December 1971): 19–26.

13. M.M. Smolen, *Multinational Product Management*, Proceedings of the American Marketing Association/Marketing Science Institute, August 1976, Report No. 76-

110, pp. X-1–X-8. B. Liander et al., *Comparative Analysis of International Marketing* (Boston: Allyn and Bacon, 1967), pp. 22–23.

14. T. Hout, M. Porter, and E. Rudden, "How Global Companies Win Out," *Harvard Business Review* (September–October 1982): 98–99.

15. A.M. Rugman, *Inside the Multinationals* (London: Croom Helm Ltd., 1981). P. Buckley and M. Casson, *The Future of the Multinational Enterprise* (London: Macmillan, 1976).

Chapter 7

1. P. Drucker, *The Practice of Management* (London: Pan Books 1968), p. 54.

2. See R.D. Buzzell, "Can You Standardize Multinational Marketing?" *Harvard Business Review* (November–December 1968): 103.

3. U. Weichman, "Integrating Multinational Marketing Activities," *Columbia Journal of World Business* (Winter 1974): 7–16. See also *Managing Global Marketing: A Headquarters Perspective* (New York: Business International Corporation, 1976).

4. See, for example, C.W. Hofer and D. Schendel, *Strategy Formulation: Analytical Concepts* (St. Paul: West Publishing Co., 1978), p. 108.

5. B. Liander et al., *Comparative Analysis of International Marketing* (Boston: Allyn and Bacon, 1967), pp. 21–27.

6. J. Leontiades, "Planning Strategy for World Markets," *Long Range Planning* (December 1970): 43.

7. A.C. Nielsen Co. Ltd., "How to Strengthen Your New Product Plan," *Nielsen Researcher* (1966).

8. B.C. Lindberg, "International Comparison of Growth in Demand for a New Durable Consumer Product," *Journal of Marketing Research* (August 1982): 364–371. W. Keegan, *Multinational Marketing Management* (Englewood Cliffs, N.J.: Prentice-Hall, 1974), pp. 190–196, 239.

9. C.R. Wasson, "The Importance of the Product Life Cycle to the Industrial Marketer," *Industrial Marketing Management* 5 (1976): 299–308. G.B. Sproles, "Analyzing Fashion Life Cycles—Principles and Perspectives," *Journal of Marketing* (Fall 1981): 116–127. George S. Day, "The Product Life Cycle: Analysis and Applications of Issues," *Journal of Marketing* (Fall 1981): 60–67.

10. R. Poli and V. Cook "Validity of the Product Life Cycle," *Journal of Business* (October 1969): 385–400. J.E. Swan and D. Rink, "Fitting Market Strategy to Varying Product Life Cycles," *Business Horizons* (January–February 1982): 72–76.

11. J. Leontiades, "Planning Strategy for World Markets," *Long Range Planning* (December 1970): 40–45.

12. R. Vernon, "International Trade and International Investment in the Product Life Cycle," *Quarterly Journal of Economics* (May 1966): 190–207.

13. The following discussion on lead-lag strategies draws on material from W.V. Rapp, "Strategy Formulation and International Competition," *Columbia Journal of World Business* (Summer 1973): 98–111.

14. *Wall Street Journal* (European ed.), February 22, 1983.

15. Y. Tsurumi, "Japanese Multinational Firms," *Journal of World Trade Law* (January–February 1973): 78.

16. *Nippon Keizai Shinbun*, December 1, 1980, cited by K. Yoshimine, "Japanese Trading Firms, Its Role in International Expansion" (M.B.A. dissertation, Manchester Business School, 1981), p. 79.

Chapter 8

1. R.Z. Sorenson and U.E. Wiechmann, "How Multinationals View Marketing Standardization," *Harvard Business Review* (May–June 1975).
2. E.A.G. Morgan, "Marketing International Brands in Cosmetics," *Chelwood Review* (1977): 29–36. R.D. Buzzell, "Can You Standardize Multinational Marketing," *Harvard Business Review* (November–December 1968): 102–113. J. Leontiades, "International Transfer of Company Strengths and Weaknesses," Working Paper No. 78-30 European Institute for Advanced Studies in Management, Brussels, July 1978).
3. P.M. Kraushar, *New Products and Diversification* (Tiptree, Essex: Anchor Press, 1977), pp. 182–183.
4. G. Hall and S. Howell, "An Economic Perspective on Experience Curves," *Strategic Management Journal*, 1984 forthcoming. W. Fellner, "Specific Interpretations of Learning by Doing," *Journal of Economic Theory* (1969): 119–140; Note on the Use of Experience Curves in Competitive Decision Making, Intercollegiate Case Clearing House No. 9-175-174, Boston, Harvard College, 1975. House of Commons, "Strategy Alternatives for the British Motorcycle Industry," report prepared by the Boston Consulting Group (London: HMSO, 1975).
5. E. Sciberras, *Multinational Electronic Companies and National Economic Policies* (Greenwich, Conn.: JAI Press, 1977), pp. 81–91.
6. *Wall Street Journal* (European ed.), August 17, 1983, p. 1.
7. Sorenson and Wiechmann, "How Multinationals," pp. 39, 42. See also W. Keegan, *Multinational Marketing Management*, (Englewood Cliffs, N.J.: Prentice-Hall, 1974), pp. 297–306. L.W. Phillips, "Explaining Control Losses in Corporate Marketing Channels: An Organizational Analysis," *Journal of Marketing Research* (November 1982): 525–549.
8. M.R. Heeler and J. Thorpe, "Developing International Advertising Strategy," *Journal of Marketing* (Fall 1980): 73–79. J.H. Donnelly and J.K. Ryans, "Standardized Global Marketing: A Call as Yet Unanswered," *Journal of Marketing* (April 1969): 73–79. J.J. Boddewyn, "Advertising Regulation in the 1980's: The Underlying Global Forces," *Journal of Marketing* (Winter 1982): 27–35. D.M. Peebles, J.K. Ryans Jr., and I.R. Vernon, "Coordinating International Advertising," *Journal of Marketing* (January 1978): 28–34.

Chapter 9

1. Y. Aharoni, *The Foreign Investment Decision Process* (Boston: Division of Research, Harvard Business School, 1966), p. 79.
2. H.I. Ansoff, *Corporate Strategy* (New York: McGraw-Hill, 1965), p. 16.
3. R.B. Stobough, Jr., "Where in the World Should We Put That Plant?" *Harvard Business Review* (January–February 1969): 129–130.

4. R.B. Stobough, "How to Analyze Foreign Investment Climates," *Harvard Business Review* (September–October 1969): 101.

5. C.W. Hofer and D. Schendel, *Strategy Formulation: Analytical Concepts* (St. Paul: West Publishing Co., 1978), pp. 73–76. See also Stobough, "How to Analyze," p. 102.

6. S.J.Q. Robinson and D.P. Wade, "The Directional Policy Matrix—Tool for Strategic Planning," *Long Range Planning* (June 1978). See also Hofer and Schendel, *Strategy*, pp. 72–86.

7. See F.M. Scherer et al., *The Economics of Multiplant Operation, An International Comparisons Study* (Cambridge: Harvard University Press, 1975), pp. 51, 387.

8. *Financial Times*, October 19, 1983.

9. G. Hall and S. Howell, "An Economic Perspective on Experience Curves," *Strategic Management Journal* (1984); W. Fellner, "Specific Interpretations of Learning by Doing," *Journal of Economic Theory* (1969); ICCH No. 9-175-174, op. cit., W. Abernathy and K. Wayne, "Limits of the Learning Curve," *Harvard Business Review* (September–October 1974): 109–119.

10. Hall and Howell, "Economic Perspectives." See also House of Commons, "Strategy Alternatives for the British Motorcycle Industry" (London: HMSO, 1975), pp. 37–52.

11. E. Seidler, *Let's Call It Fiesta* (Cambridge: Patrick Stephens, 1976), pp. 181, 182. See also interview with Ford management, July 20, 1978 and January 30, 1981.

12. Seidler, *Let's Call It*, pp. 77–83.

13. Ibid., pp. 81, 82, 83.

14. Interview with Ford management, August 8, 1980.

15. Siedler, *Let's Call It*, p. 174.

16. J. Johanson and J. Vahlne, "The Internationalization Process of the Firm—A Model of Knowledge Development and Increasing Foreign Market Commitments," *Journal of International Business Studies* (Spring–Summer 1977): 23–32. See also S. Majaro, *International Marketing—A Strategic Approach to World Markets* (London: G. Allen and Unwin, 1977), pp. 133, 134.

17. R. Vernon, "International Trade and International Investment in the Product Life Cycle," *Quarterly Journal of Economics* (May 1966): 190–207.

18. I. Ayal, "International Product Life Cycle: A Reassessment and Product Policy Implications," *Journal of Marketing* (Fall 1981): 91–96. G. Leroy, *Multinational Product Strategy* (New York: Praeger, 1976), p. 108. R. Vernon, *Sovereignty at Bay* (London: Longman, 1971), p. 107.

19. J. Leontiades, "Plant Location—The International Perspective," in *Corporate Planning and Procurement*, D.H. Farmer and B. Taylor, eds., (London: Heinemann, 1975), p. 156.

Chapter 10

1. J. Leontiades, "International Transfer of Company Strengths and Weaknesses," Working Paper No. 78-30 (: European Institute for Advanced Studies in Management, Brussels, July 1978).

2. See, for example, Y. Aharoni, *The Foreign Investment Decision Process* (Boston: Division of Research, Harvard Business School, 1966), pp. 76–121.

3. For a discussion of the initial competitive disadvantage of multinationals relative to domestic firms, see C.P. Kindleberger, *American Business Abroad* (New Haven: Yale University Press, 1969), pp. 11–18.

4. For another perspective, see R. Mazzolini, "Are State Owned Enterprises Unfair Competition?" *California Management Review* (Winter 1980): 20–28.

5. See S. Majaro, *International Marketing—A Strategic Approach to World Markets* (London: G. Allen and Unwin, 1977), pp. 132–161.

6. See M. Porter, *Competitive Strategy* (New York: Free Press, 1980), pp. 191–236.

7. See also W.E. Rothschild, "Competitor Analysis: The Missing Link in Strategy," *McKinsey Quarterly* (Autumn 1979): 42–53.

8. S. Schoeffler, R. Buzzell, and D. Heany, "Impact of Strategic Planning on Profit Performance," *Harvard Business Review* (March–April 1974): 137–145.

9. R.W. Hodgson and H. Uyterhoeven, "Analyzing Foreign Opportunities," *Harvard Business Review* (March–April 1962): 60–72.

10. C. Donaud, J. Kedzierski, and A. Bottier, "Market Research Applied to Overseas Markets: Concrete Execution," Proceedings of the European Society for Opinion and Marketing Research, Special Group Sessions, Venice (September 1976), pp. 198–199.

11. See B.C. Lindberg, "International Comparison of Growth in Demand for a New Durable Consumer Product," *Journal of Marketing Research* (August 1982). See also W. Keegan, *Multinational Marketing Management* (Englewood Cliffs, N.J.: Prentice-Hall, 1974), pp. 190–196, 239.

12. A.M. Jaeger, "The Transfer of Organizational Culture Overseas: An Approach to Control in the Multinational Corporation," *Journal of International Business Studies* (Fall 1983): 91–114.

Chapter 11

1. J. Johanson and J. Vahlne, "The Internationalization Process of the Firm—A Model of Knowledge Development and Increasing Foreign Market Commitment," *Journal of International Business Studies* (Spring–Summer 1977).

2. V. Terpstra, *International Marketing* (Hinsdale, Ill.: Dryden, 1978), pp. 319–327.

3. D. Tookey, *Export Marketing Decisions* (Harmondsworth: Penguin Books Ltd., 1975), pp. 69–73.

4. Ibid., pp. 74–82.

5. For licensing policies and practice, see F.J. Contractor, *International Technology Licensing: Compensation, Costs, and Negotiation* (Lexington, Mass.: Lexington Books, D.C. Heath and Company, 1981), pp. 55–98.

6. See J. Leontiades, "Plant Location—The International Perspective," in *Corporate Planning and Procurement*, D.H. Farmer and B. Taylor, eds. (London: Heinemann, 1975), pp. 155–168.

7. Ibid., p. 161.

8. W.H. Davidson, *Global Strategic Management* (New York: John Wiley and Sons, 1982), pp. 44–51, 57–59.

9. See also D.G. Bradley, "Managing against Expropriation," *Harvard Business Review* (July–August 1977): 81, 83.

10. M.Z. Brooke and J. Holly, "International Management Contracts," in *The Management of Headquarters-Subsidiary Relationships in Multinational Corporations*, L. Otterbeck ed. (Hampshire: Gower, 1981), pp. 297–317.

11. S.M. Robbins and R. Stobough, "The Bent Measuring Stick for Foreign Subsidiaries," *Harvard Business Review* (September–October 1973): 80–88.

12. M.E. Wicks Kelly and G.C. Philippatos, "Comparative Analysis of Foreign Investment Evaluation Practices by U.S. Based Manufacturing Multinational Companies," *Journal of International Business Studies* (Winter 1982). See also D.F. Channon with M. Jalland, *Multinational Strategic Planning* (London: Macmillan, 1979), p. 134. M.E. Wicks, *A Comparative Analysis of the Foreign Investment Evaluation Practices of U.S. Based Multinational Companies* (New York: McKinsey and Company, 1980).

13. For distinction between the practices of large and small firms, see Wicks and Philippatos, "Comparative Analysis," p. 25.

14. For practical application, see P.O. Gaddis, "Analyzing Overseas Investments," *Harvard Business Review* (May–June 1966): 115–122.

15. B. Marois, "French Firms and Political Risk Abroad," Working Paper, E.R. N 197, C.E.S.A., Jouy en Josas, France, 1982), p. 8.

16. Wicks and Philippatos, "Comparative Analysis," p. 24.

Chapter 12

1. I am grateful to Kellogg's of Great Britain for assistance in preparing the following material.

2. R. Buzzell, "Can You Standardize Multinational Marketing?" *Harvard Business Review* (November–December 1968): 103. B. Liander et al., *Comparative Analysis of International Marketing* (Boston: Allyn and Bacon, 1967), p. 22.

3. J.H. Davidson, *Offensive Marketing* (London: Cassell, 1972), pp. 246–248.

4. Liander et al., *Comparative Analysis*, p. 22.

5. R.J. Saldick, "Multinational Product Management," Proceedings of the American Marketing Association/Marketing Science Institute, Report No. 76-110 (August 1976), pp. IV-1–IV-5.

6. Buzzell, "Can You Standardize," p. 109.

7. P. Kotler, *Marketing Management* (London: Prentice-Hall International, 1984), pp. 66, 67.

8. J.R. Goodyear and M.G. Vineall, "From Hats, Rabbits and Magicians to the Present Day," Proceedings—European Society of Opinion and Marketing Research, Main Sessions, Venice (September 1976), pp. 282–286.

9. B.C. Lindberg, "International Comparison of Growth in Demand for a New Durable Consumer Product," *Journal of Marketing Research* (August 1982): 364–371. W. Keegan, *Multinational Marketing Management* (Englewood Cliffs, N.J.: Prentice-Hall, 1974), 191–194.

10. J. Leontiades, "Patterns in International Markets and Market Strategy," in *European Research in International Business*, ed. M. Ghertman and J. Leontiades (Amsterdam: North Holland, 1978), pp. 239–246.

11. See E.A.G. Morgan, "Marketing International Brands in Cosmetics," *Chelwood Review* , pp. 29–36.

12. For adaptation of marketing methods to a developing country, see N. Aydin and V. Terpstra, "Marketing Know-How Transfers by Multinationals: A Case Study in Turkey," *Journal of International Business Strategy* (Winter 1981): 35–48. Glade et al., *Marketing in a Developing Nation: The Competitive Behavior of Peruvian Industry* (Lexington, Mass., Heath, 1970).

13. *Financial Times*, June 20, 1978.

Chapter 13

1. Stephen J. Kobrin, "Political Risk: A Review and Reconsideration," *Journal of International Business Studies* (Fall–Spring 1979): 67–80. Stefan H. Robock, "Political Risk: Identification and Assessment," *Columbia Journal of World Business* (July–August 1971): 6–20. J.V. Micallef, "Political Risk Assessment," *Columbia Journal of World Business* (Summer 1981): 48.

2. Raymond Vernon, *Sovereignty at Bay* (London: Longman, 1971), p. 46.

3. Ibid., p. 54.

4. Thomas A. Poynter, "Government Intervention in Less Developed Countries: The Experience of Multinational Companies," Working Paper Series No. 238R1 (London, Ont.: Research and School of Business Administration, University of Western Ontario, December 1980), p. 16.

5. Ibid., pp. 25–28.

6. R. Rummel and D. Heenan, "How Multinationals Analyze Political Risk," *Harvard Business Review* (January–February 1978): 69.

7. Ibid., p. 70–75.

8. Hans Schollhammer, "Identification, Evaluation and Prediction of Political Risk from an International Business Perspective," in *European Research in International Business*, M. Ghertman and J. Leontiades, eds. (Amsterdam: North Holland, 1978), pp. 91–109.

9. Rummell and Heenan, "How Multinationals," p. 71.

10. Ibid., p. 71.

11. Bernard Marois, "Organizational Structures Set Up by French Firms to Manage Political Risk In Foreign Investment," Working Paper Cr N 213/1982, C.E.S.A. Jouy en Josas, France 1982), pp. 32, 35.

12. D.G. Bradley, "Managing against Expropriation," *Harvard Business Review* (July–August 1977): 81, 83.

13. Ibid.

14. Ibid., p. 82.

15. Marois, "Organizational Structures," p. 12.

16. Poynter, "Government Intervention," pp. 16, 17.

Chapter 14

1. A.P. Sloan, *My Years with General Motors* (London: Pan Books, 1967), p. 145.

2. W.K. Brandt and J.M. Hulbert, "Patterns of Communication in the Multinational Corporation: An Empirical Study," *Journal of International Business Studies* (Spring 1976): 57–64.

3. W. Keegan, "Multinational Marketing: The Headquarters Role," *Columbia Journal of World Business* (January–February 1971): 88. See also C.A. Bartlett, "Multinational Structural Change: Evolution versus Reorganization," in *The Management of Headquarters-Subsidiary Relationships in Multinational Corporations*, L. Otterbeck ed. (Hampshire: Gower, 1981), p. 128.

4. G. Hofstede, "Alienation at the Top," *Organizational Dynamics* (Winter 1976): 44–60.

5. For a description of the capital budgeting process in multinational firms, see Y. Aharoni, *The Foreign Investment Decision Process* (Boston: Division of Research, Harvard Business School, 1966), pp. 142–172.

6. J.L. Bower, *Managing the Resource Allocation Process* (Boston: Division of Research Harvard Business School, 1970), p. 43.

7. *American Marketing News* (American Marketing Association), July 16, 1976, p. 5.

8. Ibid.

9. Some firms refer to centers of excellence; see *Managing Global Marketing: A Headquarters Perspective* (New York: Business International Corporation, 1976) p. 67.

10. Ibid., p. 122.

11. The material in this section is based on personal interviews within a U.S. multinational firm operating in Europe.

12. Hofstede, "Alienation," p. 56.

13. See A.M. Jaeger, "The Transfer of Organization Culture Overseas: An Approach to Control in the Multinational Organization," *Journal of Business Strategy* (Fall 1983): 93–95.

14. A. Edstrom and J. Galbraith, "Transfer of Managers as a Coordination and Control Strategy in Multi-National Organizations," *Administrative Science Quarterly* (1977): 248–263.

15. H.V. Perlmutter and D.A. Heenan, "How Multinational Should Your Top Managers Be?" *Harvard Business Review* (November–December 1974): 121–132.

Chapter 15

1. J. Johanson and Jan-Erik Vahlne, "The Internationalization Process of the Firm—A Model of Knowledge Development and Increasing Foreign Market Commitments," *Journal of International Business Studies* (Spring–Summer 1977): 23–32.

2. Y. Tsurumi, *Multinational Management* (Cambridge, Mass.: Ballinger, 1977), pp. 502, 503.

3. Y. Tsurumi, *The Japanese Are Coming* (Cambridge, Mass.: Ballinger, 1976), p. 145.

4. K. Yoshimine, Op. Cit., pp. 68, 83, 84.

5. L.G. Franko, *The European Multinationals* (London: Harper and Row, 1976), p. 203.

6. Ibid., p. 87.

7. Ibid., pp. 198–200.

8. See also D. Channon with M. Jalland, *Multinational Strategic Planning* (London: Macmillan, 1974), pp. 31–33.

9. W.H. Davidson and P.C. Haspeslagh, "Pitfalls of the Global Product Structure," INSEAD Working Paper No. 81/15 (1981), p. 13.

10. Ibid., pp. 17–35.

11. Ibid., pp. 17, 31.

12. *Financial Times*, October 17, 1979.

13. Ibid., October 25, 1982, p. 14.

14. See J. Stopford and L. Wells Jr., *Managing the Multinational Enterprise* (London: Longman, 1972), pp. 63–72. See also, J. Stopford, "Growth and Change in the Multinational Firm (D.B.A. dissertation, Harvard University, 1968), pp. 133–138.

15. Y.L. Doz and C.K. Prahalad, "Headquarters Influence and Strategic Control in MNCs," *Sloan Management Review* (Fall 1981): 20–23. See also C.K. Bartlett, "Multinational Structural Change: Evolution versus Reorganization," *The Management of Headquarters-Subsidiary Relationships in Multinational Corporations*, L. Otterbeck ed. (Hampshire: Gower, 1981), p. 128.

Index

Accounts and accounting practices, 22, 49, 121

Administration: costs of, 180; day-to-day tasks of, 12

Advertising: agencies, 176; aspects of, 5, 7, 34, 79, 86, 144, 150–151, 163; budgets, 93–94; campaigns, 93; companies, 67

Advice and assistance: financial, 132; governmental, 62; provision for, 16–17

Africa, 33, 61, 72, 75, 122, 189; developing countries in, 126. *See also* South Africa

Agents and agencies: advertising, 176; external, 162, 164; governmental, 61; independent, 92, 130–133; research, 61; sales, 22, 32

Agreements and allegiances, 134, 136, 169

Agriculture: companies, 39; equipment, 4, 126; products, 132

Aharoni, Yair, cited, 96

Aircraft industry, 5, 133

Alaska, 4

Allocation: of capital, 169, 173; of resources, 14–15, 18, 39, 46–49, 107, 144, 171–174

Allowances for depreciation, 121

Ambiguity, tolerances for, 129

American Express, 59

Americanization, definition of, 79

Analysis: financial, 137, 172; preliminary, 142–143; risks, 138; sensitivity, 138; switching of, 139–140

Andean Group, factor of, 5

Andrews, Kenneth, cited, 7–8

Ansoff, Igor, cited, 7, 96

Antitrust legislation, 119, 126

Appraisal(s): environmental, 113–117; managerial, 112–113; resource, 124–126; strategic, 111–114

Arbitration, third-party, 165–166

Argentina, 44, 75, 145, 150, 162

Asia, 33–34, 75, 189; investment in, 44. *See also* Southeast Asia

Assets: definition of, 40; divestment of, 166; financial, 169; national, 166; ownership of, 153; and sales, 120; transfer of, 103

Associations: industrial, 55; national, 59

Attitudes: consumer, 79, 145; customer, 126; governmental, 49, 55, 97–98, 119, 157; managerial, 18; national, 70; political, 158–159

Australia, 34, 39, 79, 150, 158

Austria, 22

Authority: central, 32; decentralized, 175; fixing of, 189; hierarchical, 32; primary, 196–198

Automobile industry, 3, 5, 77, 103; market for, 24–26, 33–34; and small cars, 25–29; world sales in, 25

Autonomy: degrees of, 15, 18, 32, 180, 189, 191, 196; local, 175–176

Avon, policy of, 92

"B" car concept, 25–29

Backgrounds: managerial, 126–127; national, 181

Balance of payment figures, 72, 151

Balance of power and trade, 104, 196

Bank of America, 66

Bankruptcy, problem of, 63

Banks and banking institutions, 5, 132, 187; domestic, 67; international, 67, 124; retail, 124

Bargaining positions and powers, 156, 164–165

Barriers: border, 5–6, 134; of distance, 3; entry, 56, 82, 111, 133, 136; institutional, 5–6, 9; international, 11, 22; national, 33–35, 55–59, 64, 80, 98; overcoming of, 6; protective, 80; tariff, 98, 134; trade, 18, 53, 133

Bavarian Motor Works (BMW), 65

Beckett, Jerry, cited, 23

Behavior patterns: buying, 72; managerial, 17

Belgium, 9, 22

Board of directors, activities of, 31, 39

Bobcat program, 28–32, 35

Boeing, 107

Bolivia, 153

Bonds and bonus payments, 40, 182

Borders: barriers to, 5–6, 134; national, 48, 95, 103; restrictions on, 55

Boston Consulting Group (BCG), 46–47

Boundaries: geographical, 18–19; national, 4, 6, 9, 11, 19, 49, 52, 55, 126, 169

Bowman, E., cited, 8

Brand names, importance of, 24, 163

Brands and branding, company, 69, 86

Brazil, 5, 34, 44, 75, 96, 105, 126, 162

Brewing companies and beer production, 8–9, 77, 118

Brown, Richard C., cited, 75

Brussels, Belgium, business in, 132

Bubble charts and matrices, 40–41

Budgets and budgeting, 18; advertising, 93–94; capital, 171–177; decisions on, 171; on research and development, 61; resource allocation, 171–174

Building materials, 8, 112

Bureaucracy, problems of, 15, 18, 154, 202

Burger King Corporation, 102

Business(es): acquisition of, 14; alternative, 39; cash-rich, 47; environment, 4–7, 113–114, 149, 153, 202; high-risk, 40; international, 6; low-growth, 46–47; national, 69; opportunities, 44; trends in, 178. *See also* Strategic business units (SBUs)

Buying patterns and buy-out clauses, 72, 136

Buzzell, Robert, cited, 147

Cadbury Schweppes, 174–177

Cameroon, 122

Campaigns: advertising, 93; promotional, 30–31, 93, 138

Canada, 25, 46, 141–145, 149, 158, 191

Capital, 5; allocation of, 169, 173; budgeting, 171–175, 177; commitment of, 50; controls on, 49, 98; costs, 67; earnings, 47; formation, 25, 31, 160, 172; indigenization of, 154–155; investments, 135, 137, 172; local, 162; new outlays of, 134, 172; shortage of, 151

Career paths, 41, 181

Cash: flow of, 39–40, 137; management services, 47, 66

Central: authority, 32; controls, 16, 177; information, 71; office headquarters, 12–13

Centralization policies, degrees of, 11, 71, 187, 196

Chandler, Alfred, cited, 12, 34, 199

Changes: environmental, 122; force of, 5–7, 11, 73, 173; in host government, 158–161; industrial, 8; international patterns, 122; political, 159–161, 165; productivity, 90; in taxation policies, 154–155; technological, 6

Chemical industry, 4, 120, 132

Chile, 41, 153; copper industry in, 156

China, 21

Chrysler, Walter P., cited, 59, 162

Ciba-Geigy, 190

Citibank, 66

Climate: conditions of, 19, 147; economic, 44, 99; industrial, 100; investment, 114–115

Clinics, effectiveness of, 30

Coca-Cola, 94

Collusion, factor of, 119

Colombia, 44

Commercials, television, 144, 151

Commodore International, 92

Communication facilities: cross-national, 16; direct, 6, 33, 171; face-to-face, 3; improvement in, 93, 171, 195; intercompany, 181; international, 67, 84; limitations in, 4, 196; lines of, 3, 56, 134–135; telephone, 3

Community formation, European, 5, 18–19, 24, 33, 57, 62, 132

Comparison studies: data on, 72; international, 147; strategic, 148–150

Competition and competitors: constraints on, 152; domestic, 111; environmental, 61; European, 24; external, 98; factor of, 9, 45, 143, 173, 178; foreign, 7, 62, 83; global, 14, 51, 57–59, 80–82; head-on, 54; international, 52–59, 66–67, 119; intracompany, 89; Japanese, 120, 180; major, 41; national, 4, 6, 80–82; performance, 3, 120; portfolios, 46; potential, 107, 129; price, 89, 92, 132; product, 30, 32, 145; protection against, 83; regional, 14; spheres of, 4–6; strategies, 51–56; technological, 101

Computer industry, 5, 92; British market, 62; softwares in, 60

Concentration and coproduction, industrial, 107, 119

Concessions, factor of, 164

Confidentiality, lack of, 67

Conflict of interest, problem of, 17, 133

Conglomerates, rise of, 39

Constraints: financial, 15; governmental, 152; legal and political, 7, 47, 152

Construction projects, 133

Consumer: attitudes, 79, 145; durables, 92, 177; goods, 85–86, 147; income, 147; purchasing patterns, 147; rural and urban, 144; tastes, 102, 142–143; testing policies, 143

Contingency plans, development of, 178–179

Contracts and contractual obligations, 107, 129, 132, 136

Control(s): bureaucratic, 15; on capital, 49, 98; central, 16, 177; financial, 17, 47, 124; fragmentation of, 135; governmental, 23, 32; issue of, 133–135, 181; loss of, 103; managerial,

89; pollution, 67; on prices, 33, 154–155

Coordination and coordinating principles: cross-national, 35, 56–57, 196; decisions, 70; discretionary, 175–176; international, 88, 179, 201–202; in marketing, 69–70, 87–88; regional, 24–25; strategic, 9, 16

Corning, 193

Corporate: diversification, 39; hierarchy, 169, 181–182, 196; identity and reputation, 93, 182; image, 67, 93, 165; international knowledge, 33; marketing policies, 75; meetings, 31; resources, 59; risks, 95; strategy, 7–8, 11; structure, 7, 188

Cosmetic industry, 39

Cost(s): administrative, 180; capital, 67; efficiency formulas, 89, 194; fixed, 57; investment, 25; labor, 102, 105; pricing, 62; production, 34, 89; reductions, 24, 90, 92, 102; research, 54, 56, 80; short-term, 90; transportation, 83, 98, 104, 133–134, 136; wage, 53, 82–83

Country of origin, factor of, 3, 126

Credit cards, use of, 73, 124

Cross-border contacts and transfers, 32, 35, 48, 56, 103, 137

Cross-checking, importance of, 70–71

Cross-national strategy, 16, 32, 126

Cuba, 153

Culture: development of, 181–183; differences in, 22, 64, 126–127; factor of, 70, 114–115, 169

Currency. *See* Money

Customer(s): attitudes, 126; international, 69, 187, 191; national, 71; potential, 7, 60, 71, 106, 121; preferences, 18–19, 33, 41, 56; relations, 9, 88, 180; services, 60, 66; and suppliers, 118

Customs. *See* Traditions and customs

Cyert, R.M., cited, 21

Data: accumulation of, 72, 129; backup, 174; gathering of, 70–77, 199; lack of, 99; multicountry, 71; social, 70

Dealers and dealerships, network of, 24

Decentralization, policy of, 11, 169–172, 175, 189, 202

Decisions and decision-making process, 16, 22, 87, 105, 107, 141, 179, 193, 198; budgeting, 171; coordinative, 70; investment, 47, 95–96; management, 119; marketing, 69, 85, 107; portfolio, 14; predetermined, 85; study of, 21–22

Defense expenditures, 160

Delivery delays, problem of, 134

Delphi technique, use of, 160

Demand(s): level of, 130; local, 134; product, 5, 104; and sales volume, 92; shift in, 71; and supply, 17

Demography, factor of, 72

Denmark, 22, 198

Depreciation: allowances for, 121; problem of, 50

Design(s): duplicate, 86; of goods and services, 57; product, 24, 30, 121; research, 52

Developed countries, 86, 104–105; affluence of, 150

Developing countries, special situations in, 4–5, 9, 73, 82, 105, 118, 122, 126, 150–152, 157, 162

Development: of business firms, 11–12; of contingency plans, 178–179; of corporate images, 67, 93, 165; economic, 5, 77, 80; industrial, 4; investment costs of, 25; management, 180; market, 77; product, 29, 62, 80, 83, 86–88, 141, 171–172

Dior, Christian, cited, 55

Direct: communications, 6, 33, 171; investment, 3–4, 79, 95, 129, 133, 157–158; sales force, 71

Discounts and discount home centers, 82, 118

Distance, problems created by, 3, 22

Distribution: channels of, 118–119, 142; door-to-door, 92; geographic, 44, 72, 180; income, 147, 160; levels of, 18, 32, 79–80, 89–93, 145, 188; marketing, 30, 187; outlets, 130; products and producer, 92, 118

Diversification and voluntary divestiture, corporate, 39, 166

Domestic: banks, 67; companies, 41; competitors, 111; markets, 72, 185

Drucker, Peter, cited, 7–8, 69

Dumping strategy, company, 131–132

Duplication: avoidance of, 18, 61; of designs, 86; forms of, 193; of sales, 187; of research, 16

Durable products, factor of, 92, 145, 177

Earnings: capital, 47; per share, 137; regulations on, 49

Economies of scale: advantages of, 45, 63; major, 60; presence of, 80–82; restricted, 86

Economists and the economy: activities of, 44, 66, 70–71; characteristics, 147; conditions of, 44, 99, 114–115; development of, 5, 71, 77, 80; growth of, 100; national, 157–159; and political power, 153; status of, 72; supermarket, 150; world, 3

Educational institutions, support of, 165

Efficiencies of scale, use of, 34, 66, 101–102, 196

Efficiency formulas: cost of, 89, 194; internalization of, 67; production changes in, 90, 102

Electrolux, 52–53, 111, 119

Electronic industry, 14, 53, 62, 88; component products of, 60, 151; systems developed by, 3; and timepieces, 82

Employment: factor of, 30, 104, 156; local, 107

Engineers and engineering products, 8, 28

England. *See* Great Britain

English Electric Computers, 60

Entry: barriers, 55–56, 111, 133, 136; choice of, 133; of exports, 133; generic strategies, 129–133; national, 55, 113–114

Environment: business, 4–7, 113–114, 149, 153, 202; changes in, 32, 122; characteristics of, 147; competitive, 61; evaluation of, 12, 102, 113–117; external, 7, 70; knowledge of, 33, 35; market, 71; national, 8–9, 11–12, 17–18, 21, 102, 111, 113–117, 130, 172, 181; operational, 4, 12, 21; political, 153

Equipment: agricultural, 4, 126; engineering, 8; industrial, 71; office, 5;

telecommunications, 105; use of, 63, 136, 171

Equity: foreign-based, 135–136; investments, 135, 162; ownership, 60; risks, 162

Escort car model by Ford, 26–29

Ethnocentric factors, approach to, 32

Europe, 92, 177; competition from, 24; community countries of, 3, 23–24, 32–34, 47; Ford plant in, 25–30; markets of, 24, 26, 63; multinational firms in, 189–190; tariffs of, 24. *See also* Western Europe

Exchange: foreign, 151; rate of, 32, 49, 103, 138

Executives: board level, 39; experienced, 69; flow of, 31; key, 189–191, 200; marketing, 69; regional, 69; travel of, 18

Exiting privileges, freedom of, 132

Expansion: geographical, 11–12; industrial, 3, 11; international, 3, 11, 32, 63; in manufacturing, 105; of railroads, 12; of traditional exports, 3

Expenditures: defense, 160; design, 52; media, 174; research, 52, 55. *See also* Cost(s)

Experience: accumulation of, 21; curve effect of, 90–92, 102; marketing, 69, 73–75; transfer of, 16, 66, 73–75; use of, 17

Expertise and consultants, 159–160, 166

Exports and exporting activities, 11, 30, 95, 99, 104, 130, 133, 135, 137, 185–188, 191; Japanese, 52–53, 82

Expropriations, problem of, 164

External: agencies, 162, 164; competition, 98; environment, 7, 70

Extractive industries, 66

Family and family life, factor of, 126

Far East, 6, 61, 82

Fast-food outlets, popularity of, 5, 73, 102

Feasibility studies, importance of, 130

Feedback, need for, 104, 133–134, 196

Ferranti, 65

Fiat car model, production of, 26

Fiesta car model by Ford, 30, 88

Finances and financial methods, 70, 95; advice on, 132; analysis, 137, 172; assets and bonds, 40, 169; controls on, 17, 47, 124; institutional, 9, 111; markets, 67; performance, 14, 18, 121; resource constraints, 15; services, 54, 59, 73

Flexibility: degrees of, 49; geographical, 135

Follower countries, 82–83

Food industry: animal, 72; breakfast, 39, 142; franchises in, 5; outlets for, 5, 73, 102; packaged, 4, 105; products, 150; Swiss based, 69

Ford, Henry, cited, 21–23

Ford, Henry, II, cited, 25

Ford of Europe, establishment of, 24–25, 28, 31

Ford Motor Company, 21–23, 25, 88; European production facilities, 23–30; international automotive operations, 22–24, 29, 34; management, 28, 103; market share by, 26; national subsidiaries, 30; organizational structure, 34–35; Product Planning and Research staff (PP&R), 28; regional coordination, 24–25, 28–29; in Spain, 30–32, 102–103; strategic planning, 25–31; union policies, 23

Foreign: competition, 7, 62, 83; exchange, 151; markets, 72, 86, 131; ownership, 136; production facilities, 82, 84, 134–135; subsidiaries, 70–71, 169; supply sources, 16

Fortune 500 industrial companies, 40

Fragmented industries, 119, 135

France, 12, 22–23, 30, 59, 165; market in, 26

Franchises: agreements on, 5, 95, 134, 136; fast-food, 5

Franko, Larry, cited, 189

Free trade areas, 133

Friction, sources of, 16–17, 24, 93, 180

Fujitsu, 62

Funds and funding policies, 155, 169

Furnaces for electric steel, 6

General Agreement on Tariffs and Trade (GATT), 6, 131, 166

General Dynamics, 107

General Electric Company, 5, 99

General Engineering, 60, 71
General Motors Corporation, 24, 52, 67, 169; tradition in, 34
Generic entry strategies, factor of, 129–133
Generic International Competitive strategies, 51–56
Geography and geographic factors: boundaries, 18–19; concentration, 60; differences, 41; dispersion, 64; distribution, 44, 72, 180; distances, 22; expansion, 11–12; flexibility, 135; location, 39, 41; scope of, 6, 70, 133, 147, 170, 176, 181, 189; specialization by, 55
Geopolitics, aspects of, 56–58
Germany, 22–24, 30, 88, 119. *See also* West Germany
Global: competition, 14, 51, 57–59, 80–82; concepts, 6–7, 70, 170; logistics, 101–107; market shares, 54; objectives, 17; opportunities, 41; perspectives, 19; pricing policies, 14; strategies, 8, 21, 34, 51–52, 62–65
Good citizen policies, value of, 164–165
Goods: consumer, 85–86, 147; durable, 145; industrial, 122–123; physical, 95; and services, 57
Government: aid, 62; attitude, 49, 55, 97–98, 113–115, 119, 157; competition, 152; controls, 23, 32; equity ownership, 60; incentives, 57; loans, 62; objectives, 156–157; policies, 18; preferential treatment, 56, 60–62, 134, 152, 157; private insurance, 164; protection, 82; regulations, 103, 122–123, 151–152; research agencies, 61; restrictions, 137, 152
Grants, awarding of, 60
Great Britain, 21–24, 30, 88, 118, 141–143, 149–150; manufacturing base, 98; markets in, 59–63
Greece, 77
Gross national product (GNP), 72
Growth: business, 40, 46–47; economic, 100; in Japan, 59; opportunities, 46; potential for, 39; sales, 131; share matrixes, 41
Grundig, 107
Guinness, 149

Habits. *See* Traditions and customs
Handicapped workers, hiring of, 164
Haspeslagh, Philippe, cited, 40
Hazards of international standardization, 64
Headquarters: directives of, 17; functions of, 12–18, 70, 85; management of, 70–71; marketing role, 69; planning by, 170; prices set by, 90; subsidiary relationships, 14
Heenan, D., cited, 160
Hewlett-Packard, 119
Hierarchy: authority by, 32; corporate, 169, 181–182, 196; levels of, 12, 18, 170, 196; management, 70
History, factor of, 41
Hitachi, 84, 188
Hodgson, R., cited, 121
Hofer, C.W., cited, 8
Hofstede, Geert, cited, 181
Holding companies, role of, 14–18, 49, 56, 101, 137, 189
Holland, 22, 111
Home: appliances, 4; market, 22, 83, 86, 126
Honda, 65
Hong Kong, 5, 57, 157
Hospitals and health and medical science, 71
Host governments: changes within, 158–161; guarantees of, 164; role of, 165, 180
Household appliance industry, 3, 53
Hunsicker, J. Quincy, cited, 198

IBM, 17, 52, 54; in Japan, 61; in Latin America, 61; marketing operations, 60–61; return on investment, 63
Identity: corporate, 93, 182; national, 181
Image, national and international, 51, 180
Imports: factor of, 30, 95; from Nigeria, 137'
Incentives: governmental, 57; investment, 134; schemes, 30, 151, 157–158; tax, 157
Income: averaging of, 73; consumer, 147; distribution, 147, 160; levels of, 86, 92, 96, 100; national, 160; per capita, 96, 100, 104, 145, 160

Independent: agencies, 92, 130, 132–133; management, 16–17
India, 21, 44, 96, 150, 157
Indigenization programs, 162; capital, 154–155; industry, 157; management, 154–155
Indonesia, 4, 44
Industrial: countries, 3, 73, 119, 150, 157, 164; development, 4; equipment, 71; products, 77; relations, 100; sites, 158; uniform standards, 6
Industrialization, levels of, 80, 119, 135
Industrialized countries, 6, 120
Industry: associations, 55; changes in, 8; fragmented, 119, 135; indigenous, 157; infant, 158; rationalization of, 6
Infant mortality, problem of, 71
Inflation, adjustments for, 121
Information: centralized, 71; demographic factor of, 72; market, 33; processing of, 180; publication of, 72; systems, 182–183
Insurance: government and private, 5, 164, 166
Integration: economic, 23–24; international, 16, 162–163; strategy of, 17–18
Intelligence, marketing, 70–77, 187–188
Intercompany and intercountry comparisons, 73, 181
Interdependence: international, 64; portfolio, 49–50
Interest payments, 121, 124, 162. *See also* Rate of return
International: automotive operations, 22–24, 29, 34; banking, 67, 124; business barriers, 6, 11, 22; career paths, 41, 181; change patterns, 122; communications, 67, 84; competition, 4–5, 51–59, 66–67, 119; coordination, 88, 179, 201–202; corporate meetings, 31; customers, 69, 187, 191; distribution policies, 92–93; expansion, 3, 11, 32, 63; image, 51; integration, 16, 162–163; interdependence, 64; logistics network, 101–104; market interpretations, 71–72; sourcing, 66; strategies, 25–31
International Computers Limited (ICL), 59–61; competitive position, 62;

marketing methods, 65; research and development, 62
International Monetary Fund (IMF), 6, 166
International Service Systems (ISS), 198
Internationalization, early efficiencies of, 4–5, 22, 51–54, 67, 85
Intracompany price competition, 89
Intuition, factor of in business, 129, 138
Inventions, number of, 6
Inventory policies, established, 121, 126, 151
Investment(s): in Asia, 44; capital, 135, 137, 172; codes, 114–115, 166; costs, 25; decisions, 47, 95–96; direct, 3–4, 79, 95, 129, 133, 157–158; equity, 135, 162; foreign, 22, 47, 95–96, 156, 165; incentives, 134; increase in, 13; large-scale, 7, 104; local, 103; national, 133; new, 50, 101, 103, 137, 143, 156; opportunities, 173; plant, 101, 103; return on, 30, 44, 49, 63, 95, 112, 137–138, 172; small-scale, 104
Iran, 159
Ireland, 149, 151
Italy, 14, 26, 46, 53, 150

Japan, 3–4, 41, 46, 57, 79, 106, 119; competition from, 120, 180; exports of, 52–53, 82; IBM in, 61; motorcycle production, 82; products growth, 59, 65; television production, 52–53, 84; trading companies in, 187–188
Jobs, union reaction to, 32
Joint ventures, factor of, 135–136, 158, 162

Kellogg's of Great Britain, introduction of new product, 141–145, 149
Knowledge: accumulation of, 21; environmental, 33, 35; of local conditions, 4
Kraushar, Peter, cited, 87

Labor: costs, 102, 105; force, 51, 66, 111; legislation, 126; union involvement, 32
Laboratories, research and development, 61
Language: common, 171; schools for, 30

Latin America: activities in, 26, 33–34, 44, 47, 57, 72, 79, 92, 197; countries of, 75; IBM in, 61
Laws: company, 154; national, 126
Lead-lag patterns and strategies, 79, 122
Leader countries, location and markets of, 79–80, 83
Learning curve, effects of, 102
Leasing policies, factor of, 134
Legal: constraints, 7, 47, 152; institutions, 9
Legislation: antitrust, 119, 126; effects of, 118; product, 145; worker, 126
Less developed countries, problems of, 80, 82, 104–105, 152, 188
Leverage, use of, 156–157
Licenses and licensing: agreements, 106–107; and contracts, 129–130; policies, 11, 52, 95, 99, 134, 136, 193; regulations on, 126; sales to Nigeria, 137; of technology
Life cycles: patterns of, 77; product, 72–73, 80–83, 90, 122; specialization by, 55
Lloyds of London, 164
Loans, 118; government, 62; research, 60
Lobbying and lobbyists, efforts of, 62
Local: autonomy, 175–176; borrowing, 162; capital, 162; conditions, 4; demand, 104; employment, 107; investors, 103; management, 14, 69, 147; markets, 31; political risks, 136; sales branches, 134; shareholders, 126, 162; subsidiaries, 93; taxes, 89
Location: influence of, 83–84; in lead country, 80; marketing, 105; national, 44, 48; plant, 23, 95, 101–107
Logistics and logistical methods, 133–134; planning network of, 101–104
Logo, standardized business, 94
Lutz, Bob, cited, 34

Machine tools industry, 59, 85
McKinsey and Company, 99
Macroeconomics, factor of, 172
Macroenvironmental factors, national, 113–114, 178
Makita, 82
Management: appraisal by, 112–113; attitudes of, 18; cash services of, 47, 66; central, 107; complexities, 7, 11,

165; contracts, 136; control of, 89; decisions, 119; development and motivation, 180; at Ford Motor Company, 103; hierarchy, 70; independence of, 16–17; indigenization of, 154–155; international, 9, 70–71; local, 14, 69, 93, 147; nonequity, 136; philosophy and simplification, 61, 189; promotion system, 181; recruitment, 182; skills, 141, 157; subsidiary, 93; top-ranked, 7, 51, 69, 103, 171, 182, 194
Managers: backgrounds, 126–127; behavioral impact, 6, 17, 22; market strategy; 69; national, 69
Manufacturing: expansion, 105; in Great Britain, 98; standards, 154; strategy, 22, 102, 178
Mapping, usefulness of, 122–124
Market(s): access to, 6; American, 3, 59; automotive, 24–26, 29, 33–34; British, 59–63; Canadian, 141–143; conditions, 111; development, 77; entry methods, 133–134; environment, 71; European, 24, 26, 63; financial, 67; foreign, 72, 86, 131; French, 26; home, 22, 83, 86, 126; information, 33; international, 65, 71–72, 75; Italian, 26, 150; in lead countries, 83; local, 31; locations, 105; mass, 52, 75, 79, 150; money, 47; national, 5, 24, 26, 31, 45, 51, 57, 69, 77, 83, 101, 103, 106, 138, 140, 147; Nigerian, 112–113, 133; opportunities, 132, 188; penetration, 32, 106, 144–145; reference product, 115, 145, 149; regional, 178; research, 30–31, 34, 75, 87, 122, 149; shares, 4–5, 26, 41, 45–46, 54, 63, 113, 132, 171, 173, 179; Spanish, 26; specialization, 55; strategy, 143; surveys, 30; target, 141, 147; trends, 173; West German, 98; world, 57, 77
Marketing: activities, 60, 105; concepts, 69, 73; coordination, 69–70, 87–88; corporate, 75; decisions, 69, 85, 107; and distribution, 30, 187; executives, 69, 73–75; headquarters role, 69; intelligence, 70–77, 187–188; international, 69; methods, 65, 174–

175; operations, 60–61; programs, 52, 55, 69; responsibilities, 69; strategies, 69, 77–84, 106; techniques, 73; test, 144

Marketing Science Institute (MSI), 73

Marois, Bernard, cited, 163

Marsh, J.G., cited, 21

Mass: markets, 52, 75, 79, 150; media, 75, 79, 142, 151; production techniques, 22

Matrix structures, 40–41, 196–198

Media: expenditures, 174; mass, 75, 79, 142, 151

Medicines and medical services, 5, 72, 89

Mediterranean countries, 29–30

Meetings and conventions, importance of, 18, 49

Mergers, business and financial, 60

Mexico, 44, 46, 59, 75, 77, 157, 162–163

Middle East geographical area, 4, 44, 61, 160, 162, 189

Middlemen, factor of, 133; responsibility of, 130

Miner, J.B., cited, 8

Minimum efficient size (MES), 34

Mintzberg, H., cited, 8

Mitel Corporation of Canada, 63

Mobile resources, 17

Money: convertability of, 6; fluctuations in, 33, 49, 103; market, 47

Monopolies and monitoring policies, 17, 126

Morocco, 157

Mother-daughter organizational structure, 191, 196

Motorcycle industry, 59, 65; in Japan, 82

Motorola, 52

Multinational companies, 4, 12–13, 69, 189–190

Nation-states of tomorrow, 4

National: allegiances, 169; assets, 166; associations, 59; attitudes, 70; background, 181; barriers, 33–35, 55–57, 59, 64, 80, 98; borders and boundaries, 4, 6, 9, 11, 19, 48–49, 52, 55, 95, 103, 126, 169; businesses, 69; companies, 3–4; competition, 4, 6, 80–82; currency, 49; customers, 71; economy, 77, 157–159; entry

conditions, 55, 113–114; environment, 8–12, 17–18, 21, 102, 111–117, 130, 172, 181; identity and image, 180–181; income, 160; investments, 133; laws, 126; locations, 44, 48; macroenvironment, 113–114, 178; managers, 69; markets, 5, 24, 26, 45, 51, 57, 69, 77, 83, 101, 103, 106, 138, 140, 147; planning, 14, 29; sales branches, 134, 179; strategy, 13, 55, 57; subsidiaries, 11–17, 29–30, 61, 71, 141, 175–176, 189, 191, 193, 197, 200; supplies, 4; tariffs, 133; territories, 31, 83, 86, 90, 98, 101, 104, 147, 160, 164, 179, 191–193; welfare contributions, 165

Nationalization and nationalized industries, 118, 162

NEC Corporation (Japan), 3

Negotiation and arbitration, 165–166

Nestlé, 39, 190

Nigeria, 44, 114, 120, 126, 150, 159; sales to, 137–138

Nonequity managerial problems, 136

North America, 3, 14, 34, 59–60, 82

North Sea, oil production in, 4

Norton Company, 41

Novice company, 21

Objectives and goals, regional and global, 7, 17, 112–113, 156–157

Office equipment industry, 5

Oil industry, 4–5, 136; companies involved, 156–158, 162; and refinery capacities, 4

Oligopolistic situations, factor of, 119

Olivetti, 14

Open door policy, advantages of, 158

Opportunities: areas of, 51; in automotive field, 26; business, 44; growth of, 46; international, 172; investment, 173; market, 132, 188; new, 3, 6; regional and global, 41

Organization of Economic Cooperation and Development (OECD), 6, 166

Overcapacity and production, problem of, 131

Ownership: company assets, 153; factor of, 35; foreign, 136, 153, 158; government equity, 60

Packaging and packaged foods, 69, 86, 105, 163
Paper industry, products of, 75
Patent regulations, 126
Payback periods, factor of, 137
Penetration: market, 32, 106, 144–145; strategy, 130–131
Pennsylvania railroad, 12
Per capita income, levels of, 96, 100, 104, 145, 160
Performance: financial, 14, 18, 121; portfolio, 48–49; profit, 49; sales, 61; standards of, 112, 119
Personnel programs, 130, 132, 182
Peru, 44, 162
Petroleum and petrochemical industry, 3–4
Pharmaceutical: companies, 88–89, 126; industry products, 5, 39, 82, 105, 132, 150
Philippines, The, 75
Philips, 106, 190
Physical characteristics and goods, 72, 95
Pilkington Company, 134
Pittsburgh, Pennsylvania, 12
Planning: capital budget, 171–174; formal and informal, 25, 170–171; global headquarters, 21, 170; international logistical, 101–104, 133–134; long-range, 7; multinational, 12–13; at national level, 14, 29; product, 23, 177; regional, 21, 31; strategic, 12–21, 25, 177; uniform systems, 16
Plant: investment, 101, 103; location, 23, 95, 101–107; offshore, 105–107; satellite, 106
Plessey Limited, 60
Poland, 22
Politics and political conditions, 178; attitudes, 64, 158–159; constraints, 7, 47, 152; environment, 19, 153; institutions, 9, 111, 114; leverage, 156–157, 172; parties, 158; power, 153; risks, 39, 44, 133–138, 153–155, 161–166; scientists, 71, 96, 99–100; system changes, 159–161, 165
Pollution, control of, 67, 154
Population size, factor of, 96
Porter, M., cited, 8
Portfolio: assessment, 48–49; competition, 46; decisions, 14;

interdependence, 49–50; screening, 98–102; strategy, 15, 39, 40–46, 173
Potential: competitors, 107, 129; customers, 7, 60, 71, 106, 121
Power: balance of, 196; economic and political, 153
Pratt and Whitney, 5
Preferential treatment, influence of, 34, 56, 60–62, 83, 152, 157
Preliminary analysis of situations, 142–143; premarket categories, 77
Price(s): competition in, 89, 92, 132; controls, 33, 154–155; nationally based, 89–90; war on, 92
Pricing: costs, 62; experience curves, 90–92; global policies, 14, 30, 52, 79, 85; standard formula for, 89; strategic, 90
Primary: authority, 196–198; responsibility, 15, 30, 193
Procter and Gamble, 145
Producers: and distributor relationship, 118; Italian, 53; Makita hand tools, 82
Product(s): agricultural, 132; competition in, 30, 32, 145; demands for, 5, 104; design, 24, 30, 121; development of, 29, 62, 80, 83, 86–88, 141, 171–172, 180; distribution, 92; electronic, 151; food, 150; industrial, 77; Japanese, 59, 65; legislation, 145; life cycles, 72–73, 80–83, 90, 122; markets, 77, 115; new, 16, 73, 75; paper, 75; planning, 23, 177; preferences in, 72, 149; range, 19, 52, 149; safety of, 67, 85, 88–89; sources, 79, 143–144; standardization, 85–86; trends and tailoring, 75, 143
Product Planning and Research staff (PP&R) of Ford Motor Company, 28
Production: capacity, 30, 51; costs, 34, 89; efficiency, 90, 102–103; facilities, 17, 23–30, 52, 104–105, 133; foreign, 82, 84, 134–135; large-scale, 22, 34; methods, 5, 16, 33; of services, 95; specialization of, 55; techniques, 22
Profits and profitability: definition of, 121; degrees of, 5, 39, 44, 61, 95, 137, 144, 171, 179; margin, 24, 79; near-term, 131–132; performance, 49–50; record, 63, 92; and taxes, 156
Promotion: of management, 181; policies on, 18, 52, 85–86, 93–94

Promotional campaigns and material, 30–31, 67, 75, 93, 138, 144, 149
Protectionist policies: barriers, 80; era of, 33; foreign competition, 83; governmental, 82
Psychology and psychological characteristics, 72
Publishing industry and published information, 54, 72
Purchasing power and patterns, 22, 140, 147, 150

Quality, standards of, 67, 119
Quantitative methods, factor of, 160–161
Quotas, effectiveness of, 6, 55, 57, 133–134

Radios. *See* Television and radio industry
Railroad industry, expansion of, 12
Rating scales and rates of return, 32, 49, 96–98; 121, 124, 130, 137–138, 162
Rationalization of industry, 6
Raw materials, use of, 4, 51, 66, 162
Recruitment, management, 182
Red tape, problem of, 15, 34, 170. *See also* Bureaucracy
Redlich, Fritz, cited, 12
Reference markets, factor of, 15, 145, 149
Regional jurisdictions: competition analysis, 14; executives in, 69–70; Ford coordination, 24–25, 28–29; goals and objectives, 7, 17, 112–113, 156–157, 178; global logistics, 101–107; markets, 178; opportunities, 41; perspectives in, 19; strategic planning, 21, 31
Regulations: earnings, 49; government, 103, 122–123, 151–152; industrial, 149, 154
Religion, issue of, 19, 126
Renault, 26
Rents and renting activities, 134
Repatriation, definition of, 49, 137
Reputation, key role business factor, 51, 88, 93, 130, 182
Research: budget, 61–62; costs, 54, 56, 80; development, 14, 61–62, 86, 193; duplication, 16; expenditures, 52, 55; facilities, 86, 169; government agencies, 61; grants, 60; health, 71;

laboratories, 61; market, 30–31, 34, 75, 87, 122, 149
Resource(s): allocation, 14–15, 18, 39, 46–49, 107, 144, 171–174; appraisal, 124–126; commitments, 40, 67, 130; company, 126, 136; corporate, 59; financial, 15; mobile, 17; redistribution of, 40, 44; switching of, 44, 48; technological, 5–6, 65; utilization of, 67, 75, 80
Responsibility: areas of, 14, 170, 174, 178, 180; marketing, 69; of middlemen, 130; primary, 15, 30, 193; to shareholders, 171
Restrictions: border, 55; economies of scale, 86; governmental, 137, 152. *See also* Barriers
Return(s): on interest payments, 121, 124, 162; on investments, 30, 40, 44, 49, 63, 95, 112, 137–138, 172; rate of, 130, 137
Rewards, system of, 182
Rise and Shine orange drink, 142–145, 149
Risk(s): analysis, 138; approach to, 40, 161; business, 40; commercial, 172; corporate, 95; equity, 162; minimization of, 130; perceptions, 49; political, 39, 44, 133, 135, 138, 154–156, 161–166; premiums for, 138
Rolls Royce, 5, 55, 94
Rome, Treaty of (1958), 25
Rummel, R., cited, 160–161
Rural areas, factor of, 144, 150
Russia, 21–22

Safety: factor of, 154; product, 67, 85, 88–89; standards of, 113, 164
St. Louis, Missouri, 12
Sales: agents, 22, 32; and assets, 120; branches, 134; decline in, 138; demand for, 92; duplicate, 187; factor of, 18, 22, 39, 95, 132, 171; force, 71; growth in, 131; international, 5; national, 134, 179; to Nigeria, 137–138; performances, 39, 61, 121; projected, 144; representatives, 71; specialization, 121; world automotive, 25
Satellite plant operations, 106
Schendel, O., cited, 8
Schollhammer, Hans, cited, 160

Science and scientists, political, 71, 96, 99–100
Screening: methods, 96, 108; portfolio, 98–102; preliminary, 172; systematic, 158
Sears Roebuck and Company, 44
Seasonal cycles, business, 39
Segmentation: international, 72; schemes, 121–122
Sensitivity, analysis and degrees of, 138, 169, 178
Service(s): cash management, 47, 66; contracts, 136; customer, 60, 66; financial, 54, 59, 73; and goods, 54, 59, 73; industries, 57; production of, 53–54, 95
Shareholders: interests of, 41; local, 126, 162; responsibility to, 171
Shares: earnings per, 137; market, 4–5, 41, 45–46, 54, 63, 113, 132, 171, 173, 179; matrix of, 41; return on, 63
Shell Company, 11, 52, 67, 99
Sinclair Company of Britain, 107
Singapore, 5, 46, 57, 157–158
Singer, Isaac Merit and Singer Company, 3, 105
Sites. *See* Location
SKF, 52
Skills in managerial personnel, 157
Sloan, Alfred P., cited, 169
Smith, Adam, cited, 54
Snecma of France, 5
Sociology and sociologists, influence of, 30
Sony, 67, 119
Sorenson, R.Z., cited, 86
Sources and sourcing: decisions on, 105; foreign, 16; of friction, 16–17, 24, 93; product, 79, 143–144; second defined, 106–107; of supply, 16, 106
South Africa, 34
South America, 21
South Korea, 5, 44, 157
Southeast Asia, 53, 82, 89
Spain, 22, 44, 59; Ford plant in, 30–32, 102–103; markets in, 26
Specialization: advantages of, 56; degrees of, 54; geographical, 55; by life cycles, 55; market segment, 55; sales, 121; strategy, 65; technological, 54; in telecommunications, 63

Standardization and standards: hazards of, 64; international, 52, 64; performance, 112; planning, 171; pricing, 89; product, 85–86; quality, 67, 119; safety, 113, 164; uniform industrial, 6
Statistical criteria and status, economic, 72
Steel industry, 4, 132
Steiner, A., cited, 8
Stopford, John, cited, 199
Stoppage work problems, 64
Strategic business units (SBUs), 40–41, 44; foreign-based, 49
Strategy: appraisal, 111–114; competitive, 51–56, 148–150; coordination of, 16; corporate, 7–8, 11; cross-national, 32, 126; definition of, 132–133; evaluation and selection, 136–140; federal mode, 16; Ford Motor Company international, 25–31; formulation levels, 13; generic entry, 51–56, 129–133; global, 8, 21, 31, 34, 51–52, 62–65; host governments, 156–157; integrative, 17–18; international, 8–10, 51–56, 90; lead-lag, 79, 122; manufacturing, 22, 102, 178; marketing, 69, 77–84, 106, 143; national, 13, 55, 57; penetration, 130–131; planning of, 12–21, 25, 31, 177; portfolio, 15, 39, 40–46, 173; pricing, 90; product development, 141; regional, 21, 31; skim, 130–131; specialization, 65
Strikes, problem of, 25
Structure(s): Ford Motor Company organizational, 34–35; hybrid, 198; simplified management, 61
Studies and surveys: empirical, 133; feasibility, 130; market, 30
Subsidiaries: company, 14; dispersal of, 16; foreign, 70–71, 169; headquarters, 14; local management of, 93; national, 11–17, 29–30, 61, 71, 141, 175–176, 189, 191, 193, 197, 200
Success, factors involving, 122–125
Supermarkets: economy of, 150; use of, 75
Suppliers and supply, 4, 7, 16–17, 106, 118, 130

Suzuki, 65
Sweden, 22, 46, 111, 150
Switching tactics, purpose of, 139–140
Switzerland, products of, 69, 82

Tabulators, international, 60
Taiwan, 105, 157
Target markets, potential, 121–122, 141, 147
Tariffs: barriers, 98; circumvention of, 11; forms of, 9, 30, 33, 56, 80, 89, 103, 107; high, 23, 79, 98, 102, 134; national, 133; reduction in, 5–6, 19, 32–33
Taxation policies: changes in, 154–155, 157; concessions to, 164; local, 89; and profits, 156
Techniques and technical advice, marketing and mass production, 16, 22, 73
Technology: advanced, 6, 62; capability, 73; changes in, 6; competition in, 101; impact of, 6, 19, 34–35, 41, 119, 121, 134, 165, 173; industries, 16, 65, 106–107; licensing of, 165; limitations on, 22; new, 52, 156; resources, 6, 65; specialization, 54; transfer of, 95, 157, 193
Telephones and telecommunications industry, 3, 63, 105, 183
Television and radio industry, 3, 59, 82; commercials on, 144, 151; and Japanese producers, 52–53, 84
Territories: national impact, 31, 83, 86, 90, 98, 101, 104, 147, 160, 164, 179, 191–193; new distinctions of, 18–19, 44
Test marketing and consumer testing, 143–144
Texas Instruments, 14, 65, 90, 92
Textile industry products, 187
Thailand, 41
Third parties, arbitration by, 165–166
Three Rivers, 63
Times (London), cited, 25
Timex Sinclair, 1000 computer model by, 92
Timing comparisons and time, factor of, 75–77, 80, 149–150, 181
Toiletries industry, 150, 198
Top management, positions of, 7, 51, 69,

103, 171, 182, 194
Trade: balance of, 104; barriers, 18, 53, 133; free areas of, 133; international, 6–7; names, 166; world, 16, 187–188
Trademarkes, use of, 94, 163
Traditions and customs, influence of, 3, 34, 41, 59, 72, 85–86, 92, 124–127, 191
Training courses, need for, 182, 191
Transfers and transferability: of assets, 103; associated, 144; of company experience, 16, 66, 73–75; cross-border, 35, 56, 103; question of, 126; of technology, 95, 157, 193
Transportation industry and facilities, 3, 54, 82, 89; costs of, 83, 98, 104, 133–134, 136; limitations on, 4
Travel: business executives, 18; need for, 6, 25
Travelers' checks, use of, 59
Trends: economic, 178; environmental, 32, 122; international, 72; market, 173; product, 75

Unilever, 119
Unions: activities of, 55; Ford Motor Company policies with, 23; job reactions to, 32; stoppage due to, 64; and wages, 9
Uniroyal, 176
United Nations, 166
United States, 4, 21, 46, 57
Uranium, refining of, 6
Urban: areas, 151; consumers, 144
Utilization of resources, 67, 75, 80
Uyterhoeven, H., cited, 121

Valued-added term, definition of, 121
Velasco regime (Peru), 162
Vernon, Raymond, cited, 104–105, 156
Video discs, popularity of, 84
Volkswagen, 75

Wage scales: levels of, 53, 80–83, 144, 148; union, 9
Wasson, Chester R., cited, 77
Watch industry in Switzerland, 82
Welfare, contributions to, 165
West Germany, 41, 44, 98
Western Europe, 3, 30, 34, 82, 124
Wiechmann, V.E., cited, 86

Work practices and workers, 33;
    handicapped, 164; legislation on, 126
World: economy, 3; markets, 25, 57, 77
World War II period, before and after, 3,
    5, 23, 75, 105

Yamaha Corporation, 65

Zambia, 153
Zenith, 52

About the Author

James C. Leontiades is senior lecturer in international management at the Manchester Business School, University of Manchester. He has also been with the overseas division of General Motors, involved in planning international strategy, plant location, and competitor evaluation.

After joining The Wharton School in Philadelphia, he moved to Europe in 1971 as a visiting senior lecturer at the Manchester Business School. There he has worked closely with a wide number of companies engaged in planning international expansion. He spent 1973–1974 in Brussels as professor of management with the European Institute for Advanced Studies in Management.

About the author